Connecting
humanistic gerontology

Edited by
Jan Baars, Joseph Dohmen,
Amanda Grenier and Chris Phillipson

First published in Great Britain in 2014 by

Policy Press
University of Bristol
6th Floor
Howard House
Queen's Avenue
Clifton
Bristol BS8 1SD
UK
Tel +44 (0)117 331 5020
Fax +44 (0)117 331 5367
e-mail pp-info@bristol.ac.uk
www.policypress.co.uk

North American office:
Policy Press
c/o The University of Chicago Press
1427 East 60th Street
Chicago, IL 60637, USA
t: +1 773 702 7700
f: +1 773-702-9756
e:sales@press.uchicago.edu
www.press.uchicago.edu

© Policy Press 2014

British Library Cataloguing in Publication Data
A catalogue record for this book is available from the British Library.

Library of Congress Cataloging-in-Publication Data
A catalog record for this book has been requested.

ISBN 978 1 44730 089 2 paperback

The right of Jan Baars, Joseph DohmenAmanda Grenier, and Chris Phillipson to be identified as editors of this work has been asserted by them in accordance with the Copyright, Designs and Patents Act 1988.

Cover design by Qube Design Associates.
Front cover: image kindly supplied by istock.
Printed and bound in Great Britain by CMP, Poole.
Policy Press uses environmentally responsible print partners.

Contents

Notes on contributors

Jan Baars is professor of interpretive gerontology at the University of Humanistic Studies, the Netherlands. As a social theorist and philosopher he focuses on conceptual analyses of theoretical and practical approaches to ageing. He has published extensively about critical gerontology and concepts of time in theories of ageing. His most recent book is *Aging and the art of living*, published in 2012 by Johns Hopkins University Press (www.janbaars.nl).

Margreet Th. Bruens is a humanistic counsellor at the nursing home Humanitas-Akropolis in Rotterdam, the Netherlands. Her work focuses on supporting people with dementia and being with them, listening to the stories they have to tell.

Dale Dannefer is Selah Chamberlain professor of sociology and chair of the Department of Sociology at Case Western Reserve University, USA. He is the co-editor (with Chris Phillipson) of *The SAGE handbook of social gerontology* (Sage, 2010). His work is concerned with sociological aspects of cumulative advantage and disadvantage, and the analysis of gene–environment interactions.

Joseph Dohmen is professor in philosophical and practical ethics at the University of Humanistic Studies, the Netherlands. He has written several books on Nietzsche and Foucault, the art of living and self-care. He is the author of *Life as a work of art* (Ambo, 2011).

Amanda Grenier is the Gilbrea Chair in aging and mental health, and associate professor in health, aging and society at McMaster University, Canada. She is the author of *Transitions and the lifecourse: Challenging the constructions of 'growing old'* (Policy Press, 2012).

Roelof Hortulanus is professor, social interventions and social policy, at the University of Humanistic Studies, the Netherlands. He was one of the founders of LESI, the National Expertise Centre for Social Intervention in the Netherlands. He has written several books on social policy, social interventions and wellbeing.

Hanne Laceulle is a PhD student at the University of Humanistic Studies, the Netherlands. Her research focuses on self-realisation and ethics in the context of late modern ageing.

Jielu Lin is a doctoral candidate in the Department of Sociology at Case Western Reserve University, USA. Her research focuses on theoretical and methodological aspects of the problems of normativity and variability, and she is especially interested in the implications of systematic age-related changes in variability.

Anja Machielse is associate professor, humanistic meaning and ageing well, at the University of Humanistic Studies, and senior researcher at LESI, the National Expertise Centre for Social Intervention in the Netherlands. She has written several books on social isolation, social vulnerability and social interventions.

Chris Phillipson is professor of sociology and social gerontology at the University of Manchester, UK. He is the co-editor (with Dale Dannefer) of *The SAGE handbook of social gerontology* (Sage, 2010). His book *Ageing* was published with Polity in 2013.

Mo Ray is a senior lecturer in social work at the University of Keele, UK. She has worked for many years as a social worker and manager in social work teams for older people and continues her interest in training and practice development work with the social work and social care workforce. Her research interests include culture change in social care settings and social relationships in later life.

Thomas Scharf is professor of social gerontology and director of the Irish Centre for Social Gerontology, National University of Ireland, Galway. He is the co-editor (with Norah Keating) of *From exclusion to inclusion in old age: A global challenge*, published by Policy Press in 2012.

Friederike Ziegler has a background in participatory and action research in human geography. She is currently research fellow in mental health in the Department of Health Sciences at the University of York, UK. She has published on participatory mapping, older people's mobility and wellbeing, and social participation.

Acknowledgements

We would very much like to thank the staff at Policy Press for their support in the development of this book. Emily Watt was the commissioning editor and we are extremely grateful for her encouragement and interest. Laura Vickers and Laura Greaves have also made vital contributions at different phases in the production of the manuscript. We also wish to record our appreciation for the editing support provided by Marki Rickman at McMaster University. The book has also benefited from symposia organised by the British Society of Gerontology and the Gerontological Society of America.

ONE

Introduction

Jan Baars and Chris Phillipson

> Death is a dramatic, one-time crisis while old age is a
> day-by-day and year-by-year confrontation with powerful
> external and internal forces. (Robert Butler, *Why survive?
> Being old in America*)

Demographic change in the 21st century – with the rise of ageing
populations across the Global North and South – is setting moral as
well as political and economic challenges for the range of countries
involved. On the one side come complex issues about the distribution
of resources between generations and groups, with pressures placed
on the shoulders of individuals in determining how to manage life in
old age. On the other side has come a strong sense of the possibilities
of new areas of choice in later life, notably with debates around the
rise of the so-called 'third age' and the growth of leisure and cultural
industries targeted at older people. These different sides to growing
old – constraint on the one side and choice on the other – are the
subject of detailed study and exploration in the various contributions
to this book.

Ageing, meaning and social structure aims to bring together a fruitful
interface between two approaches that have been relatively insulated
from each other, although both have been shown to be highly relevant
to understanding processes of human ageing. One aspect has emphasised
the analysis of structural mechanisms such as social inequality; another
has focused on the interpretation and articulation of meaning in later
life. The former often operates under the rubric of 'political economy
perspectives on ageing' (Baars et al, 2006), the latter as 'humanistic
gerontology' or 'humanistic ageing studies' (cf Cole et al, 2010). This
volume prepares the meeting ground for these two paradigms that
have developed separately, with each drawing on their own traditional
resources. The purpose of this volume is to explore the extent to which
they presuppose and complement each other.

Critical gerontology as structural analysis

Social critiques, such as those associated with 'critical gerontology', are usually responses to structural mechanisms that work in ways that contradict official discourses that emphasise freedom, social justice or equality. The structural character of such mechanisms implies that the social problems that trigger the critique were not caused by inevitable results of senescing, or by the irresponsible actions of those who suffer from them or through mere chance, but that they have a persistent and systemic character. This does not mean that these problems could not be changed or mitigated by a particular set of actions. Usually, however, those who articulate the critique cannot bring about such changes; they have to accept that their contribution is limited to pointing out and analysing problematic constellations, demonstrating that they have serious consequences and should be changed for the better. However, researchers working in the area of critical gerontology have maintained for more than two decades that the major problems that ageing people encounter are not the inevitable result of biological senescence, nor of unfortunate decisions, but are constructed (Phillipson and Walker, 1987; Baars, 1991) through social institutions and through the operation of economic and political forces.

Discourses that target such structural mechanisms tend to be highly critical of approaches that speak all too lightly about the individualisation of life (including ageing) in late modernity. Authors who have tried to grasp some of the changes that are taking place in contemporary societies, such as Anthony Giddens (1991) or Ulrich Beck (1992), have emphasised that individuals in late modern societies are much less supported or guided by traditions or customs than before, and are burdened by the responsibility to make their own choices. However, this problem of a moral uprooting and the ensuing obligation to decide and choose should not lead to a neglect of the structural constraints that limit the options they can choose from (Baars, 2006). From the perspective of structural analysis, 'individualisation' is seen as highly problematic because it blames the victim and makes individuals responsible for what can be seen as effects of structural mechanisms. Actually, this 'individualisation' of major problems of ageing (such as insufficient income, bad housing or healthcare) was one of the issues that led to the development of critical gerontology. Other typical sources of indignation have been biomedical reductionism and the mantra 'It is your age', in answer to any problems ageing people may have.

Humanistic gerontology: articulations of interpersonal meaning in old age

In spite of this justified critique of 'individualisation', ageing is also an *existential* process in which individuals and others in their life worlds are faced with major challenges against which structural mechanisms appear to be of little direct relevance. And even if such structural mechanisms have created the problematic situations in which older people find themselves, it is usually not possible for them to wait for structural changes before resolving important issues affecting their lives. Moreover, major crises that frequently take place in human ageing, such as chronic illness or the loss of one's partner, have to be faced by individuals and cannot be delegated to others, although this does not imply that they have to struggle with them alone or that they should not be supported. The confrontation with daily limitations and existential issues invites interpretations of the ways in which people experience ageing in different structural and cultural contexts.

Another reason why interpretive approaches are needed is the underdeveloped vocabulary of ageing, which limits the possibilities to express personal feelings by older people or to articulate existential issues (Featherstone et al, 1991; Cole, 1992; Biggs, 1997, 2003). The history of religion and philosophy demonstrates that while thinking about death is abundant, by comparison, thinking about ageing is relatively scarce – especially in the context of Western culture (Baars, 2012; Baars and Dohmen, forthcoming). This situation limits the possibilities to continue to live as an 'aged' person in a meaningful way and to develop clarity regarding the priorities and preferences for an expanding phase of life that knows few inspiring examples apart from consumerist images. The main traditions in Western science, the humanities, religion and philosophy, appear to have been developed with the (structurally induced) assumption that mankind would consist of productive males who had to work until they were exhausted and that the remainder of their lives was of no real importance. A part of this problematic history has been uncovered by feminist critiques who have corrected the masculine bias, but there remains an important age bias which must be corrected. Humanistic and critical gerontology share similar perspectives in their criticism of neoliberal ideas or images of the independent 'normal adult individual' as interpretations of what is seen as important or meaningful in life appear to be inherently connected with other people. Moreover, as the motivation for a critical analysis of macro-structural processes usually arises out of personal encounters with social problems and macro-developments would catch little critical attention if they did not lead to problems for individual older people, it is clear that the two paradigms are constitutively interrelated. In the following chapters some of the main issues in this interconnection of meanings and structural contexts will be addressed.

The authors of this volume began working on this project by organising two interrelated symposia, focusing on a confrontation and integration of structural and meaning-oriented approaches at the Annual Meeting of the British Society for Gerontology in 2010. This international project was inspired by the need of more structurally oriented researchers to include dimensions of personal meaning and the need of more existentially oriented researchers to include structural backgrounds into their work. The richness of these symposia ignited the idea of an edited volume.

Critical and humanistic perspectives

In Chapter Two, Jan Baars and Chris Phillipson identify some theoretical foundations for the interconnection of structural critiques and interpersonal meanings in terms of changing relations between constitutive life worlds and systemic dynamics. After discussing how autonomy – as a source of meaning – has been identified in the main stream of modernity as independence as opposed to interdependence, they address some typical problems of late modernity. Late modern societies are confronted with the loss of relatively integrated national or regional cultures which could be seen as broadly shared life worlds, where meanings and practices were more or less self-evident and taken for granted. Although meaningful orientations still originate in life worlds that support ways of living in a pre-reflexive way, such life worlds have become much more diverse and complex. This leads to complex interactions between different cultural perspectives on ageing, and a dominant commercial culture that approaches growing old in terms of career and consumption. At the same time, the institutions which used to guide and support the life world are being transformed into systemic formations which isolate individuals and approach them as customers or clients, assuming that they all have the same possibilities for autonomous choice. Meanwhile, the systemic formations that are supposed to support and protect basic elements such as income, education or care, are at risk of becoming prey for the accelerating global markets. As a result of an overburdening shortening of spatial and temporal distances, a housing crisis in the US can turn overnight into a global financial crisis with devastating implications for the most vulnerable parts of the population, most notably for those older people who are no longer economically active and who have to rely on previously gained savings or pensions. The chapter concludes with a discussion of a range of responses to the way in which structural and global changes are exposing the vulnerabilities and frailties of older people.

In Chapter Three, Joseph Dohmen offers an ethical perspective that is presented in practical terms as an effort to help more people attain a 'good old age'. To characterise the basic moral condition of late modernity, Dohmen introduces, following Giddens (1991), the late modern shift from a politics of *emancipation* to a politics of *life*. In the latter context, the neoliberal programme of a choice biography advertises the ample opportunities to lead 'a life of your own', but it actually frustrates both meaningful perspectives on individuality and experiences of social connectedness. To prepare the ground for an inspiring perspective for later life that may bridge the gap between agency and structure, Dohmen gives an overview of the interpretations of modern life politics that have originated from different traditions in moral philosophy. As a result of these explorations he develops a moral lifestyle for later life with the thematic components of reflective distance, expropriation, appropriation, orientation, engagement, temporal integration, serenity and finitude.

An important example of a concept that is situated at the intersection of social structures and personal meaning is that of 'agency', which forms the central theme of Chapter Four by Amanda Grenier and Chris Phillipson. Their reconsideration of the concept of agency was prompted by the questions: 'How do circumstances considered typical of the "fourth age" challenge current understandings of agency?' 'How do we account for agency in situations of frailty and impairment?' Beyond the dominant focus on health or the presupposition that agency is exemplified in popular images of the third age, they explore the tensions of what it means to live in late old age. After a clarification of the construct of the 'fourth age', the major themes in the literature on agency are reviewed, followed by an account of the challenges and contradictions presented by agency and the 'fourth age'. As is the case in other chapters of this volume they question the neoliberal discourse in which agency and other forms of actions are understood as (rational) choice. They argue that the discussion of agency with regards to later life requires that focus is shifted away from binary interpretations of agency as either present or absent, and into understanding the various forms inhibiting or encouraging expressions of agency from the locations in which ageing takes place. The chapter concludes with an assessment of various ways in which agency can be understood in the context of the fourth age.

The urgency of rethinking 'agency' in relation to other basic qualities of being human becomes visible in connection with the conditions associated with cognitive change and in particular those associated with dementia. In Chapter Five, Margreet Bruens discusses how views about dementia have changed over the past few decades – in particular, from considering dementia as a sign of normal ageing (senility) to viewing it as a biomedical condition. She presents an evaluation of the work of Tom Kitwood as a framework for assessing the positive and negative aspects of these changes, emphasising in the process the intersection of structural and interpretive dimensions regarding dementia. Alongside the dominance of biomedical approaches, cultural images of dementia may be seen to reflect existential anxieties about losing one's mind. Limited resources to care for dementing people demonstrate the basic problem of recognising personhood in programmes of health and social care. Bruens argues that dementing people remain human beings deserving of respect and dignity even when their 'agentic' qualities are changing beyond what may be assumed to be 'normal'.

In Chapter Six, Hanne Laceulle explores further the late modern ideal of self-realisation and leading 'a life of your own', as applied to the lives of older people. Instead of situating this ideal in the context of ethical traditions (as developed in Chapter Three), Laceulle argues that recent work on spiritual perspectives in gerontology by Robert Atchley (2009), who continued earlier work by Thomas Cole (1992) and Lars Tornstam (1997), raises important issues about the nature of self and the possibilities for self-realisation in later life. In contrast with most discussions of such existential issues, Laceulle relates them explicitly to social inequality, societal arrangements and scripts surrounding ageing and the lack of cultural resources regarding a meaningful old age. According to Laceulle, self-realisation does not take place in a social vacuum but will be favoured or restricted in its possibilities by cultural and structural contexts. Not only will a more adequate acknowledgement of the spiritual potential of later life contribute to meaningful views of ageing in late modern contexts, it will also elicit important critical feedback on dominant societal arrangements and cultural scripts regarding ageing.

Anja Machielse and Roelof Hortulanus examine in Chapter Seven the extent to which involvement in a meaningful social network has enriching consequences both for individuals in general and for their chances of ageing *well*. They consider why meaningful relationships have a positive effect on personal wellbeing and quality of life. They then consider possibilities for social integration under the new social conditions presented in late modern societies. The chapter presents empirical data on the personal networks of Dutch older adults, the changes that are occurring in these networks, the role of major life events and the importance of social competencies when dealing with such events. Finally, a concluding section draws together a number of remarks about ageing well in contemporary society. The authors argue that adequate personal competencies are becoming more and more important to function well in this new social environment. For future generations of older adults, a balance between independence and connectedness is crucial; only then will older people enjoy individual freedom, and at the same time feel safe and protected in the face of limitations and adversity.

In Chapter Eight, Mo Ray focuses on the political marginalisation of older people with high support needs and the extent to which this is reflected in the limited range of actions with this client group. As a result of dominant agendas of independence and choice, already marginalised older people are forced to rely on their own resources, which are supposed to be the clear and just products of their responsible choices over the lifecourse. The rhetoric of individual responsibility and empowerment turns into practices of disempowerment that can only be challenged if social work concerns itself with promoting opportunities of empowerment that take account of the contexts of power and how it is exercised. This implies appreciating the pervasive importance of dependency and care over the lifecourse, and a perspective on ageing as an interdependent and relational process. Mo Ray concludes her chapter with recommendations for social work education and the development of new forms of social work practice with older people.

In Chapter Nine, Friederike Ziegler and Thomas Scharf begin with restating the theoretical arguments and practical commitment from which critical gerontology has evolved as an endeavour to challenge and ultimately change the ways in which Western societies construct ageing and shape the lives of older people (Phillipson and Walker, 1987). This value-based approach has not only influenced the substantive themes of research in critical gerontology, but it has also helped to shape the methodological approaches adopted in empirical studies. In recent years, driven by a commitment to bring about social change, critical gerontologists have increasingly engaged with participatory or participative methods of doing research. Ziegler and Scharf give a reflected account of their experiences with an interdisciplinary research project, called the Community Action in Later Life – Manchester Engagement (CALL-ME) project. They delineate the opportunities of participatory action research, such as working *with* marginalised older people *in dialogue*, rather than knowledge *on* or *about* those very people whose lives are affected by it. But they emphasise at the same time that this form of research must remain critical and radical in its approach to issues of justice and power, to prevent a neoliberal agenda from hi-jacking participation and empowerment for its own purposes. In other words, contemporary efforts to develop a critical analysis should still heed Marcuse's (1969) warnings regarding the 'repressive tolerance' of formations of power in order to prevent social scientists from becoming agents in ways they would rather avoid.

Finally, Dale Dannefer and Jielu Lin provide a commentary on the various chapters, locating their perspective within the distinction between 'contingent' and 'existential' ageing introduced by Baars and Phillipson in Chapter Two. In the case of the former, they explore the importance of structural inequalities affecting older people for the themes discussed in the book, notably in terms of the achievement of empowerment and autonomy. In respect of the latter, they highlight various approaches for understanding human needs, and the implications for considering issues such as the role of spirituality in later life. They also explore a number of questions developed in the book relating to agency as both a theoretical and practical issue, illustrating this with a number of examples drawn from work with older people in settings such as long-term care.

References

Atchley, R.C. (2009) *Spirituality and aging*, Baltimore, MD: The Johns Hopkins University Press.

Baars, J. (1991) 'The challenge of critical gerontology: the problem of social constitution', *Journal of Aging Studies*, vol 5, pp 219-43.

Baars, J. (2006) 'Beyond neo-modernism, anti-modernism and post-modernism. Basic categories for contemporary critical gerontology', in J. Baars, D. Dannefer, C. Phillipson and A. Walker (eds) *Ageing, globalization and inequality: The new critical gerontology*, Amityville, NY: Baywood Publishing, pp 17-42.

Baars, J. (2012) *Ageing and the art of living*, Baltimore, MD: The Johns Hopkins University Press.

Baars, J. and Dohmen, J. (forthcoming) *Towards an art of aging: A rediscovery of forgotten texts*, Baltimore, MD: The Johns Hopkins University Press.

Baars, J., Dannefer, D., Phillipson, C. and Walker, A. (eds) (2006) *Ageing, globalization and inequality: The new critical gerontology*, Amityville, NY: Baywood Publishing.

Beck, U. (1992) *Risk society: Towards a new modernity*, London: Sage Publications.

Biggs, S. (1997) 'Choosing not to be old? Masks, bodies and identity management in later life', *Ageing & Society*, vol 17, pp 533-70.

Biggs, S. (2003) 'Age, gender, narratives, and masquerades', *Journal of Aging Studies*, vol 18, pp 45-58.

Butler, R. 1975. *Why Survive? Being Old in America*. New York: Harper and Row

Cole, T.R. (1992) *The journey of life*, New York: Cambridge University Press.

Cole, T.R., Ray, R. and Kastenbaum, R. (eds) (2010) *A guide to humanistic studies in aging*, Baltimore, MD: The Johns Hopkins University Press.

Featherstone, M., Hepworth, M. and Turner, B.S. (eds) (1991) *The body: Social process and cultural theory*, Newbury Park, CA: Sage Publications, pp 371-89.

Giddens, A. (1991) *Modernity and self-identity: Self and society in the late modern age*, Cambridge: Polity Press.

Marcuse, H. (1969) 'Repressive tolerance', in R.P. Wolff, B. Moore, Jr and H. Marcuse, *A critique of pure tolerance*, Boston, MA: Beacon Press, pp 95-137.

Phillipson, C. and Walker, A. (1987) 'The case for a critical gerontology', in S. Di Gregorio (ed) *Social gerontology: New directions*, London: Croom Helm, pp. 1-15.

Tornstam, L. (1997) *Gerotranscendence: A developmental theory of positive aging*, New York: Basic Books.

TWO

Connecting meaning with social structure: theoretical foundations

Jan Baars and Chris Phillipson

> Life's but a walking shadow, a poor player,
> That struts and frets his hour upon the stage,
> And then is heard no more. It is a tale
> Told by an idiot, full of sound and fury,
> Signifying nothing. (Shakespeare, 'Macbeth')

Introduction

Although these words remind us of the vulnerability of human life and its meanings, we rarely live according to such aloof attempts at wisdom but instead try to find, support and change meaningful orientations that may help us through our lives. Within the broad context of basic narratives, experiences are interpreted in such a way that at least some basic *orientation* results that helps in facing *situations* that are seen as important for our lives. Meaningful orientations prevent the world in which somebody lives from being experienced as a chaotically unconnected succession of impressions.

Connections play a fundamental role in the constitution of meaning. If we say that a sentence is meaningless, we usually intend to say that it is not connected, neither in itself, nor can we connect to it. And because we inevitably encounter other people and develop forms of intimacy, friendship, cooperation or conflict, meaningful orientations will include moral dimensions besides those that are cognitive. Seeing *connections* and experiencing *connectedness* with other people, with specific regions, cultures, nations or even the world, is constitutive for the experience that our lives have meaning. However, during long lives connections may become unclear or problematic, and experiences of connectedness with 'normal' adults may come under pressure because of ageist practices.

A fundamental point of departure should be the recognition that ageing people are adults and citizens like others, and that 'normality' is an elusive concept that invariably serves specific interests. This does not mean, however, that ageing is not an important process with significant consequences for individuals and societies or cultures. But the age-related demarcations (50+, 55+ or 65+) that are constructed in society to distinguish 'the aged' from other, seemingly 'ageless' adults, are quite arbitrary in light of the impressive differences within both categories of 'normal' versus 'ageing' or 'aged' adults (Baars, 2010c, 2012).

Unfortunately, however, ageing people are too often set apart and treated differently from other adults. Often such practices form part of what Binstock (1983, 2010) terms 'compassionate ageism', a mixture of protection and exclusion. For ageing people this may lead to such questions as: Am I being exiled from normal adulthood? Can ageing really be seen as a meaningful phase of life? Can I still contribute something important to society or should I be content with rather meaningless activities to keep me busy? Has *my* life, so far, been meaningful? Is my life *still* meaningful?

This chapter explores questions about meaning, systemic structures and later life in the context of theoretical discussions within philosophy and sociology. It first reviews the construction of meaning in later life, relating this to the characteristics of a late or post-traditional society. The discussion focuses in particular on trends towards 'individualisation' and the question of whether individual autonomy should be equated with independence. We consider, in particular, issues of recognition and interdependence in later life. The second part of the chapter brings a discussion of the changing interrelations between systemic worlds and pluralising life worlds in the context of globalisation and their implications for ageing people. The chapter concludes with an assessment of some of the arguments for theory and practice in critical gerontology, exploring the fundamental distinction between contingent and existential limitations.

Meaning, independence and interdependence

A starting point for the discussion is the observation that meaningful orientations are themselves unlikely to be innate in human beings. Humans, it would appear from numerous research studies, are faced with a dramatic lack of instincts that might otherwise help them to navigate through life. But the flipside of this evolutionary predicament is an impressive potential to learn which develops during the many years of dependence on care and education. From a historical perspective this has led to the development of institutions that transmit, develop and change cultural meanings in a broad sense as new generations are socialised and acculturated (Gehlen, 1988). These constitutive processes help to explain the important differences that exist between and within cultures, making it hardly possible to speak of a universal human culture or clearly delineated meanings of human life. Since the beginning of written traditions, experiences of ageing have led to widely diverging thoughts and reflections (Baars and Dohmen, forthcoming). Moreover, contemporary developments surrounding ageing in a globalising world provide a challenge to established perspectives on ageing (Phillipson, 2009).

However, although meanings in life or ageing need to be recognised in their diversity, they can be compared and reflected on. We can hardly build on indisputable scientific grounds to establish the most important or most promising forms of meaning. The natural sciences cannot give us a definite answer that would rise above the objective meaninglessness of the processes of nature because everything we may strive for 'must inevitably be buried beneath the debris of a universe in ruins' (Russell, 2009, p 48). Nor can we point to inherent meanings in history. According to the critique advanced by Karl Popper (1973), it would even be dangerous to proclaim such a meaning. This does not, however, mean that we cannot try to *learn* from history – much like Popper did – and in that perspective there are some *basic dimensions* of meaning that have emerged over the last centuries which can still serve to enhance our reflections. Moreover, the ways in which ageing is approached in contemporary contexts reflect the strengths and weaknesses of the main trends that have dominated Western modernisation. From this complex issue we discuss some main developments that also exert an important impact on ageing (cf Baars, 2012).

Roots of independence

In early modernity, the search for the *meaning* of life replaced the Aristotelian question that still dominated medieval discourse, namely, concern with what the *purpose* of life might be (Gerhardt, 1994). Modern citizens challenged conventional structures of meaning, driven by the desire to free themselves from traditional feudal and clerical world views. This modern quest begins with assuming the position of the independent rational individual who wonders whether he can find any orientation in life that can withstand critical questioning and thus replace the many unfounded opinions cherished by traditional authorities. Therefore, early modern treatises typically begin with introducing the (male) rational individual, to inspect and reconstruct his dormant rational capacities so that he may be able to clarify and master the world. Although modern philosophy originates in doubt and reaches an impressive profundity of questioning in the thought of Descartes, its aim is the *elimination* of all doubt: the rational individual who would stand, with absolute independence, on the solid grounds of methodical rationality, with 'clarity and distinction' (Descartes, 1994).

The idea of a happy coincidence of the rational individual and the rational structure of the world has been challenged by the many varieties of poststructuralist (Foucault, 1994) and postmodern thought (Lyotard, 1989; Derrida, 2010). At the same time, one of the main problems of late modern society is the continuation of the early modern idea that the *autonomy* of the individual must be grounded in his/her *independence*. The late modern culture of individualisation still cherishes the idea of independence even though it is apparent that these seemingly independent individuals are in their daily lives not only continuously dependent on activities of others but also confronted with systemic forces beyond their control.

Giddens (1991) has sketched a portrait of the reflexive nature of modern social activity and its implications for the conduct of everyday life (see also Chapters Three and Six, this volume). He argues that: 'Each of us not only "has" but *lives* a biography reflexively organised in terms of flows of social and psychological information about possible ways of life. Modernity is a post-traditional order, in which the question, "How shall I live?" has to be answered in day-to-day decisions about how to behave, what to wear and what to eat – and many other things – as well as interpreted within the temporal unfolding of self-identity'. Bauman points to two important aspects of late modern individualisation: While 'Individualization brings to the ever-growing number of men and women an unprecedented freedom of experimenting ... it also brings the unprecedented task of coping with their consequences. The yawning gap between the right of self-assertion and the capacity to control the social settings which render such self-assertion feasible or unrealistic seems to be the main contradiction of [contemporary] modernity.' (Bauman, 2000, pp 37-8). Moreover, he notes that, while 'Risks and contradictions go on being socially produced; it is just the duty and the necessity to cope with them which are being individualized.' (Bauman, 2000, p 34)

Although ageing well in late modern society requires social competences to avoid the pressures associated with social isolation and related phenomena (see Chapter Seven, this volume), many risks are not evenly distributed over society, but reflect deeply rooted inequalities. The late modern hero, the supposedly 'independent' individual with his 'unlimited choices', is often used to legitimate severe inequalities that emerge over the lifecourse, as if these would just be the outcome of the choices of those concerned.

Regarding ageing processes, emphasis is placed on the independent individual in the dominant interpretation of the lifecourse as a linear development of a 'career self' (Walzer, 1994). This neglects, however, the diverse, but meaningful relationships and commitments that play an important role in the lives of many people, especially women and those from minority ethnic groups (Walker, 1999; Chapter Three, this volume). The interpretation of the lifecourse as a career leads to a further implication in which ageing tends to be seen as the reverse of linear progress: a residual phase of deficit and regression, suitable for consumption but for very little else. Consequently, the societal position of 'the aged' as distinct from 'normal' productive adults will also tend to be seen as residual which will hit those hardest who have not been able to gather social and cultural capital during their earlier years.

Finally, the late modern amplification of the early modern emphasis on instrumental effectiveness as a means to attain independence has had mixed consequences for ageing people. On the one hand, there has been considerable progress in scientifically validated control over health and related conditions. On the other hand, there is an overemphasis on isolating age-related problems or diseases with limited concern for personal identity or integration of ageing people in society. There is a lack of qualitative forms of rationality relevant to the search for meaning, forms that were ignited in the pre-modern wisdom traditions (Baars, 2012). While such impulses remain visible in the humanities and in the major religions, the forms of rationality that are highly valued and supported are instrumentally oriented. In short, *ageing* as a process of continuing to lead a meaningful life after one has been labelled as 'old(er)' by society tends to be reduced to problems of (biomedical) *senescing* and problems of *the aged*, as distinct from 'normal' adults.

Another side of modernity

The developments thus far in this chapter need to be counterbalanced by the emergence of important, albeit neglected, domains of meaning that have also been characteristic of modernity. In this context it is important to remember the ideal of the individual who seeks his or her autonomy in a fulfilment of dreams and potentials in cooperation and connectedness with others, without treating them as mere opportunities for profit or domination. Here, individual fulfilment and autonomy are seen as embedded in interpersonal domains as individuals are dependent on recognition from others, while they support – ideally – through their actions of mutual recognition, a social climate that reflects their interdependence (Honneth, 1995).

If we play down its absolute forms the heritage of modernity opens a perspective on more modest forms of individual autonomy or authenticity (Taylor, 1991), with awareness of the importance of *other* people and *their* search for meaningful orientations. In their critical reflection of early forms of market orientations, Kant (1785/1993) and Hegel (1821/1991), for instance, emphasised that rational orientations must include the *mutual recognition* of humans who should not just be a means to attain one's goal, but should be respected as ends in themselves. Kant clearly saw that humans can use each other as a means for achieving their own goals, but warned against instrumental ruthlessness: 'Act in such a way that you treat humanity, whether in your own person or in the person of any other, never merely as a means to an end, but always at the same time as an end' (Kant 1785/1993, p 30). Unfortunately, ethical orientations that have resulted from these traditions, up to the work of Habermas (Baars, 2009), have overemphasised contractual and procedural aspects and neglected more contingent aspects of intersubjective life and experiences of connectedness.

Underlying this more modest form of autonomy there is awareness and experience of *inter*dependence, in contrast with the somewhat abstract and disruptive idea of *in*dependence. Respecting individual autonomy presupposes the existence of others who act respectfully and a society that supports such interrelations. It will be hard to develop as responsible and knowledgeable agents when individuals are not supported and recognised as such (Honneth, 2007). Growing up as an autonomous human being presupposes supportive social contexts that make this complex process possible, for example, in relation to advice, education, jobs, income, housing or healthcare.

In all of these processes, formative backgrounds, including limiting or inspiring examples of others, play an important role. For ageing people, the meanings that have been experienced as they grew up in a specific region, country, culture or urban lifestyle will probably remain important, whatever subsequent biographical changes. Here we can think of the language one has learned to speak or of the metaphors and narratives that oriented life from childhood through to adulthood. Such persistent meanings do not imply, however, that ageing people cannot continue to learn and change their ideas or perspectives. There is also no reason to make traditions immune from criticism: processes of socialisation often carry cultural messages of *familiarity* versus *strangeness* that imply practices of inclusion and rejection according to age, gender or ethnicity. With the contemporary dynamics of ageing societies in the context of globalisation comes the task to see formative backgrounds in interaction with other evenly formative contexts, appreciating them without idolising or immunising either of them from criticism or from an open confrontation with other perspectives. Globalisation may complicate mutual recognition of people but makes this more important at the same time.

Meanings in life and ageing

The tendency to approach meaning from an individualistic perspective, neglecting the constitutive importance of mutual recognition, is illustrated by the dominant perspectives in research on meanings in life (Baumeister, 1991; Baumeister and Vohs, 2005; Steger et al, 2006; Morgan and Farsides, 2009). Baumeister (1991), to cite one example, even adds an organismic foundation, or at least, an organismic flavour, to his four basic meanings of life when he presents them as 'needs', as if they would be the expressions of a 'human nature'. Baumeister (1991) distinguishes four 'needs for meaning'. The first is the need for *purpose*, which refers to a need to experience that one's life is meaningfully connected with some future goal or inner fulfilment. The second need is for *moral justification* or *moral worth*: the need to experience that the way in which one lives can be morally justified. The third concerns *self-worth*: the need to experience that one respects oneself and is respected by others, especially for what he or she has achieved or can do better than others. The fourth and last need would be *efficacy* or *perceived control*: the experience that life doesn't just happen to you but that you have some control.

Such idealisation of 'independent individuality' neglects the importance of interdependence and mutual recognition for societies, communities and individuals. Regarding the issue of meanings in life and especially in ageing, we emphasise more strongly the social constitution of meanings in life that requires attention to situational specificity and variability in outcomes. The existence of such variability does, however, not imply that we cannot make some major distinctions. In the following we briefly reinterpret the four 'needs' for meaning as proposed by Baumeister (1991), keeping in mind that ageing is a 'normal' part of life but shows some typical characteristics that deserve articulation.

Regarding the constitutive meaning of *purpose* we maintain that ageing people can still envision and pursue future goals that give meaning to their lives. However, a typical feature of ageing is that the time horizon of life is gradually changing (Carstensen et al, 2006;

Dittmann-Kohli, 2007), which can give goals a sense of urgency but also a feeling that it does not matter any more what one might try to achieve. Viewed from a social-existential perspective (Baars, 2010a,b, 2012), the finitude of life that asserts itself in experiences of ageing refers not only to an inevitable death but, in principle, to every situation in life, and this awareness may urge ageing people to appreciate the uniqueness of people and situations more deeply. Experiences of ageing can also lead to seeing oneself as part of a larger process or 'whole' that continues after one's death: recognition of the self in terms of an intergenerational, trans-generational or spiritual perspective (Achenbaum, 2007; see also Chapter Six, this volume). Bertrand Russell paints an interesting picture in this regard: 'An individual human existence should be like a river – small at first, narrowly contained within its banks, and rushing passionately past boulders and over waterfalls. Gradually, the river grows wider, the banks recede, the waters flow more quietly, and in the end, without any visible break, they become merged in the sea and painlessly lose their individual being' (Russell, 1951, p 210). It is a variation of old cultural images about a transcendence of individualism as individual lives participate like finite drops in infinite oceans of life beyond the scopes of planning and activist agendas. Ageing can also be an invitation to embrace goals that extend further than one's own life so that a meaningful participation is possible until the end. Death is the end of life, but the purposes of life can go beyond this horizon.

Issues such as *moral worth* and *self-worth* with regard to ageing summon attention regarding the ways in which ageing people are generally seen in their societies and cultures. If there is a strong emphasis on the idea that ageing people are a burden to society, instead of being a part of society, it will be more difficult to maintain both moral worth and self-esteem. Both elements may not be so problematic when they refer to the past in which one was still a 'normal' adult, but may become more burdensome in such contexts.

With longer lives come the risks that ageing people will be confronted with the effects of failing bodily functions. In such situations, it remains crucial that the people concerned are not identified with their failing bodily functions – an issue that applies to suffering humans of all ages. Respecting them as human beings means also respecting their agency, however residual this may seem to have become in terminal conditions or in advanced stages of dementia. Even if people in such situations are no longer capable of responding in ways that one would 'normally' expect, they still deserve to be respectfully recognised as people (see Chapters Five and Eight, this volume). Whereas *individual autonomy* implies throughout life some degree of *heteronomy* and *mutual recognition* will not always be possible without some degree of *objectification*, ageing processes may lead to typical changes in these domains as human vulnerability may lead to situations in which heteronomy and objectification are becoming more predominant. However, even inevitable forms of heteronomy have to serve and support the person's autonomy, and objectifying treatment must be legitimated by and embedded in interpersonal recognition.

What we can retain from the modern idealisation of individuality is respect for more modest forms of autonomy and agency: a sense of some control over what happens in one's life (see Chapter Four, this volume). Many older people now have – certainly in Western society as compared with any other historical period – more opportunities to influence the ways in which they want to live, reflecting improvements to health and financial resources over the course of the 20th century. But Settersten and Trauten (2009, p 457) make the point that: 'Being able to count on old age ... is not the same as being able to predict *how* those years will be experienced or *whether* the balance of experiences will be positive.' They further argue that:

> ... one of the primary ways in which old age today is distinct from younger life periods is that *the later years have a highly contingent quality*. The fact that old age is longer and highly variable seems to have made its contingent quality more salient. Old age is embodied with so much possibility – yet its potentials, if they are to be realised, depend on some big "ifs" that cannot be predicted or controlled.... These ... relate to life, health and resources: *if* I am (or we are) healthy, *if* I (or we) can manage financially, *if* I (or we) can live independently, *if* my (or our) children are able or willing to help, and so on. As these contingencies come undone, so too do the futures that have been counted on or taken for granted.

And, as the authors argue, how these big 'ifs' play out will also depend on the impact of social differences and social inequalities, notably those linked with social class, ethnicity and gender. This confronts us again with some important questions for linking meaning with social structure. In particular, can we, as we move through the 21st century, make ageing *less* contingent and unequal? The next section provides some reflections and observations on this important theme.

Meaning, systemic worlds and life worlds

The interpersonal dimensions discussed above cannot be missed in meaningful orientations but need to be complemented by a critical analysis of *systemic* formations that are usually legitimated because they would support and facilitate important aspects of daily life, such as communication, work, income, nourishment or care. Systemic structures, however, have a tendency to neglect these social origins so that their functioning requires constant monitoring, critique and adaptation. Problematic implications of societal structural dynamics have been a major concern of structurally oriented critiques of societies since the 19th century, when thinkers such as Karl Marx or Pierre-Joseph Proudhon tried to understand the structural dynamics which led to extreme hardship and misery for industrial workers and their families. In historical retrospect we can say that the humanist tradition of empathy with those who suffer from circumstances beyond their control, of solidarity with their fate and with efforts to improve this, became confronted with market–driven societal dynamics and their consequences.

Societal systemic dynamics cannot be fully understood if one remains at the level of individual choices. The creation of traffic jams, for instance, cannot be understood from individual decisions to go by car from A to B, but has to be addressed at a more structural or aggregated level where such data as numbers of cars and capacities of roads can lead to an understanding of the unintended systemic effects of individual actions. Individual actions can have important unexpected implications at aggregated levels, as can also be seen in the creation of environmental problems: for an individual household the produced amount of waste may not seem much, but taken together, individual actions create huge environmental problems. A personal preference to hire a young candidate instead of an older, more experienced one may not seem so important, but taken together such personal preferences create huge problems for so–called 'older workers' in the labour market. The interrelation between individual actions and structural dynamics also works the other way: processes at a structural macro–level, such as small reductions of pensions or reductions in community funding (see Chapter Nine, this volume), may seem minor issues but they can have serious implications for ageing people, especially for the most vulnerable among them.

In the contemporary world of globalisation, societal dynamics reach beyond nation-states and have major consequences for ageing as migrating workers, consumers of healthcare and leisure move around the world while governmental budgets and pensions are seriously affected by international financial turmoil. Meanwhile these dynamics create a multicentred world in which the European or Western perspective can no longer be regarded as predominant but will have to re-appraise its position and meaning.

To develop this critical perspective further, the idea of late modern societies as a constellation of 'life world' and 'systems' is taken as a point of departure (Habermas, 1984, 1987). In the work of Habermas, the systemic world refers to the economic system and the more or less bureaucratic organisations of the political system. Following the tradition of social systems theory, especially the theory of Niklas Luhmann (1996), Jürgen Habermas (1984) calls these societal representations *systems*, because they share an impersonal way of functioning which contrasts with the *life world* where people interact and communicate with each other on a more personal basis (which should not be identified with harmony or purity of motives), without merely implementing bureaucratic regulations or being driven by economic profit. According to Habermas (1984), and in contrast to Luhmann, the systemic world is enveloped by the life world: the systemic world can and needs constantly to be discussed, criticised and, if necessary, changed. If the life world, which is the domain of communicative action, cannot fulfil these tasks anymore, its *colonisation* by the systemic world is a fact. According to Luhmann, however, even this appeal to interpersonal discussions is completely outdated: the systemic world has taken over and cannot be meaningfully guided or criticised through interpersonal discussions.

There is insufficient space for a discussion of these theories but two main observations might be made. The first is that systemic formations are becoming increasingly typical of institutions outside the domain we associate with the political or economic system in a specific sense: for example, in education, health or institutional care. Such institutions are increasingly dominated by *bureaucratic policies* and *profit orientations*. The second observation is that Habermas' model presupposes a national society with a more or less unified life world and a political system that tries to regulate the nation's economic system and the interactions between the life world and the systemic world. In the turmoil of globalisation these conditions are changing rapidly: life worlds are becoming more heterogeneous and less able to support public discourse with shared assumptions. As far as political systems are still rooted in nation-states, they are not enveloped by a communicative life world but by an extremely complex, globalising economic system with many different dynamics which are hardly kept in check by the different nation-based political systems, although this is what they intend or pretend to do (Cerny and Evans, 2004).

Responses from critical gerontology: human rights and global change

From a critical gerontological perspective, a number of issues arise from the above arguments. Three in particular are reviewed here: first, the relationship between population ageing and social and cultural change; second, understanding modifications to the lifecourse; and third, issues relating to the protection of human rights in later life, both at the level of the most vulnerable life worlds and at the level of global agents. On the first of these, an important development at a macro level arises from the interplay between demographic change (notably longer life expectancy) and the trends associated with political and cultural globalisation (Phillipson, 2012). Stepping out of the boundaries of the national society into an interconnected world brings to the fore questions of cultural diversity, different understandings about what it means to age and the issue of whom we take to be an aged person. The tendency in research into ageing has been to use Western models of development to define old age, taking 60/65 as the boundary set by conventional retirement and pension systems. But in some continents (notably Sub-Saharan Africa) old age may be more meaningfully defined as starting from 50 (or even earlier). Access to pension systems to mark the onset of old age is itself a culturally specific process. This is relevant to Western contexts (although changing even here with privatisation), but has limited resonance in countries such as China, where out of 110 million people aged 65 plus, just one quarter are entitled to a pension (Lloyd-Sherlock, 2010). In a number of senses the traditional formulation of 'ageing societies' is unhelpful given global inequalities. Global society contains numerous demographic realities – an ageing Europe certainly, as compared with the increasingly youthful US, and plummeting life expectancy in Russia and Sub-Saharan Africa. Such contrasts create significant variations in the construction of ageing – national, transnational, sub-cultural – producing, as a result, new questions and perspectives for research in gerontology (Dannefer and Phillipson, 2010).

Second, research into the changing lifecourse under the complex pressures of different systemic formations and increasingly diverse life worlds will remain an important concern for work in the field of ageing (reflected in a number of chapters in this volume). An enduring question here concerns the tension between the retention of boundaries between different life stages, and opposing trends towards more open, flexible lifestyles. Social gerontology as a discipline was itself founded on the notion of people occupying roles specific to certain periods of life. Managing the transition from one role to another was viewed as crucial in a successful adjustment to ageing. This may continue as an important theme in some instances (the study of widowhood being one such example). In other instances the idea of clear transitions between different roles may break down as individuals combine work, leisure, caring and personal roles well into advanced old age. This will pose questions about the development of new forms of social engagement in later life, and the different opportunities available to individuals according to class, gender and ethnic position.

Third, following the arguments developed in this chapter, the case might also be made for re-connecting to the original vision of a welfare state with responsibility for promoting the wellbeing of all its citizens. The tendency for capitalism to convert public services into commodities (Navarro, 1976) has been vastly accelerated in the first decade of the 21st century, with the increasing penetration of multinational corporations into the health and social care systems. The dynamics of globalisation require new efforts to protect the life worlds that have become most vulnerable. The evidence suggests that the poorest elderly have been worst affected, with community services for low-income groups most vulnerable to under-funding and potential closure. Deppe (2009, p 36) draws a wider argument from this about the importance of what he calls 'protected social spaces, which are orientated to the common welfare and which cannot be trusted to the blind power of the market.' He argues that:

> We have to respect and sustain areas in which communication and co-operation is not commercialised, where services do not have the character of commodities. Such protected sectors extend from the way vulnerable groups are dealt with ... to social goals such as solidarity and equity and vulnerable communication structures – especially those which are based on confidence like the ... worker–patient relationship. Indeed, these protected social spaces form the basis for a humane social model. (Deppe, 2009, p 36)

Developing such spaces will be especially important given the need to protect people with Alzheimer's and other forms of dementia and those with major physical disabilities from the dangers of abusive relationships, both in the community and in institutional settings.

The need to embed care relationships within spaces that emphasise solidarity over market forces is an important task for gerontologists and others to address. In this context, an important argument for protecting those who are ageing must come from the adoption of the human rights perspective developed in the later writings of Peter Townsend (2007). Townsend highlighted the importance of measures such as the European Convention on Human Rights and the Universal Declaration of Human Rights as offering at the level of global agents a way of challenging the 'structured dependency' of older people. Use of such frameworks may become essential given the rise of care organisations operating across national borders, and the drive to de-regulate and privatise hitherto public services. Townsend argued that problems relating to dependency persisted as a major issue affecting older people, with these problems set to grow in many parts of the world. At the same time, he concluded that:

> Human rights instruments offer hope of breaking down blanket discrimination and of using resources more appropriately, and more generously, according to severity of need. But investment in human rights is not only a moral and quasi-legal salvation from things that are going depressingly wrong. Used best, human rights offer a framework of thought and planning [for] the 21st century that enables society to take a fresh, and more hopeful, direction. (Townsend, 2007, p 43)

Conclusion: contingent and existential limitations

Unless criticism has become an arbitrary stance, critique and meaning must be brought together in some way; even theoretically unarticulated critique originates from rudimentary impressions that certain situations are not as they should be according to the meaning that is implied in the critique. A major problem to address the intersections of existential and structural dimensions is a firmly rooted reductionism from *either* personal and interpersonal perspectives *or* more structurally oriented perspectives. Such reductionist tendencies seem to have been institutionalised, not only in markets and market-like domains of society, but also in the organisation of the disciplines where research on (inter)personal aspects (psychology, social psychology, anthropology, sociology, social work) tends to work in opposition or neglect of more structurally oriented disciplines such as economics or macro-sociology, and vice versa.

One way to undercut reductionist tendencies is to distinguish between limitations that are the inevitable results of senescing and finitude versus problems that are social in origin and can be alleviated. There are many different images and practices regarding aged people, ranging from respect to ageism and disdain. Many of the problems facing ageing people are socially constituted: they are often excluded from influencing the situations in which they live so that the situations would become more adequate regarding the meaning they have for them. Or they are not acknowledged as 'normal' people – whatever that may mean – and are treated in prejudiced ways.

Building on earlier observations in this chapter, an important distinction might be drawn between *contingent* and *existential* limitations (Baars, 2012); what is often called 'contingent', as in the quotation earlier from Settersten and Trauten (2009), is distinguished further in two kinds of limitations or challenges. *Contingent* are those limitations that are neither inherent in human life nor inevitable in senescing, such as poor housing conditions, insufficient care, social isolation, starvation or ageism. They may be the result of lack of knowledge, the (un)intended consequences of certain policies or caused by a lack of interest or respect for the wellbeing of older people. Refusing to accept such limitations and trying to make improvements remain important tasks that should not be taken lightly, and it remains an important domain for critical gerontology (Baars et al, 2006). There are, however, *existential* limitations and vulnerabilities that are inherent in human life and that will inevitably manifest themselves as people live longer. In a culture that celebrates ageing as a vital part of life, these two different kinds of limitations must be distinguished from each other or they will lead to lopsided approaches to ageing. When all limitations are seen as *existential* limitations, ageing people have to accept all circumstances, however dreadful. The mantra in response to any problem or limitations would be: 'It's your age'. For many important problems, this is too easy: often situations can be improved and people can be helped. However, when all limitations are seen as *contingent* limitations – a commercial tendency of late modernity – the illusion develops that one should not have to accept any limitation, that any problem can be solved given the time, money and the determination to do it; even senescing and death would not be exceptions (de Grey, 2005).

Both of these one-sided approaches distort the reality: either they underestimate the capacity to overcome difficulties, or they underestimate the finitude of life. This does not mean that limitations cannot shift: many of the limitations that confronted medieval Europeans, such as bad eyesight or certain infections, later turned out to be contingent and could be helped. And this does not make this distinction superfluous: if a particular problem cannot be overcome in any given situation, it manifests itself as an existential limitation and there is little comfort in the idea that they may be overcome in some distant future where people will probably still be faced with existential limitations.

The potential for change indicates that it is not always easy to make the distinction between contingent and existential limitations. For instance, people are confronted with profound questions such as: 'Will this severe chemotherapy or this highly risky surgery really lead to a better life, or should I concentrate on living the last phase of my life in my home instead of dying in a technological environment?' Deciding whether a limitation must be seen as contingent or existential will often require one to reflect with human sensitivity on people in specific situations. Celebrating ageing as a vital part of life implies recognition of the potentials *and* limitations, the pleasures *and* sufferings, the continuing vitality, competence *and* vulnerability of ageing.

Improving the quality of human ageing depends on both sides of the spectrum, and although late modern society demonstrates that life can be improved in many important ways, human life in general and human ageing in particular pose more questions than social policy or the sciences can answer. Such situations occur throughout life but will become inevitable when people live longer. Here, we need to develop meaningful ways of encountering situations in life that *cannot* be controlled. Late modern cultures of ageing often have difficulty acknowledging and *dignifying* limitations that cannot be overcome but must be respectfully and creatively integrated in ways of living. Acknowledging the dignity of *existential* limitations is essential for the quality of living with them (Baars, 2012).

Even conditions that we cannot change or did not choose do not have to *remain* meaningless. They should at least be *dignified* and, if possible, meaningfully integrated in our lives and in society. Can some harmful event that strikes us as utterly meaningless still ever be or become meaningful? How we can continue to live in a meaningful way when we are confronted with inevitable and in themselves meaningless processes of senescing, being in pain or dying? These are serious and heavy questions that will often find no answer that will allow us to accept what happened. The quality of a society, however, can also be determined by the way it cares for the most vulnerable: even existential limitations that cannot be removed require meaningful responses. When a family member is diagnosed with a severe disease – which is in itself a terrible event – it derives meaning when the family takes care of him/her and uses the unwanted opportunity to reaffirm their love for each other in acts of caring. This kind of meaning is not organised or guaranteed by 'nature', 'fate' or the 'cosmos' but comes from interhuman presence and a care for each other that also requires systemic support and facilitation. It begins with acknowledging the realities of life and asking 'How can we approach this in a meaningful way?' Often, this question will reveal its meaning when we try to find the answers. This does not mean that becoming seriously ill or disabled is meaningful in itself: only our response can give these situations some meaning. Caring for a dying person can be experienced as a precious time, although we would have given anything to avoid his or her death. However, even sincerely trying to find meaning in a situation does not grant us control. When there is no meaningful response, the meaninglessness of life as 'a fact' or as 'something that occurs' stares us in the face.

The question 'Why do we age?' can be taken up in evolutionary terms (narrowing 'ageing' to 'senescing'), trying to answer it in terms of 'disposable soma' (Kirkwood, 1999) or similar theories. We can also try to approach this question in a way that acknowledges processes of senescing but sees them in a broader perspective of human ageing.

References

Achenbaum, W.A. (2007) *Older Americans, vital communities: A bold vision for societal ageing*, Baltimore, MD: The Johns Hopkins University Press.

Baars, J. (2009) 'The crisis of credit, ageing, and the life world', Paper presented at the World Congress of Gerontology, Paris.

Baars, J. (2010a) 'Ageing as increasing vulnerability and complexity: towards a philosophy of the life course', in J. Bouwer (ed) *Successful ageing, spirituality, and meaning*, Leuven: Peeters, pp 39-52.

Baars, J. (2010b) 'Philosophy of ageing, time, and finitude', in T.R. Cole, R. Ray and R. Kastenbaum (eds) *A guide to humanistic studies in ageing*, Baltimore, MD: The Johns Hopkins University Press, pp 105-20.

Baars, J. (2010c) 'Time and ageing: enduring and emerging issues', in D. Dannefer and C. Phillipson (eds) *International handbook of social gerontology*, New York: Sage Publications, pp 367-76.

Baars, J. (2012) *Ageing and the art of living*, Baltimore, MD: The Johns Hopkins University Press.

Baars, J. and Dohmen, J. (forthcoming) *Towards an art of aging: A rediscovery of forgotten texts*, Baltimore, MD: The Johns Hopkins University Press.

Baars, J., Dannefer, D., Phillipson, C. and Walker, A. (eds) (2006) *Ageing, globalization, and inequality: The new critical gerontology*, Amityville, NY: Baywood Publishing.

Bauman, Z. (2000) *Liquid modernity*, Cambridge: Polity Press.

Baumeister, R.F. (1991) *Meanings of life*, New York: Guilford Press.

Baumeister, R.F. and Vohs, K.D. (2005) 'The pursuit of meaningfulness in life', in C.R. Snyder and S.J. Lopez (eds) *Handbook of positive psychology*, New York: Oxford University Press, pp 608-18.

Binstock, R.H. (1983) 'The aged as scapegoat', *The Gerontologist*, vol 23, pp 136-43.

Binstock, R.H. (2010) 'From compassionate ageism to intergenerational conflict?', *The Gerontologist*, vol 50, pp 574-85.

Carstensen, L.L., Mikels, J.A. and Mather, M. (2006) 'Ageing and the intersection of cognition, motivation, and emotion', in J. Birren and K.W. Schaie (eds) *Handbook of the psychology of ageing*, San Diego, CA: Academic Press, pp 343-62.

Cerny, Philip G. and Mark Evans (2004). 'Globalisation and Public Policy Under

New Labour', Policy Studies, vol. 25, no. 1 (March), pp. 51-65

Dannefer, D. and Phillipson, C. (eds) (2010) *The Sage handbook of social gerontology*, London: Sage Publications.

de Grey, A. (2005) 'Foreseeable and more distant rejuvenation therapies', in S.I.S. Rattan (ed) *Ageing interventions and therapies*, Singapore: World Scientific Publishing, pp 379-95.

Deppe, H.-U. (2009) 'The nature of health care: commodification versus solidarity', in L. Panitch and C. Leys (eds) *Morbid symptoms: Health under capitalism*, Socialist Register 2010, London: Lawrence & Derrida, J. (2010) *Voice and phenomenon: Introduction to the problem of the sign in Husserl's phenomenology*, Chicago, IL: Northwestern University Press.

Descartes, R. (1994) *Discourse on method: Meditations and principles*, London: Everyman.

Dittmann-Kohli, F. (2007) 'Temporal references in the construction of self-identity: a life-span approach', in J. Baars and H. Visser (eds) *Ageing and time: Multidisciplinary perspectives*, Amityville, NY: Baywood Publishing, pp 83-119.

Foucault, M. (1994) *The order of things: An archaeology of the human sciences*, New York: Vintage.

Gehlen, A. (1988) *Man: His nature and place in the world*, New York: Columbia University Press.

Gerhardt, V. (1994) 'Sinn des Lebens. Über einen Zusammenhang zwischen antiker und moderner Philosophie', in V. Caysa and K.D. Eichler (eds) *Praxis, Vernuft, Gemeinschaft. Auf der Suche nach einer anderen Vernunft*, Weinheim: Belz Athenäum, pp 371-86.

Giddens, A. (1991) *Modernity and self-identity*, Cambridge: Polity Press.

Habermas, J. (1984) *The theory of communicative action, Vol 1: Reason and the rationalization of society*, Boston, MA: Beacon Press.

Habermas, J. (1987) *The theory of communicative action, Vol 2: Lifeworld and system: A critique of functionalist reason*, Boston, MA: Beacon Press.

Hegel, G.W.F. (1821/1991) *Elements of the philosophy of right*, Cambridge: Cambridge University Press.

Honneth, A. (1995) *The struggle for recognition: The moral grammar of conflicts*, Cambridge, MA: The MIT Press.

Honneth, A. (2007) *Disrespect: The normative foundations of critical theory*, Cambridge: Polity Press.

Kant, I. (1785/1993) *Grounding for the metaphysics of morals* (3rd edn), Cambridge: Hackett.

Kirkwood, T. (1999) *Time of our lives: The science of human ageing*, London: Phoenix.

Lloyd-Sherlock, P. (2010) *Population ageing and international development*, Bristol: The Policy Press.

Luhmann, N. (1996) *Social systems*, Stanford, CA: Stanford University Press.

Lyotard, J.F. (1989) *The differend: Phrases in dispute*, Minneapolis, MN: University of Minnesota Press.

Morgan, J. and Farsides, T. (2009) 'Measuring meaning in life', *Journal of Happiness Studies*, vol 10, no 3, pp 197-214.

Navarro, V. (1976) *Medicine under capitalism*, New York: Prodist.

Phillipson, C. (2009) 'Reconstructing theories of aging: the impact of globalization on critical gerontology', in V. Bengston, D. Gans, N. Putney and M. Silverstein (eds) *Handbook of theories of aging* (2nd edn), New York: Springer, pp 615-28.

Phillipson, C. (2012) 'Globalisation, economic recession and social exclusion: policy challenges and responses', in T. Scharf and N. Keating (eds) *From exclusion to inclusion in old age: A global challenge*, Bristol: The Policy Press, pp 17-32.

Popper, K. (1973) *The open society and its enemies*, New York: Routledge & Kegan Paul.

Russell, B. (1951) *New hopes for a changing world*, London: George Allen & Unwin.

Russell, B. (2009) *Mysticism and logic: And other essays*, Ithaca, NY: Cornell University Press.

Settersten, R. and Trauten, M. (2009) 'The new terrain of old age: hallmarks, freedoms and risks', in V. Bengston, D. Gans, N. Putney and M. Silverstein (eds) *Handbook of theories of aging* (2nd edn), New York: Springer, pp 455-70.

Steger, M.F., Oishi, S. and Kashdan, T.B. (2009) 'Meaning in life across the life span: levels and correlates of meaning in life from emerging adulthood to older adulthood', *The Journal of Positive Psychology*, vol 4, no 1, pp 43-52.

Taylor, C. (1991) *The ethics of authenticity*, Cambridge, MA: Harvard University Press.

Townsend, P. (2007) 'Using human rights to defeat ageism: dealing with policy-induced "structured dependency"', in M. Bernard and T. Scharf (eds) *Critical perspectives on ageing societies*, Bristol: The Policy Press, pp 27-44.

Walker, M.U. (1999) 'Getting out of line: alternatives to life as a career', in M.U. Walker (ed) *Mother time. Woman, ageing, and ethics*, Lanham, NJ: Rowman & Littlefield, pp 97-112.

Walzer, M. (1994) *Thick and thin: Moral argument at home and abroad*, Notre Dame, IN: University of Notre Dame Press.

THREE

My own life:
ethics, ageing and lifestyle

Joseph Dohmen

Life is a battle. (Seneca)

Introduction

In recent decades there has been a shift from what may be termed a politics of emancipation to a politics of life. In a post-traditional society, late modern people, young and old, are individualised and forced to lead a life on the basis of a reflexive lifestyle. Key aims for older people include those associated with positive health and successful ageing. In this chapter I present a moral lifestyle for later life as an alternative to the dominant neoliberal concept of the choice biography. The first part discusses the transition to a politics of life as a daily struggle for a life of one's own. I then show how current moral philosophy responds critically to this modern development. In the last part, I develop a lifestyle for later life. Through a moral lifestyle, older people will be better able to relate to the cultural dictates that confront them, and may together try to reappropriate their own lives.

From emancipation to life politics

Years of emancipation

In 1958, during the Cold War, social liberal Isaiah Berlin published 'Two concepts of liberty'. He pointed at the great importance of *moral* directives for the development of Western culture, and focused on one of the most fundamental concepts of modernity: liberty. Among the many varieties of liberty, he distinguished between two central concepts: negative and positive freedom. Berlin understood negative freedom as non-interference:

> I am normally said to be free to the degree to which no man or body of men interferes with my activity.[...] The criterion of oppression is the part that I believe to be played by other human beings, directly or indirectly, with or without the intention of doing so, in frustrating my wishes. By being free in this sense I mean not being interfered with by others. The wider the area of non-interference the wider my freedom. (Berlin, 1958, p 3)

Berlin's interpretation of the concept of positive freedom is characterised by the notion of self-direction, and produces an uncommonly striking description of late modern self-awareness:

> I wish my life and decisions to depend on myself, not on external forces of whatever kind. I wish to be the instrument of my own, not of other men's, acts of will. I wish to be a subject, not an object; to be moved by reasons, by conscious purposes, which are my own, not by causes which affect me, as it were, from outside. I wish to be somebody, not nobody; a doer – deciding, not being decided for, self-directed and not acted upon by external nature or by other men as if I were a thing, or an animal, or a slave incapable of playing a human role, that is, of conceiving goals and policies of my own and realising them. (Berlin, 1958, p 8)

Because he feared paternalism from party, state and church, Berlin himself preferred a notion of freedom as non-interference. His book was meant to be a statement and did not further deal with a number of important questions, such as, how does negative freedom enable modern individuals to resist 'external' forces and make their own decisions? How can modern people formulate their own goals, realise their strategies and shape their personal autonomy (developing positive freedom via self-direction)?

Over the past few decades the idea of negative freedom has become stronger in Western societies. For 'the free West', the 1960s and 1970s meant the end of so-called natural, hierarchical relations. Freedom movements abounded: workers, students, patients, women, gay people and many other 'suppressed' groups, united to fight for their cause. The interference of employers, professors, the medical order, men and heterosexuals was seen as arbitrary, and their rules were no longer accepted as imperatives. The claim of liberty as a rejection of *every* form of interference was, both in the public and in the private domain, considered more and more self-evident. By the second half of the 20th century freedom had practically become identical to an attitude of '*anything goes*'.

Turn to life politics

Leading sociologists and philosophers such as Zygmunt Bauman, Ulrich Beck, Anthony Giddens, Jürgen Habermas and Charles Taylor, characterise our current age as a 'post-traditional' or 'secular society' (Habermas, 1985; Giddens, 1991; Beck, 1991; Bauman, 1997, 2001; Beck and Beck-Gernsheim, 2002; Taylor, 2007). Western culture has arrived at a new phase of a post-traditional society in which the influence of tradition, religion and morality has been losing its strength. Within this society, public morality has seen an important turn. Giddens characterises this turn as 'the emergence of life politics' (1991, p 209ff). Traditional society has been replaced by an 'improvisational society' in which people are being systematically individualised, and each individual is supposed to develop a lifestyle of his or her own. This raises the question about the conditions of negative and positive freedom once more. According to the individualisation thesis put forward by Beck, postmodern individuality is less concerned with 'being individual', and more with the complex process of 'becoming individual' and the task of leading one's own life (Beck, 1991; Beck and Beck-Gernsheim, 2002).

> There is hardly a desire more widespread in the west today than to lead "a life of your own." If a traveller in France, Finland, Poland, Switzerland, Britain, Germany, Hungary, the USA or Canada asks what really moves people there, what they strove and struggle to achieve, the answer may be money, work, power, love, God or whatever, but it would also be, more and more, the promise of "a life of one's own." [...] It would be only a slight exaggeration to say that the daily struggle for a life of one's own has become the collective experience of the Western world. It expresses the remnant of our communal feeling. (Beck and Beck-Gernsheim, 2002, p 22)

Although emancipation battles still exist in certain contexts, a clear shift can be identified from a *struggle for emancipation* to a *life politics*, the latter involving questions relating to the meaning of one's own identity. New life questions concern orientation and identity: who am

I? What is my origin? Who do I want to be and how should I shape my existence? It is not easy to find answers to these questions without the interference and support of others. Modern individuals need support in learning how to relate to the new post-traditional and secularised order in which new life forms are being individualised, and the question of how modern they can succeed in this struggle for a life of their own has become urgent.

Life politics and ageing

The developments described above also affect the process of ageing. The 'struggle for a life of one's own' means that, nowadays, every single individual has to grow old *in his or her own way*. The notion of a lifecourse in three, four or seven stages or phases – all pre-modern 'cosmic' classifications – has been abandoned once and for all. The new development concerns more ambitious plans for old age, as a result of the neoliberal story of a biography of choice. At the same time there is a lack of obvious examples of how modern old age might be shaped. This leads to a fundamental question: how can we grow old in a *good* way? Or, as it is nowadays usually expressed, how can we 'age well'?

According to Giddens (1991), a late modern life politics is fundamentally concerned with three key problems: on what experts and expert knowledge should we base our lives, with whom do we connect and which lifestyle do we choose. Answering these questions is indispensable for late modern individuals to obtain self-assurance and mutual respect. Lifestyle is the key concept from which people choose experts, develop relations and form their identity.

The question of late modern identity also applies to ageing individuals. Moreover, a number of supplementary conditions of a demographic, social-economic and cultural nature are applicable. First, there are demographic factors such as a longer and healthier life expectancy. We observe here a double dynamics of ageing: a significant number of people getting older and a growing number getting older than ever before (Baars, 2012). Moreover, older people are remaining more vital and healthy for a longer time, with the deferring of those conditions associated with dependency. Second, a diversity of social and economic factors is at play. Historically, government policy has been centred round the male career and the woman's focused on the provision of care. The modern course of life has greater variations in social roles, and demands far more improvisation. Finally, there are cultural factors that influence the lifestyles of older people. More and more people are diverging from the standard lifecourse in terms of learning–working–resting and want to live 'with a wider scope'. The most notable divergence is the choice biography. Modern individuals prefer to live a varied life and do not want to be focused just on their families or careers. They prefer to combine a great number of activities, such as learning, working, caring, travelling and enjoying leisure activities. Modernisation and individualisation imply a continuous process of *deskilling* and *reskilling*, and learning has become an activity extending throughout the whole lifespan: 'lifelong learning'. 'Anything goes' and 'the sky is the limit' are famous post-traditional slogans.

Struggle for a life of one's own: opportunities and risks

Although the post-traditional order offers many opportunities, the individual is not automatically capable of coping with this complicated multitude of choices. At one level, there is an increase of freedom, with people's fate no longer traditionally fixed by class, gender or ethnicity. Identity now also depends on how someone develops him or herself and the orientation and lifestyle chosen. The democratic constitutional state basically guarantees our liberty, equality and safety, and because of higher standards of living, many people are well educated, can earn sufficient money, acquire goods, travel, entertain themselves; in brief, they do whatever they want. This is, of course, the neoliberal story. In reality, numerous social scripts, forms of system pressure, economical and socio-cultural rules frame individual lives and determine the limits of people's possibilities to create their own lifestyles. The ideology of the choice biography does not automatically lead to equal opportunities for choosing (Bauman, 2001; Beck, 2002; Baars, 2006b).

Recent moral philosophical reflections on life politics

Since the 1970s and 1980s, modern ethics and moral philosophy have been subject to a number of important and very different reactions to the progressive de-traditionalisation, secularisation and individualisation, and in particular to the dominant neoliberal morality of self-determination. These reactions consist of new moral perspectives on the development of Western culture, life politics and the quality of life, illustrated in areas such as: the ethics of self-care (Foucault, 1985), the ethics of autonomy (Frankfurt, 1988), the ethics of authenticity (Taylor, 1991), the ethics of virtue (MacIntyre, 1981/1985) and the ethics of care (Gilligan, 1982).

Part of this debate, particularly the conflict between the ethics of autonomy and the ethics of care, has been reviewed in 'Ethics and old age' (Holstein, 2010a, p 630ff). Holstein observes that the bio-ethical perspective has been dominant since the beginning of the 1980s. This perspective focuses on the value of autonomy, and the moral principles of beneficence, non-maleficence (no harm) and justice (Beauchamp and Childress, 1980). Informed consent forms the basis for this approach. The question of how respect for autonomy can best be expressed as older people are increasingly less able to make their own decisions (Agich, 1990, 1995; Dworkin, 1993) takes central place in discussions in this area. Holstein points out that for many individuals and families, autonomy is a myth. The discussion on the absence of social and economic conditions that make autonomy nearly impossible for large numbers of older people, '[has] received far less attention than did individual choice' (Holstein, 2010a, p 632). 'While I view autonomy as important, [...] I do not see it as a property of isolated individuals but as the product of, and bound up with, relationships' (Holstein, 2010a, p 631). Holstein herself prefers the (feminist) perspective of the ethics of care, where care instead of autonomy is considered the most important moral value. This is also consistent with the ideas of critical gerontology, which stress the social context of late modern individuals. She concludes her overview with an urgent plea, 'that we see ethics as an ally in whatever efforts we make to help more people achieve a good old age. At the end of life as at the beginning, we need love and support as much or more than we need the chance to decide' (Holstein, 2010a, p 638).

Many important points are developed in the above view; equally, however, a number of complex issues are left unresolved. To consider these, the next section presents a brief survey of a number of normative ethical perspectives. Each moral philosophy can be shown to highlight specific aspects of a moral lifestyle. Following this discussion, a moral lifestyle for later life is developed, framed within the philosophical perspectives reviewed in this chapter.

Ethics of self-care

'So we are all artists on our lives – knowingly or not, willingly or not, like it or not. To be an artist means to give form and shape to what otherwise would be shapeless or formless' (Bauman, 2008, p 125). Bauman is the representative of a recent moral philosophical tradition that propagates the art of living and self-care (Shusterman, 1992; Hadot, 1995; Nehamas, 1998; Schmid, 1998; Kekes, 2002; Ziguras, 2004; Dohmen, 2007, 2010, 2011; Höffe, 2007; Bauman, 2008; Sloterdijk, 2009). This ethical approach is based on the later work of Michel

Foucault, who considered self-care from four connected points of view: the 'moral ontology': *what do you care for?* The 'moral deontology': *what urges you to care for yourself?* The ethical work or 'moral ascetics': *how do you care for yourself?* Finally, the 'moral teleology': *for what purpose do you care for yourself?* Self-care is thus a layered concept, in which subject, object, context, methods and goals are united. Foucault (1997) specified this ethics of self-care as a *practice of freedom*, and he had an autonomous and vital lifestyle in mind: practice self-care and remain open to change and renewal in a dynamic society.

Ethics of autonomy

The concept of autonomy is currently used in different ways. It is seen as the capacity or the power of self-rule, as a condition, a character ideal and as a right (Feinberg, 1989). The discussion about the interpretation of positive freedom is about autonomy as capacity and as a condition. Notable proponents of this type of ethics include Harry Frankfurt (1971, 1988), Ronald Dworkin (1989), Diana Meyers (1989), Thomas Cole (1992) and Peter Bieri (2006). Theories about positive freedom define autonomy as the result of the development of personal will. Ultimately, positive freedom is concerned with the capacity to give one's own life direction and meaning. Frankfurt (1971, 1988) has searched for the most characteristic definition of a person. According to him, this definition has to be found in a certain structure of personal will. People can desire for a desire. Frankfurt calls the ordinary desires *first order* desires. *Second order* desires are the desires to have a certain desire or not. A person, then, is somebody who can form second order desires: volitions. People are pre-eminently characterised by the fact that they may want to be different in their preferences and goals than they are at the moment. Having second order desires requires reflective self-evaluation (Frankfurt, 1988, p 11ff.)

Bieri further elaborated this theory in *Das Handwerk der Freiheit* (2006). According to Bieri there are three dimensions to this 'handwork of freedom': articulation, understanding and approving. Articulation relates to a correct expression of what one wants. Understanding addresses the fact that our desires are often non-transparent to ourselves and require further clarification. Finally, approval from the self is required: one has to agree with what one wants. In this way one becomes an autonomous person.

Ethics of authenticity

According to Taylor, authenticity is the foremost important moral ideal of our time. This ideal stems from Romanticism and can be characterised with the following quote: 'There is a certain way of being human that is *my* way. I am called up to live my life in this way, and not in imitation of anyone else's. But this gives a new importance to being true to myself. If I am not, I miss the point of my life, I miss what is being human for *me*' (Taylor, 1991, p 28). Taylor, however, rejects pure self-centredness and the inner monologue. He claims that authenticity should have two qualities. First, the authentic self should be fundamentally prepared to enter into a dialogue with others. Authenticity presupposes a dialogue about *hypergoods*. And second, we have to make *strong evaluations* (Taylor, 1985). To be autonomous it is sufficient to base one's acting on second order desires. Taylor underscores the importance of evaluating these desires in terms of value – strong evaluations presuppose an evaluating language that ranks these values in a certain hierarchy. Such a language uses contrasting concepts such as high and low, better and worse, integrated and fragmented. Personal choices based on dialogue and strong evaluations create an authentic way of life.

Ethics of virtue

Two schools have dominated political ethics during the past few decades: liberalism and communitarianism. Political liberalism looks on society as an assembly of individuals (Rawls, 1971; Dworkin, 1993), whereas communitarianism emphasises people embedded in society and tradition (Etzioni, 1996; Kekes, 2002; MacIntyre, 1981/1985). The communitarian Alasdair MacIntyre saw man as a social being, that is, morality founded within the community, and people forming a political community from a shared history. According to MacIntyre, Western society has lost any comprehension of morality. Modern Western culture not only lacks an all-embracing and integrated morality, but also an understanding of the meaning of morality for human life as such. The purpose of MacIntyre's *After virtue* is to retrieve this lost notion of morality, and he returns to the virtue ethics of Aristotle (see Aristotle, 1984). Aristotle observed a teleological pattern in reality and in human action: everything was goal-oriented. He argued that all human goals were hierarchically ordered, eventually serving one ultimate goal or purpose, and the purpose of life was to fulfil oneself in a good society; this was called happiness.

MacIntyre rejected the metaphysical biology of Aristotle, and tried to integrate the virtues into social practices such as the sciences, the arts, family life and sports. The participants in such a practice agreed on the goals and the common good of their practice. The virtues then served the practice, the participants and the tradition from which this practice sprang. In contrast to MacIntyre, most modern virtue ethicists are not anti-modernist (Slote, 1992; Ruddick, 1989; Sennett, 1998). The ethics of virtue is a modern form of moral education, directed at the formation of character with virtues such as discipline, integrity, openness, respect, responsibility, tolerance and care.

Ethics of care

Carol Gilligan's book *In a different voice* (1982) is often mentioned as a starting point for the ethics of care. Gilligan's book stimulated heated debates in moral philosophy, because many women (and men) recognised a large number of moral aspects in her descriptions which had been missing in the accepted morality of autonomy and justice. These include the priority of the value of care and engagement over the value of autonomy; context (*bottom up*) and a concrete practice instead of principles (*top down*), and abstract, non-functional theorising; to have an eye for relations, vulnerability and dependency instead of a focus on independence and strength; the importance of emotions; connection instead of separation; and preference for matching virtues of attention and mutual responsibility. All these aspects became object of study in a new *ethics of care* (see Noddings, 1986; Ruddick, 1989; Tronto, 1993; Baier, 1994; Held, 1995, 2006; Kittay, 1999; Walker, 2007; cf also Held, 2007). The ethics of care is a situated and contextual, practice-related ethics, emphasising relations, processes, virtues and attitudes that put separate situations and actions in a specific moral perspective. The main point of care ethics is not *what* you are living for, but *with whom* and *for whom*. It is an ethics of responsibility.

Ethics, ageing and lifestyle

Ethics and the struggle for one's own life

The current moral debate which has developed since the 1980s between the ethics of self-care, the protagonists of autonomy and authenticity, the ethics of virtue and the ethics of care, is the outcome of philosophical reflexions on the post-traditional order, the dominance of the market, and late-modern individualisation. The consequences of the neoliberal discourse, both for the quality of society and for personal life, are the starting point of diverging moral-philosophical reflections. Modern individuals are increasingly disengaging from 'history, nature, society, the demands of solidarity' (Taylor, 1991: 40). Many well-known complaints are shared by these different moral views: heteronomy, commodification, inauthenticity and the lack of engagement. Yet the solutions vary radically.

In a general sense many critical questions are asked about the concept of one's 'own life' and the neo-liberal preference of choice and self-determination. Giddens' (1991, p 81) frequently quoted statement: 'the only choice we have is to choose' implicates that choice is rather a matter of necessity than of freedom. There are numerous social scripts for later life, so it is not true that people can grow older *unconditionally* in their own way (Baars, 2006b; Dannefer and Kelley-Moore, 2009). If Berlin's premise is correct that one is free 'when not interfered', then modern people are not free at all when one considers the interference of structural arrangements concerning ageing. An individual's struggle to lead his or her own life and to grow older in his or her own way would then be a lost cause from the start. In spite of this, people often *believe* that they are radically free to lead their own lives and feel that they themselves are in fact responsible for their course of life. When they do not reach their goals and their lives are painful, they may feel guilty because they think that they have made the wrong choices. Since welfare state arrangements are increasingly being cut back, people are increasingly held responsible for their ways of life (accommodation, work, income, education, health), without adequate conditions for good citizenship. In brief: there are always conditions that are rather expropriating, and conditions that obstruct the appropriation of one's own life

Finally, it is important to ask: *what does it mean to lead a life of one's own?* Again, in a general sense this expression seems to refer to a state of independence and maybe even invulnerability. The struggle to lead one's own life means the struggle to act and live as independently and unhindered by others as much as possible. This is precisely the ideological impression of things 'in the American context, where individualism and independence are central to national self-identity' (Holstein, 2010a, p 632)

One's own ageing

In 1933, the psychiatrist Carl Gustav Jung wrote an essay entitled 'The stages of life'. In this essay he came to the conclusion that adults

generally 'started the second half of their life completely unprepared.'
(Jung, 1933). Young people were educated to discover future goals to
focus on and develop skills to achieve them. Older people may or may
not have already reached their goals and were therefore not in need
of further training and education. Subsequently, they went on with
their lives with very outdated 'existential' programmes and as a result,
many suffered from depression. According to Jung, 'the afternoon of
life should also possess its own meaning and purpose. Growing old
in a meaningful way was not just looking back at one's life, but also
looking ahead, to set oneself new goals and to aim at further wisdom.

Four decades later, Simone de Beauvoir complained, in *The coming
of age* (1972), about the way in which old age took shape in Western
culture. She criticised philosophers in the process and concluded:

> Morality preaches a calm resignation to the evil that science
> and technology cannot avoid: pain, illness, old age. Even the
> effort to bear our decay courageously is, one says, a way
> to grow mentally. But that is only word play. Projects refer
> only to our activities and to experience your age is not an
> activity. To grow up, mature, grow old and die: the passage
> of time is your destiny. (de Beauvoir, 1972, p 540)

De Beauvoir preferred as a conclusion a much more activist approach
than even Jung:

> In order to prevent that old age becomes a ridiculous
> travesty of our previous life, there is only one possibility:
> to pursue a goal that gives meaning to our life. To devote
> oneself to people, groups of people, an activity, social,
> political, intellectual, creative work. It is to be hoped, and
> this goes right against the advice of the moralists, that our
> passions remain sufficiently strong at an older age to prevent
> that we turn inward. (de Beauvoir, 1972, p 540)

Half a century later, we might ask ourselves whether we really do
have a culture of good ageing, either in an active sense or in a more
detached way, or a combination thereof. We have the half romantic,
half neo-liberal 'invitation' to age in our own way in 'the third age'
(Laslett, 1989; see also Chapter Four, this volume). And we have the
invitation to develop a more careful attitudes toward vulnerable older
people. Although we might hope to receive support from experts and
significant others, in the end we all are urged to make our own choices.

But how, and why? The next section of this chapter develops a moral lifestyle for later life, based on recent moral philosophy.

A moral lifestyle for later life

Ageing is both a natural and a culturally determined process with a complex relation between pros and cons. In the current post-traditional society, people are encouraged to grow older in their own way. The lifestyle concept may serve, possibly supported by experts and significant others, to give direction to ageing in a morally responsible way. What should such a moral lifestyle for later life look like? The arguments below integrate elements from the moral debate elaborated thus far in this chapter. The discussion develops a new idea of lifestyle as a fundamental concept to bridge the gap between agency and structure.

According to Giddens, lifestyle is a typical post-traditional phenomenon. It only occurs at a time when people no longer live by traditional role patterns, and have a great number of choices. Giddens gives several definitions of lifestyle: 'A lifestyle can be defined as a more or less integrated set of practices which an individual embraces, not only because such practices fulfil utilitarian needs, but because they give material form to a particular narrative of self-identity.' (1991, p 81). A lifestyle therefore refers to a collection of reflexively organized routines and practices regarding, for example, food, clothing, and ways of trading and meeting. In this way, a lifestyle provides coherence and gives shape to someone's physical and mental life. A lifestyle, as a pattern of behaviour, offers orientation and guidance, and always takes place within the so-called *lifestyle sectors*: time-space 'slices' in which certain practices are shaped, such as the way people spend their weekends. Life choices also always presuppose certain life chances, and thus a certain degree of emancipation. Thanks to a lifestyle, people can plan their lives and design their own future. Partly due to the modern pluralisation of social spheres, where people from all kinds of different milieus can meet, late-modern lifestyles are in principle subject to change. Lifestyles are created through the market and the media, through peer pressure, and through role models holding up their life choices as an example to the public. Lifestyles create a relative measure of autonomy in late modernity, where making a choice is inevitable.

In a further development within social gerontology, Hendricks and Hatch (2009) proposed to use the concept of lifestyle to bridge the gap between the concepts of agency and structure. They show that agency is generally connected with 'life choices', whereas structure is linked to 'life chances'– or the lack of these. Agency is often presented in terms of positive concepts like choice, empowerment and reflexivity, whereas structure is associated with limitations, power and repression. Older people have little agency ascribed to them in the social and scientific discourse. When they are discussed, the emphasis lies more on their limitations. The concept of 'lifestyle', according to Hendricks and Hatch, can pre-eminently show the interaction between life choices and life chances. On the one hand, someone's lifestyle is the expression of the personal choices he or she made in his or her life, on the other hand, the available possibilities of choice as perceived by someone, are from the start influenced by the structural factors that determine his or her situation.

Hendricks and Hatch (2009) apply the concept of lifestyle as a mediating concept between agency and structure that embodies the various ways in which people are ageing, particularly to choices of behaviour in relation to one's health. The approach taken in this chapter differs in two important respects: first, lifestyle is taken to be a fundamentally holistic *moral* concept, and the suggestion is that it should be used in a much broader context than health alone. Second, the discussion will show that the concept of lifestyle, understood as the practice of freedom, could be meaningful in a broad view of 'ageing well'

Reflective distance

Currently, there exist many views about ageing which work in an expropriating way for older people, either because they deem them incapable of meaningful activities, or because they want to discipline them in a certain way. Older people get a lot of advice, which varies from *skilling* and *deskilling* to being actively successful or detaching oneself. They are continuously exposed to a commercial lifestyle supposedly attending to their needs. Even the appeal to shape one's life and to grow old in one's own way is a cultural matter and not at all self-evident. The first task of a moral lifestyle for later life should thus be to critically distance oneself from all directives about how one should grow older. The late modern course of life has, time and again, been portrayed as a biography of choice, which is quite complex because social scripts are drawn up and implemented everywhere by the government, sciences and the market. For a late modern lifestyle it is first of all important to explore our conditional freedom and the limits of our manoeuvring space.

Expropriation

Growing older can be understood as a continuous process of expropriation and appropriation. Growing older with a moral lifestyle not only assumes the awareness of the general conditions of life, but also the investigation of one's own particular biographical circumstances. People can be heavily disciplined during their lives by their parents, the church, or by a certain ideology. Take, for example, the woman who has always followed her husband. He always selected the holiday locations, he chose hotels, restaurants, menus. This woman did not really live in her own time, but in *his* time. Look at the compulsive philosopher who has been working feverishly, but without pleasure, on his own oeuvre. Suddenly he realises that his father's voice has kept him all those years from doing something completely different. He realizes that he has always lived in a time of expectation. For these reasons Isaiah Berlin wrote his plea for non-interference: the sharp delineating of a domain of negative freedom and self-determination.

Ageing means, in this aspect of a late modern lifestyle, trying to free oneself gradually from influences that have been dominant over earlier phases of the life course. Other examples are people who have become addicted during their youth or people with little self-control. A certain degree of inner freedom means a more open way of life and a new experience of time. An important instrument to remove inner obstacles may be identified in terms of narratives or life-reviews (Butler, 1963, 1974; Bendien, 2010, Bohlmeiyer and Westerhof, 2010). This second aspect of lifestyle concerns the importance of discovering one's own forms of expropriation. If one succeeds in this, the future may restore the past, in one way or another.

Appropriation

It is important for older people to remain vital and to set goals for themselves. The question is, however, *what* goals, and why? The principal recommendation of the protagonists of autonomy is to discover one's own scope. The formation of personal will occurs within a space that has not been created by the individual. Our wishes and which of them will eventually lead to action, depend on many things that are not within our control. Society opens the space for our desires; the rest is up to the individual.

At this point important questions are raised such as: *where do I stand? How did I reach this point? What do I still expect from my life and in which way do I want to proceed from here?* Reflective control of our will remains of great importance in later life. Gauguin left his wife and four children and went to paint on an island in the South Pacific. Not many people can and will make such a radical new start. Yet ageing means trying to make your life really your *own* life. Self-care and the art of living apply to concrete actions taken throughout the life course.

We have to make many substantial decisions in our life: to marry or not; to have children or not; to pursue an ambitious career or to study, or just hang around, to travel or to stay at home, to live a healthy life or not. It is important to keep living in view of an open future, and therefore to examine our desires and determine what we really want. This aspect of late modern lifestyle is about appropriation of our self, our own will. Some important substantial choices everybody needs to make for later life are: to be ambitious or more detached; to be either withdrawn or play a more public role; to live alone or with others; to focus on your own well-being or on also taking care of others; to be either mild or severe on yourself; to live a fragmented or an integrated life; and last but not least, to struggle with finiteness or to live with a peaceful mind.

Orientation

The question remains whether such an autonomous lifestyle is sufficient for a meaningful life. Taylor (1991, p 40) rejects the late-modern tendency 'to bracket out history, nature, society, the demands of solidarity, everything but what I find in myself.' Therefore he pleads for authenticity, based on dialogue and a moral horizon. An autonomous lifestyle differs from an authentic lifestyle. The main distinction being that the autonomous individual makes weak evaluations and brings his own desires reflectively under control, whereas the authentic individual tries to make strong evaluations by asking himself what the value of his own desires is. People who evaluate strongly, orient themselves and think about what sort of life they want to lead and which desires are sufficiently valuable to give depth to their life. To make contact with a *hypergood* of a dominant value horizon, and to subsequently use this value as a guiding principle, is an important condition for a meaningful human life. Taylor calls this 'personal resonance'. A further aspect of the late modern lifestyle is the quest for what makes our own lives really valuable and therefore meaningful. Moreover, each authentic individual requires his own virtuousness. A strong evaluation requires patience, attention, discipline, courage, enduring tensions and dealing with mistakes.

Engagement

Neo-liberal morality of self-determination and non-interference arouses a fear of paternalism rather than an atmosphere of mutual engagement. In opposition to an individualistic concept of agency, the care ethicist Margaret Walker (2007) developed a theory of agency in terms of engagement and responsibility. During our life course we participate in a variety of relationships: as a child at home and in school; later as an adult, in relationships and organisations; as a citizen, volunteer, or as care-receiver and caretaker. Hence we are time and again confronted with our own and other people's responsibilities. Although we cannot simply make claims on others or vice versa, we do, in fact, live in a sphere of mutual expectations and trust, which refer to our previous relationships We are dependent on the decisions of others, just like others depend on our decisions. In Walker's view the concept of one's own life does not refer to a story of self-fulfilment. Rather, one's own life refers to a series of dynamic and social practices, which are lived and described from the evaluative perspectives of all concerned. Neither autonomy nor authenticity, but engagement and responsibility should be the most important *hypergoods* of a moral lifestyle.

A very important and substantial decision for older people living a moral lifestyle is to lead an engaged life. This might include being an adviser or counsellor to young people, working in non-governmental organisations (NGOs), a career in politics, the care of children and grandchildren, or voluntary work. It is important to respect the chain of generations, and to devote oneself to the fate of future generation. (McAdams, 1993; Erikson, 1997; de Lange, 2010). Looking at myself from the end of my life, this question is of major importance: how involved and engaged was my life?

Integration and time

'Our society lacks a concept of a life as a whole.' This is a famous dictum from Erik Erikson (1997). Life as a whole is, however, a precarious notion, since late modern life in a post-traditional order often leads to fragmented rather than well-integrated lives. Yet even a late modern lifestyle needs to be concerned with creating and maintaining a certain coherence in one's own life.

'My own life' refers to my biography, to my life from the past to the present and into the future. Many biographies are situated on a continuum between maximal integration and abandoning the idea of integration. Personal identity, time and morality are inherently connected. For autonomous thinkers minimal integration is sufficient and it will do when desires for later life have a certain coherence with the past. When I make a substantial decision, I do so because my will fits best with my identity 'until now'. Williams (1981) took a further step by linking integration with the idea of constitutive projects, that give direction and coherence to our life. Taylor (1989, 2007) takes it even further with a holistic vision that aims at maximal integration. Personal identity is about our *entire* life. Coherence within our life is formed by our orientation on what we consider to be our own highest or deepest values. Integration, then, is a goal-oriented movement and refers to an ever-deepening fulfilment.

Female authors in particular have opposed this type of 'whole life ethics' in general (Meyers, 1989; Strawson, 2004; Walker, 2007). The diachronic picture of life as a coherent whole on the basis of a reflexive lifestyle, a constitutive project or a hypergood, does not correspond with the episodic nature of many people's experiences, in particular women and people from a lower social class (Walker, 1999). The subjective story of 'my own life' needs to be replaced by a relational vision on agency based on intersubjectivity, in which justice is done to the interconnectedness of the various small and large histories of people. The idea of integration as the coherence of an individual life should be abandoned in favour of a local reliability and responsibility for each other.

For a late modern moral lifestyle for later life it is important to safeguard the connection of one's own life with others, especially with a view about a meaningful life. In my view, autonomy, authenticity, care and responsibility do not mutually exclude each other. Each of us has to solve the tensions between these different moral values of our life in his or her own way.

Serenity

Taking distance, autonomy, authenticity, engagement and responsibility are the active modes of a contemporary moral lifestyle. They are indispensable to a meaningful life, yet lack an important dimension: the tragic. Ageing well also means considering 'the fragility of goodness' (Nussbaum, 1986). Ageing is not only a matter of control, but also of understanding the fundamental fragility of human life.

First of all, life is tragically subjected to the blind course of 'world events'. Setbacks and misfortune may happen beyond our control and without our fault. When we enter emotional bonds with friends, beloved ones and family members, all mortal beings, our life also depends on such irreplaceable ties of affection. Our happiness in life is just as vulnerable as those ties themselves. As we grow older, the chance that our network of loved ones will disintegrate becomes larger and larger. There is no possible control over this part of human condition. Another reason why human vulnerability cannot be undone is that valuable matters in our life are not necessarily commensurable; we often have to make resolute assessments. This may bring us into situations where we have to choose between two loyalties, values or even obligations that do not support each other. Growing old is full of difficult life choices and the 'right' choice is a matter of moral luck.

Finally, a human life can be destroyed from within. Passions we cannot control may darken our vision, which lead us to take the wrong decisions or even to act immorally. Since nearly everybody is beset by such passions at some fateful moment, we need to practice remorse. True remorse is the pain and regret about this period during which we have temporarily lost our rational control (Bieri, 2006).

Ageing well is thus not only a matter of an active lifestyle, but also of a certain resignation and serenity. As we grow older and have left the largest part of our lives behind us but still have a limited time to live, we experience time differently. When life offers more memories than expectations, what, then, will be our fundamental mood? We may try to reconcile ourselves with our past, but this might not always succeed. We have to gradually develop a lifestyle of serenity, in which acceptance, peace of mind and letting go play an increasingly larger role. The backbone of a late modern lifestyle is to find a balance between active control and resignation. The greatest joy of life may lie in something we have not actively pursued, but that befalls us.

Finitude

Finally, late modern people have to learn the *ars moriendi*, originally a Roman, early Christian and medieval art. Because of our active and ambitious lives we are not easily prepared to accept finiteness. At the same time everything in our life is finite: our youth, parenthood, love, friendship, knowledge, meetings, results, and even fame. Baars (2012) describes this in terms of 'finitisation', which implies a continuous dynamic between mourning and accepting our losses and new beginnings. At the real end of life we meet death. What kind of a person should we have been? What do we want to leave behind for our beloved ones, for society, or even for our planet? Maybe we have the courage to realise how we lived our life. If we discover why we have lived, and realise our moral luck and our stupidities, we may be able to reconcile ourselves with death.

Conclusion

Following Holstein (2010b), we must see ethics as the effort to help more people achieve a 'good old age'. The aim of this chapter has been to propose a moral lifestyle for later life in the context of a post-traditional society. I have shown that in the past half-century, the dominant politics of emancipation in Western society has given way to a politics of life. Although the aspect of emancipation will never fully disappear, and must be addressed from the point of view of justice over and over again, mainstream thinking and acting today circles around a politics of identity. The new questions are: *who am I? What kind of life do I want to lead? To whom should I relate?*

In the daily struggle for one's own life, the late modern individual looks for safety and control, resilience and empowerment. The actual struggle is also about relationship, engagement and finding one's position in a larger entity. Resilience and engagement are two important aspects of the late modern lifestyle. The question of how modern individuals succeed in this struggle for a life of their own has attained great urgency. The main problem here is: what does it mean to 'succeed' in this struggle? Today's life politics, especially the widely acclaimed notion of 'a life of one's own', has been interpreted in a strongly individualist manner, partly due to the dominant culture of neoliberalism. Many late modern individuals have become very self-centred and are susceptible to commodification.

For a number of decades, moral philosophy has exerted two kinds of critical responses to neoliberalist thought. One of these critiques is precisely a defence of individualism. The commonsense view of the current choice biography does not make people autonomous or authentic. This critique is thus aimed at the lack of resilience of the individual. The other critique is also very anti-liberal but anti-individualist. The liberal choice biography does no justice to people's longing for community and connectedness. The idea of negative freedom does not inspire engagement and responsibility.

In the context of ageing, the struggle for a life of one's own means that every single individual nowadays has to grow old in his or her own way. This struggle goes on, and hence, doesn't suddenly end when people reach middle age. Moreover, the struggle is thus not just about health or successful ageing, and definitely not about commodification. So, in this chapter, I have developed a broad moral lifestyle for later life, which is pluralist in the sense that resilience and engagement are closely linked.

The moral philosophical debate on the content of a moral lifestyle is partly about what the starting point should be: autonomy or care? Martha Holstein states: 'I do not see it as a property of isolated individuals but as the product of, and bound up with, relationships' (2010a, p 634). I definitely agree with the latter half of that remark – autonomy is bound up with relationships. But autonomy is most certainly not just the product of relations. And the caregiver decides for himself/herself whether and when he/she takes care of another or not. Therefore, both these moral values – care and autonomy – are of vital importance in later life. After all, authenticity is quintessential for late modern people, since no lifestyle can be durable if one does not believe, truly and from within, in what one thinks and does. The truth of virtue ethics is that values need practical maintenance, for example, through attention, discipline, patience and respect. Just as it is wrong to vote for either autonomy or care, it is equally dangerous to argue for either an active or a passive lifestyle. An active lifestyle is necessary, but every human life knows its own tragedies, and the only remedy for that is serenity.

In conclusion, a moral lifestyle must also be an ethics of finitude. With every ownership (a life of one's own) comes learning to accept loss. The discussion here suggests that it is important to hold on to the notion of a life of one's own as a core concept for late modernity. But this notion deserves a different, better interpretation than the neoliberal interpretation in terms of negative freedom. My proposal is that we should try to live our own lives with a moral lifestyle, a theme that has been reviewed in a range of arguments developed in this chapter.

References

Agich, G. (1990) 'Reassessing autonomy in long-term care', *Hastings Center Report*, vol 20, no 6, pp 12-17.

Agich, G. (1995) 'Actual autonomy and long-term care decision making', in L.B. McCullough and N.L. Wilson (eds) *Long-term care decision: Ethical and conceptual dimensions*, Baltimore, MD: The Johns Hopkins University Press, pp 113-36.

Aristotle (1984) 'The Nicomachean ethics', in *The complete works of Aristotle, The revised Oxford edition* (edited by J. Barnes), Princeton: Princeton University Press, Part II, 1729-1867.

Baars, J. (2006a) 'Beyond neomodernism, antimodernism, and postmodernism: Basic categories for contemporary critical gerontology', in J. Baars, D. Dannefer, C. Phillipson and A. Walker (eds) *Aging, globalization and inequality: The new critical gerontology*, Amityville, New York: Baywood Publishing, pp 17-42.

Baars, J. (2006b) *Het nieuwe ouder worden. Paradoxen en perspectieven van leven in de tijd* (2nd edn) [The new ageing: Paradoxes and perspectives of living in time], Amsterdam: SWP.

Baars, J. (2012) *Aging and the art of living*, Baltimore, MD: The Johns Hopkins University Press.

Baier, A. (1994) *Moral prejudice: Essays on ethics*, Cambridge, MA: Harvard University Press.

Bauman, Z. (1997) *Life in fragments: Essays in postmodern morality*, Oxford: Blackwell Publishers.

Bauman, Z. (2001) *The individualized society*, Cambridge: Polity Press.

Bauman, Z. (2008) *The art of life*, Stafford: Polity Press.

Beck, U. (1992) *Risk society: Towards a new modernity*, London: Sage Publications.

Beck, U. and Beck-Gernsheim, E. (2002) *Individualization: Institutionalized individualism and its social and political consequences*, London: Sage Publications.

Bendien, E.M. (2010) *From the art of remembering to the craft of ageing*, Rotterdam: Stichting Humanitas Huisdrukkerij.

Berlin, I. (1958) 'Two concepts of liberty', in I. Berlin (1969) *Four essays on liberty*, Oxford: Oxford University Press, pp 118-72.

Bieri, P. (2006) *Das Handwerk der Freiheit: Über die Entdeckung des eigenen Willens* [The craft of freedom: About the discovery of one's own free will], Frankfurt am Main: Fischer-Taschenbuch-Verlag.

Bohlmeijer, E.T. and Westerhof, G.J. (2010) 'Reminiscence interventions. Bringing narrative gerontology into practice', in G. Kenyon, E.T. Bohlmeijer and W.L. Randall (eds) *Storying later life*, New York: Oxford University Press, pp 273-93.

Butler, R.N. (1963) 'The life review: An interpretation of reminiscence in the aged', *Psychiatry*, vol 26, pp 65-76.

Butler, R.N. (1974) 'Successful ageing and the role of the life review', *Journal of the American Geriatrics Society*, vol 22, pp 529-35.

Cole, T. (1992) *The journey of life: A cultural history of aging in America*, Cambridge: Cambridge University Press.

Dannefer, D. and Kelley-Moore, J.A. (2009) 'Theorizing the life course: New twists in the path', in V. Bengtson, M. Silverstein and N. Putney (eds) *Handbook of theories of aging*, New York: Springer, pp 389-412.

de Beauvoir, S. (1972) *The coming of age,* New York: Putnam.

de Lange, F. (2010) *Waardigheid. Voor wie oud wil worden*, [*Dignity: for those who want to grow old*], Amsterdam: SWP.

Dohmen, J. (2007) *Tegen de onverschilligheid. Pleidooi voor een moderne levenskunst* [*Against indifference: Plea for a modern art of living*], Amsterdam: Ambo.

Dohmen, J. (2010) *Brief aan een middelmatige man* (*Letter to a mediocre man*), Amsterdam: Ambo.

Dohmen, J. (2011) *Het leven als kunstwerk* [*Life as a work of art*], Amsterdam: Ambo.

Dohmen, J. and Baars, J. (2010) *De kunst van het ouder worden: De grote filosofen over ouderdom* [*The art of ageing. The great philosophers on ageing*], Amsterdam: Ambo.

Dworkin, R. (1993) *Life's dominion: An argument about abortion, euthanasia and individual freedom*, New York: Knopf.

Erikson, E.H. (1997) *The life cycle completed*, New York: International Universities Press.

Etzioni, A. (1996) *The new golden rule: Community and morality in a democratic society*, New York: Basic Books.

Feinberg, J (1989) 'Autonomy', in *Harm to self: The moral limits of the criminal law*, (vol 3) Oxford: Oxford University Press, pp 27-46

Foucault, M. (1985) *The care of the self*, New York: Random House.

Foucault, M. (1997) *Ethics* (edited by P. Rabinow), London: Penguin Press.

Frankfurt, H. (1971) 'Freedom of the will and the concept of a person', *Journal of Philosophy*, vol 67, no 1, pp 5-20.

Frankfurt, H. (1988) *The importance of what we care about: Philosophical essays*, Cambridge: Cambridge University Press.

Giddens, A. (1991) *Modernity and self-identity: Self and society in the late modern age*, Cambridge: Polity Press.

Gilligan, C. (1982) *In a different voice*, Cambridge, MA: Harvard University Press.

Habermas, J. (1985) *The philosophical discourse of modernity*, Cambridge, MA: The MIT Press.

Hadot, P. (1995) *Philosophy as a way of life*, Oxford: Blackwell.

Held, V. (1995) *Justice and care: Essential readings in feminist ethics*, Boulder, CO: Westview Press.

Held, V. (2006) *The ethics of care: Personal, political and global*, New York: Oxford University Press.

Held, V. (2007) 'The ethics of care', in D. Copp (ed) *The Oxford handbook of ethical theory*, New York: Oxford University Press, pp 437-566.

Hendricks, J. and Hatch, L.R. (2008) 'Theorizing lifestyle: Exploring structure and agency in the life course', in V. Bengtson, M. Silverstein, N. Putney and D. Gans (eds) *Handbook of theories of aging*, New York: Springer, pp 435-54.

Höffe, O. (2007) *Lebenskunst und Moral. Oder macht Tugend glücklich?* [*Art of living and morality. Does virtue make people happy?*], München: Verlag C.H. Beck.

Holstein, M.B. (2010a) 'Ethics and old age: the second generation', in D. Dannefer and C. Phillipson (eds) The Sage handbook of social gerontology, London: Sage Publications, pp 630-9.

Holstein, M.B. (2010b) 'Ethics and aging, retrospectively and prospectively', in T.R. Cole, R.E. Ray and R. Kastenbaum (eds) *A guide to humanistic studies in aging*, Baltimore, MD: The Johns Hopkins University Press, pp 244-70.

Jung. C.G. (1933) 'The stages of life', in C.G. Jung, *Modern man in search of a soul*, New York: Harcourt, Brace & Co.

Kekes, J. (2002) *The art of life*, New York: Cornell University Press.

Kittay, E.F. (1999) *Love's labor: Essays on women, equality and dependence*, New York: Routledge.

Laslett, P. (1989) *A fresh map of life: The emergence of the third age*, London: Weidenfield & Nicholson.

MacIntyre, A. (1981/1985) *After virtue: A study in moral theory*, London: Duckworth.

McAdams, D.P. (1993) *The stories we live by: Personal myths and the making of the self*, New York: Guilford Press.

Meyers, D.T. (1989) *Self, society and personal choice*, New York: Columbia University Press.

Nehamas, A. (1998) *The art of living: Socratic reflections from Plato to Foucault*, Berkeley, CA: University of California Press.

Noddings, N. (1982) *Caring: A feminine approach to ethics and moral education*, Berkeley, CA: University of California Press.

Nussbaum, M. (1986) *The fragility of goodness: Luck and ethics in Greek tragedy and philosophy*, Cambridge: Cambridge University Press.

Rawls, J. (1971) *A theory of justice*, Cambridge, MA: Belknap/Harvard University Press.

Ruddick, S. (1989) *Maternal thinking: Towards a politics of peace*, Boston, MA: Beacon Press.

Schmid, W. (1998) *Philosophie der Lebenskunst* [*Philosophy of the art of living*], Frankfurt: Suhrkamp.

Sennett, R. (1998) *The corrosion of character: The personal consequences of work in the new capitalism*, New York/London: W.W. Norton & Co.

Shusterman, R. (1992) *Pragmatist aesthetics: Living beauty, rethinking art*, Oxford: Blackwell.

Slote, M. (1992) *From morality to virtue*, Oxford: Oxford University Press.

Sloterdijk, P. (2009) *Du mußt dein Leben ändern* [*You have to change your life*], Frankfurt am Main: Suhrkamp.

Strawson, G. (2004) 'Against narrativity', *Ratio (New Series)*, vol 17, December, pp 428-52.

Taylor, C. (1985) 'What is human agency?' in C. Taylor (ed) *Philosophical papers 1: Human agency and language*, Cambridge: Cambridge University Press, pp 15-44.

Taylor, C. (1989) *Sources of the self: The making of the modern identity*, Cambridge: Cambridge University Press.

Taylor, C. (1991) *The ethics of authenticity*, Cambridge: Cambridge University Press.

Taylor, C. (2007) *The secular age*, Cambridge, MA: Harvard University Press.

Tronto, J. (1993) *Moral boundaries: A political argument for an ethics of care*, New York: Routledge.

Walker, M.U. (1999) 'Getting out of line. Alternatives to life as a career', in M.U. Walker (ed) *Mother time: Women, aging and ethics*, Oxford: Rowman & Littlefield Publishers, Inc, pp 97-113.

Walker, M.U. (2007) *Moral understandings: A feminist study in ethics* (2nd edn), Oxford: Oxford University Press.

Williams, B. (1981) *Moral luck*, London: Cambridge University Press.

Ziguras, C. (2004) *Self-care: Embodiment, personal autonomy and the shaping of health consciousness*, London: Routledge.

FOUR

Rethinking agency in late life: structural and interpretive approaches[1]

Amanda Grenier and Chris Phillipson

Introduction

Over the course of the 1990s and 2000s, debates in gerontology focused around the period of the 'fourth age' as a complex socio-cultural construct. These contributions have moved beyond the long-standing use of the 'fourth age' as an uncritical age-based criterion in research samples (for example, 80+) or simply as a marker of eligibility for services. At the same time, however, they have produced a new set of challenges for interpretations of the fourth age, and in particular, concerns about the extent to which agency may be said to operate within this period of the lifecourse. The assumption that agency is either present or absent is one that plays out in academic debates and organisational practices. Although the focus on older people at advanced ages with impairments is long overdue, concerns with regards to the role of agency within late old age are also beginning to emerge.

Agency, and the enactment of agency through participation and activity, is often assumed in the public and social context. As populations live longer, healthier lives, policy discourses and socio-political interventions are increasingly organised around models of 'active', 'successful' and 'productive' ageing (Katz, 2000). Frameworks for 'growing old' are ordered around 'third age' issues of health and wellness with older people expected to live out their later years as productive and active citizens. The academic literature has captured this trend by focusing on the changing lifestyles and patterns of consumption of older people (Featherstone and Wernick, 1995; Gilleard and Higgs, 2000). Linked with this are calls to empower older people in social and health services as well as to encourage participation and the inclusion of their 'voice' in research (see Chapter Nine, this volume). While such positive involvement of older people is desirable, the altered contemporary context that focuses almost exclusively on health raises new challenges for debates around agency and the 'fourth age'.

Forms of agency that are constructed as dependent on a degree of health that is less likely to be present in the 'fourth age' create discrepancies for older people with impairments. The dominant focus on health tends to assume that agency is possible, and in doing so, implicitly establishes agency as an objective of involvement and vice versa, whether on the social or practical level. In doing so, the implied message is that health, activity and independence are necessary for agency. What it actually means for older people to become involved, both symbolically and in the implementation of policy or research, remains unaddressed. The implicit – and unreflective – coupling of health and more specifically, participation, as an enactment of agency fails to address the limitations that could be experienced from social locations such as those of the 'fourth age'. Also overlooked are the ways in which embedded associations with dependency and decline serve to disrupt healthy and success-based models for late life, particularly where agency is concerned. As such, both the strategies that encourage voice and participation without accounting for constraints, and the failure to consider the specific interpretations of the 'fourth age' risk that active, individual and healthy definitions of agency become 'taken for granted' in policy discourse and research on ageing. Such underlying assumptions serve to reinforce a troublesome division between the 'third' and 'fourth age' where agency is concerned – the idea that agency is only possible through health, activity and independence that is typical of the 'third age'.

Our reconsideration of the concept of agency was prompted by the questions: *how do circumstances considered typical of the 'fourth age' challenge current understandings of agency? How do we account for agency in situations of frailty and impairment?* We set out to explore agency from a standpoint that questioned the view that 'voice' and 'participation' automatically gives rise to a sense of empowerment and control, and the seemingly contrary notion that older people in the 'fourth age' were often deemed to be 'unagentic'. Exploring agency with regards to the social and cultural constructs and practices, however, revealed the extent to which our analysis would require interdisciplinary perspectives drawing both on structural analysis and interpretations of experience in old age. This chapter uses a framework derived from critical gerontology (Phillipson, 1998; Estes et al, 2003; Katz, 2005) in order to articulate the tensions and contradictions inherent in the concept of agency with regards to the 'fourth age'. We argue that the discussion of agency with regards to late life requires that researchers shift their focus away from binary interpretations of agency as either present or absent (see Shilling, 1997, 1999;Wray, 2003), and into understanding the possible forms, inhibiting or encouraging conditions, and expressions of agency from various locations. The chapter is divided into the following: first, the construct of the 'fourth age' is clarified; second, themes in the literature on agency are reviewed; third, the challenges and contradictions presented by agency and the 'fourth age' are outlined together; finally, the chapter concludes with a review of issues for further research and development.

The 'fourth age' defined

The 'fourth age' is a concept used to demarcate experiences that occur at the intersection of advanced age and impairment. The application of this concept ranges from an uncritical age- or stage-based notion used to distinguish groups of respondents in research investigations, to a signifier of impairment or chronic condition, and further, to a socio-cultural construct aligned with frailty. In this chapter, we use a broad notion of the 'fourth age' to discuss the ideas and expectations that occur at the intersections of age and impairment. Originally coined by Laslett (1989), the concepts of the 'third age' and the 'fourth age' were intended to distinguish healthier groups of older people from those more prone to impairment and decline. Writing in a context where ageing was understood through a lens of dependency, the 'third age' was intended to counter age-based discrimination by focusing on the active, healthy and productive aspects of ageing. The resulting articulation of the 'third' and 'fourth age' distinction, however, has been criticised for overstating the potential of the 'third age', defining illness and impairment as negative, and for pushing the stigmatising aspects of ageing into the 'fourth age' (Bury, 1995; King, 2003;Vincent et al, 2008).Yet, while problematic in this sense, the ways in which these constructs continue to represent and sustain negative impressions and practices which define the 'third age' as freedom and the 'fourth age' as decline require further investigation.The concept of 'fourth age' is an important discursive and symbolic marker of the boundaries between health and impairment in late life, and by extension, what is expected with regards to agency in late life (see Kaufman, 1994; Grenier, 2007).

In recent years, researchers in gerontology have reappraised frailty and the 'fourth age' in a variety of ways (Grenier, 2007; Gilleard and Higgs, 2010, 2011). In biomedical studies and geriatrics, the constructs of frailty and the 'fourth age' are used to refer to a diagnosis or medical condition and to target services accordingly (Fried et al, 2001; Rockwood and Mitniski, 2007). In the social sciences, 'frailty' and the 'fourth age' have been considered as socio-cultural constructs, examples of practices used to classify and determine eligibility in public health and social care services, and symbolic and meaningful locations in late life (see Lloyd, 2004; Gilleard and Higgs, 2010; Grenier, 2012). While the recent focus on frailty and the 'fourth age' as social and cultural constructs has shifted the debate beyond the application as uncritical research criterion or descriptive markers, the renewed focus on this concept has produced new conflicts and challenges. The underlying assumptions of dependency and decline that are inherent in the construct of the 'fourth age' can be problematic in relation to the application of discussions around agency.

The current conceptualisation of the 'fourth age' raises a number of issues in relation to debates around agency. In 2007, Grenier drew attention to the importance of the symbolic associations of decline that are made with regards to 'frail' older bodies in health and social care practices of risk and frailty, and later, to the ways in which these beliefs, when considered in the broader socio-cultural context, resulted in a growing polarisation between the 'third' and 'fourth age' (also see Grenier, 2009a, 2009b, 2012). Extending this, Gilleard and Higgs (2010, 2011) have suggested that the 'fourth age' is a 'social imaginary' that is void of potential. In other words, the 'fourth age' is a space or phenomenon that is, in many ways, empty in comparison compared to that of the 'third age.'[2] As such, social and cultural interpretations of the 'fourth age' not only stand in stark contrast to the 'third age', but are created in part by these distinctions from the potential for freedom and definition in the 'third age'. In more recent work, they have based their theorisation of the 'fourth age' directly on the foundation of 'ageing without agency' (Gilleard and Higgs, 2010, 2011). An important distinction thus exists between the interpretation of Gilleard and Higgs (2010, 2011) and Grenier (2009a) that we feel is important to this debate. While both highlight the socio-cultural interpretations of risk, fear, dependency/decline and disgust, only Grenier's (2009a) interpretation retains the possibility of expression, communication and agency in the 'fourth age'. In considering agency, it would seem that the failure to disentangle the question of agency in the 'fourth age' from that of dependency and decline as negative states, and from dominant active, healthy and independent interpretations of agency, has led Gilleard and Higgs (2010, 2011) to an articulation of the 'fourth age' as unagentic. Such an assertion seems problematic. This chapter is concerned with the understanding and operation of agency in the lives of older people located at the intersections of advanced age and impairment. It focuses on both the structural features and conditions that shape and have an impact on late life and the ways in which such locations are experienced. We turn now to approaches to understanding agency in order to ground the analysis developed in this chapter.

Approaches to agency

The agency and structure debate

Agency, and in particular the relationship between agency and structure, has received attention from different theoretical perspectives and from a variety of disciplines. Classic and interpretive approaches within sociology have debated what is viewed as the 'elusive' nature of structure and agency (Hendricks and Hatch, 2009, p 437; see Marshall and Clarke, 2010, for a review). Running through these debates were questions about the extent to which experiences could be attributed to either structure or agency, and to what point agency was possible from within particular structural conditions. Giddens (1985) presented the two elements as a dualism, with agency creating social structure and social structure enabling and constraining agency. This approach underlined Settersten's (1999) argument that agency always operates within specific settings, what he terms 'agency within structure', with the further observation that: '... this recognition only enhances the significance of agency because it makes clear that agentic action is essential and constitutive of social relationships and social context' (Dannefer and Settersten, 2010, p 7; see further below).

Introducing time and context as a means to understand constraints, Dannefer and Kelly-Moore (2009) take the view that 'human activity is generically "*agentic*"' but that agency is also inhibited by other forces operating from the beginning of the lifecourse onward. They note how: '... social structure can be said to precede individual agency in human development and continues to frame the range of choices across the life course' (p 392). In this, the power of the structure and the individual cannot be considered equal. Dannefer (1999) emphasises the importance of social relations and social structure on the individual. He states that while 'actions of individuals play an important role in the social system, they have less effect on the system than the system on the actor' (Dannefer, 1999, p 115). This power imbalance is important for our consideration of issues relating to agency and the 'fourth age'. While the 'fourth age' does not represent a structure per se, it is a social construct that exists at the intersections of powerful structures, organisational practices and constraints experienced by the older person. Our concern is, therefore, to understand the extent to which approaches to agency can account for differential power relations that exist within and between older people and the structures they encounter, and the enactment of agency at micro and macro levels, both across time and into late life.

A key challenge for understanding agency in late life is that while there is a large body of scholarship on agency, this literature remains separate from the consideration of older people considered to be in the 'fourth age'. In policy and research on ageing, one of the central problems is that agency is often assumed to be a natural part of human experience, with the expected expression of this agency rooted in claiming a voice and/or enacting change in ways consistent with successful ageing. The social gerontological literature and policies targeted toward older people assume the duality between agency and structure, and as a result appeal to the inclusion of voice and experience as the means to achieve empowerment. In most cases agency is viewed as either absent or present (Wray, 2003), with this dilemma becoming increasingly apparent in the current debates surrounding the 'fourth age'. Challenges for understanding agency thus take place at a number of levels: first, the conceptual definition of agency; second, the strength of the socio-cultural associations of dependency and decline that underlie interpretations of the 'fourth age'; and third, the extent to which agency is understood as active behaviour linked to rational desires, choices and independent physical actions.[3] While we consider agency and change as important to retain with regards to the study of ageing, current approaches to these concepts are too closely aligned with expectations of choice and voice, and imply that agency in the 'fourth age' is improbable. A critical reassessment of the realities and constraints that influence the lives of older people in late life is required in order to address the dilemmas of agency with regards to the 'fourth age'. To develop these we turn next to arguments put forward from interpretive perspectives within social science, also linking these with perspectives from critical gerontology.

Interpretive and psycho-dynamic perspectives on ageing

The question of agency has also become a central theme in the approach taken by interpretive sociologies. Rooted in phenomenology and symbolic interactionism, these highlight the importance of meaning and the relationship between 'the I and the me' as a central link between the self and society. Several authors argue that agency can be identified in everyday experiences and narrated accounts (McAdams et al, 1996;

Biggs et al, 2003). Gubrium and Holstein (1995) argue that agency is located in ordinary, everyday practices used to create and sustain the self. They make the point that: 'Theoretically, we accept that in constructing agency people make use of what is shared and available in their immediate circumstances, such as the concepts a particular group, profession, or organization might conventionally use in everyday description' (Gubrium and Holstein, 1995, p 558). They suggest three categories of resources for the construction of selves: (1) the locally shared; (2) biographical particulars that participants bring with them; and (3) meaningful available material objects. Interpretations made within a socio-cultural and environmental context thus become important to how individuals experience or enact agency (for discussions of agency and culture, see also Archer, 1988; Hays, 1994). Agency, in their view, is a construction based on making meaning of experiences, some of which may be partially structured by the environment, but also occur through relationships with the self, context and meaningful objects. Such work suggests that the locations and expressions of agency, the authority to define what agency means, and the context within which agency is seen to occur, may differ from current understandings.

The elements of time highlighted through interpretive frameworks (see, in particular, Emirbayer and Mische, 1998; Baars, 2010) are important to considering agency in the 'fourth age'. Hitlin and Elder (2007), for example, argue that individuals exercise different forms of agency depending on their temporal orientation. They outline four types of agency – existential, identity, pragmatic and lifecourse – with the existential form underlying the last three. Linking time with social psychology, they argue that actors use different processes at different points in time, and that these diverse processes result in varied forms of agency. They argue that:

> Actors' temporal orientations are shaped by situational exigencies, with some situations calling for extensive focus on the present and others requiring an extended temporal orientation. Agentic behaviour is thus considered to be influenced by the requirements of the interaction. As actors become more or less concerned with the immediate moment versus long-term life goals, they employ different social psychological processes and exhibit different forms of agency. (Hitlin and Elder, 2007, p 171)

Acknowledgement of the importance of time and situation is shared by other perspectives within the social sciences. Giddens (1991) and

Elder (1994), for example, writing from a lifecourse perspective, discuss how agency can be linked to 'fateful moments' or 'turning points' in people's lives. The emphasis on time, or temporal frameworks, stresses how interpretive processes occur in relation to events and constraints that are experienced through the lifecourse. In doing so, interpretive frameworks confront the 'naturalness' of agency as a part of human experience, demonstrating that although agency may appear natural, this may be more a function of the way it is defined than the way it is exercised. In this sense, agency – and the form in which it is enacted – may also be a function of the time whereby agency may depend on shared experiences, contexts and relationships to objects and/or humans.

Drawing on interpretive frameworks of time suggests that the agency expressed or experienced from locations such as the 'fourth age' may be – or perhaps may appear – different than previously conceptualised earlier in the actor's life. They may also differ as one ages or moves through the lifecourse. For example, the agency expressed may not be a 'choice' as such, may not be independent, and possibly not even active. In many cases, structural features and power relations may have contributed to processes that restrict the choices or actions of the actor across the lifecourse. In response, we may argue that the focus on agency needs to shift toward a more fluid interpretation whereby older people in the 'fourth age' may, as Gubrium and Holstein (1995, p 558) suggest, 'make use of what is there'. Concrete examples of this in practice might include agency as expressed through touch or voice, rather than language, as well as acts that may be difficult to interpret.

The emphasis on relationships in the interpretative approaches, and the challenge to agency as rational or conscious choice, leads us to consider the non-rational models of subjective experience. Psychodynamic thinking highlights the complex emotions and irrational elements that can occur at the crossroads of structure and experience. *Psycho-social perspectives* that consider the emotions, fears, anxieties and destructive moments that may be a part of expressions such as agency have been used in relation to social policy and social welfare (see Hoggett, 2000; Clarke et al, 2006). Hoggett (2001), for example, argues that understandings of agency must be broadened in order to include subjects located within the experiences of powerlessness and psychic injury. He suggests that: 'A robust model of agency must also confront the subject's refusal of agency or the assertion of forms of agency which are destructive towards self and other, and that it is both possible and necessary to explore such "negative capacities" while maintaining a critical and realist stance' (Hoggett, 2001, p 38). This could include, for example, self-harming practices such as addiction, or experiences of depression, and so forth. Hoggett's view challenges the expectations of choice, rational action, and more important, the assumption that the agency expressed by individuals and/or groups is, in all cases, positive and empowering. It also challenges the understanding that the agency expressed is immediately available and understood by the person or situation to which it is directed. Although our focus is more on reading agency within conditions of reduced capacity than a refusal of agency per se, Hoggett's (2001) articulation of agency allows for expressions from within difficult or painful locations, such as those considered inherent to the 'fourth age'.

Drawing lessons from the psycho-social perspective allows for a non-rational model of the subject that can include contradictions, as well as fears, anxieties and destructive moments. Taking account of such moments reveals how constraints that challenge agency may be rooted in difficult experiences across the lifecourse, or take place through reconstructed notions of the self. While our intent is not to focus on the expression of agency as an indicator for therapeutic intervention, nor to suggest that individuals hold sole responsibility for altering their conditions, the challenges articulated by the psycho-social perspective can be useful for the purpose of understanding agency with regards to the 'fourth age'. When combined with an analysis of structures and social relationships, the psycho-social perspective can help us to clarify the role of agency in the 'fourth age'. In particular, it can provide direction from which to reconsider forms of communication that are currently interpreted as disturbing, and to ponder these as expressions of agency. Reaching across boundaries of structural, interpretive and psycho-dynamic perspectives has drawn our attention to the complexity of experience, the implications of lifelong trajectories and the variety of responses produced that create possibilities for reconsidering understandings of agency in late life.

Reframing agency in the fourth age

Our inquiry was led by the questions *how do circumstances such as those characteristic of the 'fourth' age challenge current understandings of agency? How do we account for agency in situations of frailty and impairment?* In exploring these questions, we must bear in mind that the circumstances brought about by the intersections of age and impairment create a number of challenges with regards to agency and late life. The circumstances and actions associated with older people in the 'fourth age' confront our established sets of knowledge and expectations, and may fundamentally threaten what we know and assume about agency and late life. For example, older people in the 'fourth age' may experience multiple impairments or illness, be homebound or institutionalised, and have limited strength or mobility that may inhibit their participation in new definitions of ageing. They may also have altered forms of verbal communication, physical activity or mental capacity compared to earlier in the lifecourse. As researchers, we are thus faced with a number of contradictions when we attempt to apply current understandings of agency to the 'fourth age'. In this section we explore three specific challenges with regards to the 'fourth age'. These challenges deal, first, with the issue of 'choice'; second, that of 'active action'; and third, rational conscious awareness and 'control'.

Challenge one: choice

Current approaches to agency in the academic literature and organisational practices of policy and health services have created a paradoxical situation with regards to agency and the 'fourth age'. Dominant expressions of ageing and late life equate agency with expectations of health and participation as exercised through choice. Agency for the majority is assumed to be an activity or chosen action (for discussions of agency as choice, see Kontos, 2004; Marshall, 2005; Jolanki, 2009). At the same time, serious impairments in late life tend to be overlooked or marginalised in discussions. Older people – especially those in the category of the 'fourth age' – have been aligned with a decline narrative whereby they are either expected to participate in the same way as the general population, or are deemed incapable of the same amount of change as those in earlier periods of the lifecourse. As such, responding to the questions raised by the 'fourth age' requires consideration of the complex relationship between structured experiences and meanings. This includes accounting for the altered realities of impairment in late life, the ways in which these change the contexts within which agency is exercised, and the expectations of late life. Older people with impairments may experience more severe or additional constraints than those experienced throughout the lifecourse. As their level of function decreases, they may be less socially mobile, and/or rely on care support services or family/kin. *In these cases, how do we account for agency when the expected forms of agency are defined as choice?*

Theoretical perspectives on agency and choice address these issues differently. Within critical gerontology, the study of *structures* and *social relations* can be used to illustrate the rising economic and social disadvantages that occur as an older person enters late life, including the intersections of impairment and late life. Focus on the structures, organisational practices and social constructs that shape and define the 'fourth age' can draw attention to the widening gap between those in the 'third' and 'fourth age', and to the marginalisation or exclusion of 'frail' older people (Grenier, 2009a, 2009b). Yet such perspectives can leave little room for agency or choice. Further, the expected forms of agency from structural perspectives tends to be articulated as active and often targeted to a macro level, which is much less clear where the realities of the 'fourth age' are concerned (see Grenier and Hanley, 2007, on resistance). To account for this, one could look to the individual approaches such as the *lifecourse perspective* (see Elder, 1985, 1994; George, 1993) to address such concerns. The issue here, however, is that this approach might be said to overemphasise 'action' and 'choice'. The lifecourse perspective inadequately addresses structures and constraints, and fails to articulate how agency might occur. It is for these reasons that Dannefer and Uhlenberg (1999) have argued that the acceptance of 'choice' in the lifecourse perspective is problematic and cannot be defended. This limitation is even greater when the pressures of multiple impairments, constraints and conditions for adaptation that face people in the 'fourth age' are considered. Finally, perspectives that emphasise 'cultural lifestyles' also rely heavily on a rational type of agency that is aligned with choice and consumer resources that are used to refashion the lifecourse. Limited access to the lifestyles of health and activity, combined with a dualistic understanding of agency and structure, have led Gilleard and Higgs (2010) to stress the lack of agency in the 'fourth age'. From all perspectives, the underlying implication of choice and the idea that agency is either present or absent that is embedded in current understandings represents an ongoing dilemma where the 'fourth age' is concerned.

Challenge two: active action

Contemporary interpretations of agency in academic research and public policy tend to consider agency as an active form of participation, an act of strength or a form of *resistance* (see Joas, 1996; Dannefer, 1999; Barnes, 2000; Tulle, 2004). However, agency that is defined as an independent physical act of strength and defiance can be problematic in late life, and in particular with regards to the 'fourth age' (for a discussion of what counts as action, see also Dannefer, 1999,). Interpretations of agency that are based in active participation or resistance can mean that older people in the 'fourth age' appear powerless and 'unagentic'. Older people in the 'fourth age' may not have the strength or resources to carry out changes in 'expected' ways, may require support and assistance and may have altered forms of communication. In such understandings, agency from within the 'fourth age' is thus considered nearly impossible by means of its inverse association with healthy ageing. With impairment and decline considered antonyms of successful ageing, the 'fourth age' is automatically deemed 'unsuccessful' by means of its proximity to illness and death. Any expression of agency from the 'fourth age' may therefore be difficult to understand. At present, the only available forms of agency for this period are those 'rejecting' impairment and decline and/or making use of a youthful identity or anti-ageing products (see Gilleard and Higgs, 2000; Calasanti, 2007). However, these seem to have little relevance or 'believability' where socio-cultural interpretations of the 'fourth age' are considered. We do not mean to suggest here, as is sometimes argued, that older people may not exercise a form of agency in the 'fourth age'; rather, that the current means of understanding agency is confined to active interpretations that limit what is recognised as 'agentic' in the 'fourth age'.

The failure to critically assess forms or expressions of agency from within the 'fourth age' is a major concern. Agency that is akin to voice, adaptation developed in response to impairment or participation in a social or public context, may not capture the experiences of older people in the 'fourth age'. In this sense, the problems with the concept of agency are similar to that of resistance, in that it is understood as a direct action against a situation or person, and is therefore problematic for older people who are more seriously impaired (Grenier and Hanley, 2007). Expectations of agency as such are difficult to achieve from within the 'fourth age', especially where the context is not adapted to the specific needs required for participation. Similarly, interpretations focused on individual models of development that do not account for impairment provide limited direction with regards to understanding agency from within the 'fourth age'. While psychological models of agency focus on addressing decline by drawing on psychological mechanisms, such as coping and resilience, have been articulated, these developmental tasks are considered to be difficult to achieve in the 'fourth age' (see Baltes, 1997; Baltes and Smith, 1999). Even psychological models of agency articulated along the lines of coping or adaptation have become aligned with productive and successful interpretations of age realised through fitness, health or material success (Katz, 1996, 2005; Tulle, 2004). The active strategies used throughout the lifecourse, including those of agency, become problematic in relation to the intersections of age, illness and impairment that is characteristic of the 'fourth age'. What is needed for the 'fourth age' is a model that detaches agency from physical activity and action.

Challenge three: rational conscious awareness and 'control'

Finally, current interpretations of agency assume awareness and control on the part of the individual (see Marshall, 2005; Jolanki, 2009). Dominant interpretations of agency are conceptualised as positive and independent acts of strength and control that can be difficult to achieve by older people with severe impairments. In most definitions, agency is considered to be an act of control over circumstances and choices that are natural, or at least appear natural (see Wendell, 1996). Consider Sewell's (1992) definition of agency as an example of the implied control over social relations, and processes of change. He argues that:

> To be an agent means to be capable of exerting some degree of control over the social relations in which one is enmeshed, which in turn implies the ability to transform those social relations to some degree ... agency arises from the actor's control of resources, which means the capacity to reinterpret or mobilise an array of resources in terms of schemas other than those constituted the array. Agency is implied by the existence of structures. (cited in Marshall and Clarke, 2010, p 296)

Similarly, Giddens' (1991) notion of agency is also rationalistic in that it requires a knowledgeable and capable subject. The majority of available definitions and uses of agency continue to be rooted in versions of choice, strength and independent control that are problematic for older people with impairments of either a physical or cognitive type.

The question of control, however, has been raised both in disability studies and in studies of ageing. Scholars writing in relation to the former have criticised the control and able-bodied assumptions that are embedded in agency (Wendell, 1996). Similarly, the rational behaviour and assumption of cognitive competence that are implied in definitions of agency have also been the subject of critique with regards to late life (Kontos, 2004; Jolanki, 2009). In the context of cognitive impairment, for example, Kontos (2004) considers whether dementia precludes one from exercising agency. We may ask similar questions with regards to the 'fourth age', and particularly in situations where mobility and/or communication are strained or difficult. In this sense, the perspectives on disability and impairment problematise the state of the literature in social gerontology that is increasingly moving toward accepting the 'fourth age' as a period characterised by a lack of agency. This critique of rationality, action and control is also supported by the previously discussed psycho-social perspective that highlights how the expression of agency may not always be a positive act (see Hoggett, 2001). In the cases of welfare recipients for example, the psychological injury sustained may mean that individuals reject agency altogether, and/or express forms of agency that are resistant or even harmful to their selves. Yet, in the cases outlined by Hoggett (2001), even the negative or self-harming acts of agency may rely on cognitive capacity or a physical act – both of which could be criticised with regards to impairment. Nonetheless, each of the three viewpoints challenges the assumption of rationality, action and control embedded in definitions of agency.

Attention to the 'unintentional', 'less controlled' or 'harmful' aspects of agency that are made apparent from a psycho-social perspective can help to reconsider agency with regards to the 'fourth age'. Such interpretations provide the possibility to explore destructive acts that may be expressed from within the 'fourth age', as well as forms of communication that may be less well understood. Consider, for example, what is often referred to as 'responsive behaviours' whereby older people with dementia react to the context or situations around them in order to reach out, communicate or deal with disengagement or boredom (Vance and Johns, 2003; Bourbonnais and Ducharme, 2010). Acts therefore may include anger, defiance toward workers or other older people, as well as less recognised or confusing forms of communication such as screams, cries or moans. Moving away from viewing these acts as behaviours, such actions may be read as attempts to communicate. Although increasingly viewed as unagentic – and portrayed as disturbing – these responses suggest a desire for involvement and communication. Rather than suggesting that agency cannot exist from within the locations of the 'fourth age', we consider how the location of the 'fourth age' can challenge current understandings of agency, and suggest a reconsideration that is capable of identifying and understanding alternative forms and expressions. In this, it becomes increasingly possible that existing conceptualisations of agency are not capable of addressing differences such as impairment in late life. It is also possible, however, that we need to alter definitions of agency so that they are more attuned to the complex realities of the 'fourth age'.

New approaches to agency in the fourth age

Our review of agency with regards to late life leads to a reconsideration and reconceptualisation of agency in the 'fourth age'. From the standpoint of a critical perspective on trends in social gerontology that depict the 'fourth age' as unagentic, this chapter has outlined tensions between structural and interpretive perspectives, the realities of impairment in late life and understandings of agency. While the concept of the 'fourth age' that is currently being put forward is intended to refer to a social imaginary rather than an uncritical application of age- or stage-based markers of late life, the inherent power relations – including the implication that the 'fourth age' is unagentic – are created, sustained and reinforced through organisational practices that polarise the 'third' and the 'fourth age'. *A concept of the 'fourth age' that is based on 'ageing without agency' risks sustaining or even increasing the existing polarisation between health and impairment.* Nowhere are the contemporary contradictions and challenges of understanding ageing more clear than the case of agency in the 'fourth age', and the growing practical and symbolic acceptance of the 'fourth age' as unagentic. We wish to suggest that agency may be possible in the 'fourth age', but that the forms or expressions of this agency likely differ from that currently understood.

Drawing on a critical approach combining structural and interpretive understandings of agency has produced substantive questions about agency in the context of the 'fourth age' (on the attempt to combine macro and micro level change, see also Hays, 1994; Hendricks and Hatch, 2008). Our analysis has pointed to the importance of identifying structures, circumstances or relationships – including those located in the body – that may constrain and/or allow older people to communicate and enact change. This is combined with the importance of considering the meanings, expectations, time and contexts within which agency may be experienced or expressed (see also Gubrium and Holstein, 1995). An important tension can be found where expectations of rational, independent and active agency come into conflict with the realities of impairments in late life that may lead particular groups, such as the 'fourth age', to be considered as left with little to no scope for agency. Marshall and Clarke (2010, p 301) have argued for a 'duality of structure' approach that 'combines agency with a view of structure that includes resources', and includes 'intentionality, resources, behaviour, and the social and physical structuring of choices' (Marshall and Clarke, 2010, p 301). However, similar to many of the available interpretations, this model seems to underemphasise lived experience, how structures and events can influence decisions/motivations and the importance of meaning-making across time and in particular contexts, such as those of long-term care, for example. It also implicitly suggests a rational model that, as we have outlined, can be problematic. These considerations reveal how the question of agency and the 'fourth age' bring to light complicated tensions that underlie our theoretical and practical approaches to late life.

Our analysis suggests the need to reconceptualise agency with regards to the 'fourth age'. One approach would be to conceptualise agency in the 'fourth age' around coping or compensation, drawing insights from Baltes' (1997) model of selective optimisation and compensation. This could, for example, mean adapting to bodily changes or lowering expectations in late life so that they are more in line with the realities of chronic impairment, illness or decline that may occur at advanced ages (see Jolanki, 2009). Yet, Hoggett (2001) highlights the problem in equating agency with constructive coping as reinforcing normative notions of agency as good and the absence of agency as bad (see also Clarke et al, 2006). Challenging this thinking is certainly relevant with regards to the 'fourth age', where those in the category are considered unagentic, and therefore devalued. He argues:

> ... we need a model which can provide space for non-reflexive as well as reflexive forms of agency, for acting on impulse as well as on the basis of conscious intent and calculation. We also need a model that can contain the idea of self-as-object as well as self-as-agent, for it is impossible to conceive of agency without also conceiving of its opposite. (Hoggett, 2001, p 43)

This requires a model based in a both/and perspective where agency is possible at the intersections of age and impairment, rather than either agentic or unagentic. An interesting example of agency in the context of the fourth age can be found in the work of Shura et al (2011) who use participatory action research to understand culture change practices in long-term care. In this research, the authors highlight how when involved, residents generate creative ideas for improvement and reform. This example directly confronts the hierarchical and professional tendency within organisational reform, but also the view of older people in long-term care as unagentic. Yet the majority of theoretical and methodological interpretations of agency rely on models that overlook this potential. Hoggett (2001) critiques the standpoint of Giddens (1991) for its reliance on the 'how to do it' culture of self-management, and highlights how realities such as the suffering, decay and death of bodies challenges such optimistic perspectives of change. He challenges the reliance on the active voice that is present within Giddens' approach to agency, and suggests that 'accounting for a passive voice may better account for the stressful and disempowering environments that welfare subjects can experience' (Hoggett, 2001, p 45). Yet, within the various constraints, Hoggett (2001) emphasises the idea that 'even within the most crushed and fragmented psyche there is a subject which can be called upon to place thought before enactment and a commitment to life and development before fear or despair' (Hoggett, 2001, p 54). Such is likely true of older people in the 'fourth age', who may exercise agency in a variety of forms – some of which, depending on the perspective being put forward, may not be fully recognised as agentic. The work of Shura et al (2011) provides a powerful example that illustrates the extent to which agency and change may be expressed from within the 'fourth age'.

While there is no one clearly defined path from which to move forward, what has emerged from the exploration of agency in the 'fourth age' is the need to closely examine the 'age-appropriate' versions of agency that are created and sustained in social and cultural discourses. Jolanki (2009), for example, has explored whether 'being old' itself is constructed as an agentic position, finding that while participants did describe themselves in agentic terms, agency became problematic whenever the category of old was used. This raises questions about powerful associations that are inherent in the constructs of advanced age, including that of the 'fourth age'. The relationships between social structures, socio-cultural discourses and the interpretation of experience with regards to agency thus require greater attention, especially in cases where constructs such as the 'fourth age' are considered to leave little room for accounting for agency in late life. Drawing on versions of critical gerontology that bridge structural and interpretive interpretations allow researchers to move closer to understanding the challenges inherent in the 'fourth age'. This includes the power relations and structural features of impairment and late life, the socio-cultural constructs of 'being old' or 'in decline', the ways in which each may shape or alter expectations and experiences of agency in late life, as well as the forms of communication used by older people in the 'fourth age', or in contexts such as care. Two options for reconceptualising agency in late life emerge from this analysis: that agency may be reduced or constrained in late life; and that agency may be present but look different than currently conceptualised.

The first option, that agency may be *reduced* as a result of physical or cognitive constraints, needs to be more carefully considered. Here, several opportunities for development are available in relation to the body, marginalisation and vulnerability, and the built environment. The argument that agency may be reduced as a result of constraints can serve to normalise impairment across the lifecourse and in late life, as well as to expand interpretations of agency so that they are less focused on independent, rational, actions. Moving away from the binary absence or presence of agency, this interpretation suggests that agency exists on a continuum. The drawback is that by articulating agency in late life as reduced, we implicitly reinforce the idea of control and action, and the idea of a gradual slope into late life (see Baltes, 1997) whereby the older person moves closer to an unagentic position over time. Doing so sustains the problematic trend that is emerging in late life – that an increase in impairment (physical and cognitive) is associated with a decrease in agency. However, grounding such an interpretation in arguments put forward by the disability movement or the psycho-social perspective would create the conditions to emphasise the need for an altered built environment and/or efforts to understand the changing needs, conditions and contexts that would allow agency to be both expressed and recognised over time (also see Shura et al, 2011). There is also the possibility that these constraints are both structural and constructed through relationships, interactions and associations (see further, Dannefer and Settersten, 2010). Attention to agency as reduced or diminished in late life – and/or constructed as reduced – draws attention to the importance of analysing and addressing power relations where increasing marginalisation and vulnerability are concerned.

The second option that emerges from our analysis suggests that agency may *look different* in late life than currently conceptualised. This viewpoint – that the forms or expressions of agency from within the 'fourth age' may differ from those which we currently know and expect of agency – is a serious challenge to the state of knowledge in gerontology and the social sciences more generally. What we suggest is based on social relations, socio-cultural expectations, time and context: the agency of someone who is in the 'fourth age', possibly bed-ridden and ill, is likely very different from an able-bodied young person. Acts may be non-verbal or take place through forms of communication that are often difficult to understand (for example, cries, moans or screams) (Bourbonnais and Ducharme, 2010). They may also take the form of outright resistance or disruptive acts, as suggested by the psycho-social perspective on agency. What we can say, however, is that agency from locations such as the 'fourth age' are likely not characterised by a physically active and public act of collective social change, as is implied in dominant definitions. Nor may they be about a 'lifestyle' per se. As we have recently suggested, one form that these expressions could take in this period is that of hope, will or contentment (Grenier, 2011). Yet, despite similarities that exist with regards to constraints to choice, the literature on agency does not adequately account for the forms of agency that may occur at the intersections of impairment and advanced age. Here, the example of agency expressed from within long-term care institutions is likely the most immediately available example that we can attempt to understand. In such settings, older people have reduced bodily and/or mental capacities, and their choices/actions may be constrained within routinised structures. The agency expressed from such locations may thus be unrecognisable or interpreted as disturbing, as is suggested by the literature, as well as possibly different from what they wish to enact. This question to both rationality and intentionality is crucial to considering how agency in the end stages of life may look different than currently conceptualised. That is, the altered contexts, experiences and timing of being in the 'fourth age' may result in expressions that are both unfamiliar and challenging. An analysis that takes account of interpretation, forms of expression and context may allow researchers to account for the complexities of late life, and in doing so, provide evidence of the ways in which agency in late life may be different rather than invisible. This perspective can move us closer to accounting for agency from within locations of bodily or cognitive impairment that can characterise the 'fourth age', and allow researchers to reconsider expressions that are currently being depicted as disturbing or unagentic.

Conclusion

Our critical analysis of the concept of agency has left us with a number of questions and concerns. We conclude this chapter with four interrelated paths for further exploration. First, does, or how does, the cultural construct of 'age' reduce expectations of agency? Why is the experience of physical impairment in late life considered to lead to the loss of an agentic position? Are we missing or misunderstanding the forms and expressions of agency in late life? Second, what is the relationship between dominant expectations of agency across the lifecourse, in late life? How can we understand these expectations with regards to powerful social relations, socio-cultural discourses such as health and decline, and the organisational practices and lived experiences that take place within and between such locations? Further, how do similarly complex locations such as extreme deprivation, cognitive impairment or vulnerability challenge what we believe, think and know about agency? Third, 'what counts as agency'? Is agency always active? Is it possible to disentangle agency from the independent/dependent binary? How might we recognise agency in locations of 'dependency' or decline? And finally, how does 'social structure' continue to shape and influence processes through the middle and later phases of the lifecourse? How can we study the 'long arm' of social structure as it operates throughout the lifecourse? With these questions in mind, we wish to open the debate on agency as it is expressed from one of the most challenging locations of impairment in late life.

In exploring the contemporary issue of agency in the 'fourth age', this chapter points to the importance of critical perspectives that reach across disciplines to better understand conceptual and practical implications of thinking around constructs such as agency. Our exploration of agency has produced insights with regards to linking structural and humanistic thinking in social gerontology. It highlights how challenges such as understanding agency in a contemporary context requires that we work across interdisciplinary boundaries in order to better understand the phenomenon and experience at hand. It reinforces the importance of a critical project that questions taken-for-granted and underlying assumptions within current concepts and practices, and demonstrates that an approach linking structural and interpretive features can open the debates and create the space for new scholarship that is more in line with older people's experiences. The analysis that was made possible through attention to structural and interpretive features draws attention to the need for fresh interpretations of agency in late life. We need a model that is capable of accounting for differences within the context and constraints of social relations and cultural practices, including experiences of marginalisation, impairment and decline. Models are required that integrate more passive and/or less active notions of agency, that take account of constraints ranging from the structural to the personal, and that challenge the underlying assumptions of health, control and independence that are increasingly promoted in current perspectives.

Notes

[1] An earlier version of this chapter was presented at the annual meeting of the British Society of Gerontology in 2010.

[2] In their 2010 article, Gilleard and Higgs described the fourth age as a 'black hole'.

[3] Disciplinary differences exist. Where sociology has tended to focus more on social relations arising from and linked with social structures, and in particular, ethnicity, gender and social class, psychology has tended to focus on individual behaviours, adaptive features and understandings of social actors (for example, motivations, choices, goals).

References

Archer, M.S. (1988) *Culture and agency: The place of culture in social theory*, Cambridge: Cambridge University Press.

Baars, J. (2010) 'Time and aging: enduring and emerging issues', in D. Dannefer and C. Phillipson (eds) *The SAGE handbook of social gerontology*, New York and London: Sage Publications, pp 367-76.

Baltes, P. (1997) 'On the incomplete architecture of human ontogeny: selection, optimization, and compensation as foundation of developmental theory', *American Psychologist*, vol 52, pp 366-80.

Baltes, P. and Smith, J. (1999) 'Multilevel and systemic analyses of old age: theoretical and empirical evidence for a fourth age', in V.L. Bengston and K.W. Schaie (eds) *Handbook of theories of aging*, New York: Springer Publishing Company, pp 153-73.

Barnes, B. (2000) *Understanding agency: Social theory and responsible action*, London: Sage Publications.

Biggs, S., Lowenstein, A. and Hendricks, J. (2003) 'The need for theory in gerontology', in S. Biggs, A. Lowenstein and J. Hendricks (eds) *The need for theory: Critical approaches to social gerontology*, Amityville, NY: Baywood Publishing, pp 1-14.

Bourbonnais, A. and Ducharme, F. (2010) 'The meanings of screams in older people living with dementia in a nursing home', *International Psychogeriatrics*, vol 22, no 7, pp 1172-84 (http://journals.cambridge.org/action/displayAbstract?fromPage=online&aid=7910220).

Bury, M. (1995) 'Ageing, gender and sociological theory', in S. Arber and J. Ginn (eds) *Connecting gender and ageing: A sociological approach*, Buckingham: Open University Press.

Calasanti, T. (2007) '"Bodacious berry," "potency wood," and the "aging monster": gender and age relations in anti-aging ads', *Social Forces*, vol 86, no 1, pp 335-55.

Clarke, S., Hoggett, P. and Thompson, S. (eds) (2006) *Emotion, politics and society*, Basingstoke: Palgrave Macmillan.

Dannefer, D. (1999) 'Freedom isn't free: power, alienation, and the consequences of action', in J. Brandstadter and R. Lerner (eds) *Action and self-development*, Thousand Oaks, CA: Sage Publications, pp 105-31.

Dannefer, D. and Kelly-Moore, J.A. (2009) 'Theorizing the life course: new twists in the paths', in V. Bengston, D. Gans, N.M. Putney and M. Silverstein (eds) *Handbook of theories of aging*, New York: Springer, pp 389-412.

Dannefer, D. and Settersten, R.A. (2010) 'The study of the life course: implications for social gerontology', in D. Dannefer and C. Phillipson (eds) *The Sage handbook of social gerontology*, London: Sage Publications, pp 3-19.

Dannefer, D. and Uhlenberg, P. (1999) 'Paths of the life course: a typology', in V. Bengston and K.W. Schaie (eds) *Handbook of theories of aging*, New York: Springer, pp 306-26.

Elder, G. (1985) *Life course dynamics: Trajectories and transitions*, Ithaca, NY: Cornell University Press.

Elder, G. (1994) 'Time, human agency, and social change: perspectives on the life course', *Social Psychology Quarterly*, vol 57, no 1, pp 4-15.

Emirbayer, M. and Mische, A. (1998) 'What is agency?', *American Journal of Sociology*, vol 103, no 4, pp 962-1023.

Estes, C.L., Biggs, S. and Phillipson, C. (2003) *Social theory, social policy and ageing: A critical introduction*, Maidenhead: Open University Press.

Featherstone, M. and Wernick, A. (eds) (1995) *Images of aging: Cultural representations of later life*, London: Routledge.

Fried, L., Tangere, C., Walston, J., Newman, A., Hirsch, C., Gottdiener, J., Seeman, T., Tracy, R., Kop, W., Burke, G. and McBurnie, M.A. (2001) 'Frailty in older adults: evidence for a phenotype', *Journals of Gerontology, Series A*, vol 56, no 3, M146-M157.

George, L.K. (1993) 'Sociological perspectives on life transitions', *Annual Review of Sociology*, vol 19, pp 353-73.

Giddens, A. (1985) *The constitution of society: Outline of the theory of structuration*, Berkeley, CA: University of California Press.

Giddens, A. (1991) *Modernity and self-identity: Self and society in the late modern age*, Standford, CA: Standford University Press.

Gilleard, C. and Higgs, P. (2000) *Cultures of ageing: Self, citizen and the body*, New York: Prentice Hall.

Gilleard, C. and Higgs, P. (2010) 'Aging without agency: theorizing the fourth age', *Aging and Mental Health*, vol 14, no 2, pp 121-8.

Gilleard, C. and Higgs, P. (2011) 'Ageing abjection and embodiment in the fourth age', *Journal of Aging Studies*, vol 25, no 2, pp 132-42.

Grenier, A. (2007) 'Constructions of frailty in the English language, care practice and the lived experience', *Ageing & Society*, vol 27, no 3, pp 425-45.

Grenier, A. (2009a) 'Critical perspectives on "frailty" in late life', Paper presented in the symposium, 'New departures in critical gerontology: Multi-level perspectives on power and inequality', 19th International Association on Geriatrics and Gerontology (IAGG) World Congress of Gerontology and Geriatrics, Paris, 6 July.

Grenier, A. (2009b) 'Les femmes âgées et la fragilité: la résistance face aux pratiques de soins de santé et de services sociaux', in M. Charpentier and A. Quéniart (eds) *Femmes, vieillissement et société: Regards pluridisciplinaires* [*Women, ageing and society: Multi-disciplinary perspectives*], Montréal: éditions du remue-ménage, pp 249-70.

Grenier, A. (2011) 'Frailty: the connection between policy and lived experience', Paper presented in the symposium 'Theorizing ageing embodiment as social critique', Theorizing Age, Challenging the Disciplines Conference, Maastricht University, The Netherlands, 6-9 October.

Grenier, A. (2012) *Transitions and the life course: Challenging the constructions of 'growing old'*, Bristol: The Policy Press.

Grenier, A. and Hanley, J. (2007) 'Older women and "frailty": aged, gendered and embodied resistance', *Current Sociology*, vol 55, no 2, pp 211-28.

Gubrium, J.F. and Holstein, J.A. (1995) 'Individual agency, the ordinary, and postmodern life', *The Sociological Quarterly*, vol 36, no 3, pp 555-70.

Hays, S. (1994) 'Structure and agency and the sticky problem of culture', *Sociological Theory*, vol 12, no 1, pp 57-72.

Hendricks, J. and Hatch, L.R. (2008) 'Theorizing lifestyle: exploring structure and agency in the life course', in V. Bengston, M. Silverstein, N. Putney and D. Gans (eds) *Handbook of theories of aging*, New York, NY: Springer, pp 435-54.

Hitlin, S. and Elder, G.H. Jr (2007) 'Time, self, and the curiously abstract concept of agency', *Sociological Theory*, vol 25, no 2, pp 170-91.

Hoggett, P. (2000) *Emotional life and the politics of welfare*, Basingstoke: Palgrave Macmillan.

Hoggett, P. (2001) 'Agency, rationality and social policy', *Journal of Social Policy*, vol 30, no 1, pp 37-56.

Joas, H. (1996) *The creativity of action*, Chicago, IL: University of Chicago Press.

Jolanki, O.H. (2009) 'Agency in talk about old age and health', *Journal of Aging Studies*, vol 23, no 4, pp 215-26.

Katz, S. (1996) *Disciplining old age: The formation of gerontological knowledge*, Charlottesville, VA: University Press of Virginia.

Katz, S. (2000) 'Busy bodies: activity, aging, and the management of everyday life', *Journal of Aging Studies*, vol 14, no 2, pp 135-52.

Katz, S. (2005) *Cultural aging: Life course, lifestyle, and senior worlds*, Peterborough, ON: Broadview Press.

Kaufman, S.R. (1994) 'The social construction of frailty: an anthropological perspective', *Journal of Aging Studies*, vol 8, no 1, pp 45-58.

King, C. (2003) 'Imagining the third age: symbolic exchange and old age', *Health Sociology Review*, vol 12, no 2, pp 156-62.

Kontos, P. (2004) 'Embodied selfhood: redefining agency in Alzheimer's disease', in E. Tulle (ed) *Old age and agency*, New York: Nova Science Publishers, pp 105-21.

Laslett, P. (1989) *A fresh map of life: The emergence of the third age*, Cambridge, MA: Harvard University Press.

Lloyd, L. (2004) 'Mortality and morality: ageing and the ethics of care', *Ageing & Society*, vol 24, pp 235-56.

McAdams, D.P., Hoffman, B.J., Mansfield, E.D. and Day, R. (1996) 'Themes of agency and communion in significant autobiographical scenes', *Journal of Personality*, vol 64, no 2, pp 339-77.

Marshall, V. (2005) 'Agency, events, and structure at the end of the life course', *Advances in Life Course Research*, vol 10, pp 57-91.

Marshall, V.W. and Clarke, P.J. (2010) 'Agency and social structure in aging and life course research', in D. Dannefer and C. Phillipson (eds) *Handbook of social gerontology*, London: Sage Publications, pp 294-305.

Phillipson, C. (1998) *Reconstructing old age: New agendas in social theory and practice*, London: Sage Publications.

Rockwood, K. and Mitniski, A. (2007) 'Frailty in relation to the accumulation of deficits', *Journals of Gerontology, Series A*, vol 62, no 7, pp 722-7.

Settersten, R.A. Jr (1999) *Lives in time and place: The problems and promises of developmental science*, Amityville, NY: Baywood Publishing.

Shura, R., Siders, R.A. and Dannefer, D. (2011) 'Culture change in long-term care: Participatory action research and the role of the resident', *The Gerontologist*, vol 51, no 2, pp 212-25.

Sewell, W.H. Jr (1992) 'A theory of structure: duality, agency, and transformation', *The American Journal of Sociology*, vol 98, no 1, pp 1-29.

Shilling, C. (1997) 'The undersocialised conception of the embodied agent in modern sociology', *Sociology*, vol 31, no 4, pp 737-54.

Shilling, C. (1999) 'Towards an embodied understanding of the structure/agency relationship', *The British Journal of Sociology*, vol 50, no 4, pp 543-62.

Tulle, E. (2004) 'Rethinking agency in old age', in E. Tulle (ed) *Old age and agency*, New York: Nova Science Publishers, pp 175-89.

Vance, D.E. and Johns, R.N. (2003) 'Montessori improved cognitive domains in adults with Alzheimer's disease', *Physical & Occupational Therapy in Geriatrics*, vol 20, no 3, pp 19-36.

Vincent, J., Tulle, E. and Bond, J. (2008) 'The anti-ageing enterprise: Science, knowledge, expertise, rhetoric and values', *Journal of Aging Studies*, vol 22, no 4, pp 291-4.

Wendell, S. (1996) *The rejected body: Feminist philosophical reflections on disability*, New York: Routledge.

Wray, S. (2003) 'Women growing older: agency, ethnicity and culture', *Sociology*, vol 37, no 3, pp 511-27.

FIVE

Dementia: beyond structures of medicalisation and cultural neglect

Margreet Th. Bruens

Introduction

The past few decades have seen major changes in scientific views about dementia (Ballenger, 2006). Dementia was first viewed as a sign of normal ageing accompanied by an inevitable deterioration of cognitive functions. Alongside this came its designation as a biomedical condition. Accompanying this was the collection of a large body of scientific knowledge and a substantial increase in research funding in Europe and North America, dedicated to understanding the causes of the disease. There were, however, negative consequences that arose from the scientific and medical interventions in the field of dementia. In particular, the person experiencing the disease became largely neglected given the dominance of approaches associated with medicalisation. However, as a critical response, a humanistic and psychosocial approach began to emerge. One of the key people in developing this was Tom Kitwood, who introduced a new paradigm emphasising the person over the disease (Brooker, 2007). This more humanistic approach shifted perspectives from 'the dementia sufferer' to 'the *person* with dementia'.

A number of models of care have been developed in response to Kitwood's perspective. Different quality-criteria have emerged with changes introduced in a range of care settings. Such developments have done much to improve our understanding of the experience of dementia. At the same time, significant limitations are still apparent. The gap between the ideal and actual care for people with dementia is still considerable, with evidence for continuing stigmatisation (Taylor, 2007; Innes, 2009; Bartlett and O'Connor, 2010). Quality of care is one outstanding issue, but other concerns are of equal importance, in particular, the question of making *society* aware of people with dementia and their subjective experience *as well as* ensuring both the person and the illness remain a central part of social life (Bond et al, 2004). As Bartlett and O'Connor (2010, p 25) argue: '... the need to extend understanding of the dementia experience to capture a more dynamic, contextualised perspective is now emerging.' To achieve social inclusion requires the empowerment of people with dementia. The question is if and how this can be achieved. And is society ready for such a change (Boyle, 2008)?

This chapter first describes some of the key elements of Kitwood's work, and the influence of his approach in the field of dementia. Second, the chapter considers some of the limitations of his model and introduces a number of critical perspectives. Third, the work of Kitwood is taken a step further by introducing ideas linked with 'social citizenship' (Bartlett and O'Connor, 2010), and how the social inclusion of people with dementia might be implemented. In doing so, the chapter emphasises the ways in which humanistic approaches and societal structures can be brought together to further stimulate the empowerment and social acceptance of people with dementia.

Beyond medicalisation: the 'Kitwood shift'

The term 'dementia', coming from Latin and literally meaning 'away from one's mind', has throughout history been used to identify people considered as being beyond normal society (George and Whitehouse, 2010). Many older people with unpredictable behaviour were, in consequence, sequestered in institutions. From a somewhat vague notion that mental decline was an inevitable and normal part of ageing, it was not until the late 19th century that a specific biomedical condition was identified for mental decline which necessitated accurate diagnosis and treatment. As a result, dementia became defined by a distinct set of clinical and pathological features with the goal of diagnosis being to identify methods of treatment and prevention (Berchtold and Cotman, 1998). This biomedical approach has remained the dominant model, with emphasis placed on the neurodegenerative processes of the disease (Boiler and Forbes, 1998).

Criticism of the dominant paradigm came as early as the 1940s and 1950s, with the case made for a bio-psychosocial model of care (George and Whitehouse, 2010). In many ways these critics, who emphasised psycho-social approaches and rights to good quality care (Brooker, 2007), were the forerunners to the person-centred, humanistic approach that has emerged over the last few decades (Whitehouse and George, 2008; Bartlett and O'Connor, 2010). A key development in this shift from the focus on dementia as a medical condition to a focus on the person with dementia came with the work of Tom Kitwood (see, for example, 1990a, 1990b). He contributed an alternative perspective on both the process and experience of dementia by bringing together ideas and ways of working with the subjective experience of people diagnosed with dementia. He did so by broadening the understanding of the condition beyond that of a neurological impairment to include psychological and social dimensions, emphasising that the interaction of these different aspects plays a crucial role in forming a person's condition (Kitwood, 1990a, 1990b; Clare et al, 2003). Kitwood stated that people with dementia needed to be recognised as individuals; in order for this to happen, it was of utmost importance for the people around them to consider the perspective of the person with dementia, with an emphasis on trying to understand the person's needs as an individual (Kitwood, 1993; Stokes, 2000).

Kitwood built on his theoretical work with a number of practical initiatives. Specifically, he developed 'person-centred care', formed the Bradford Dementia Group and created dementia care mapping, an observational method for evaluating quality of life and care. The latter was based on an attempt to take the standpoint of the person with dementia, using a combination of empathy and observational skill (Kitwood, 1997a). His aim was to improve the lives of those living with dementia in order to recognise 'their full humanity' (Kitwood, 1997a, p 7). A central concept is that of 'personhood', defined as 'a standing or status that is bestowed upon one human being by others in the context of relationship and social being; it implies recognition, respect and trust' (Kitwood, 1997a, p 8). Kitwood held the view that the self could change over time, but would also persist throughout the dementia process. Central to this view is that the person with dementia remains valued as a person (a self) in the eyes of others, throughout the progression of the disease.

Kitwood argued that the conventional approach to dementia was: '… medically based, deficit-focused and therapeutically nihilistic' (quoted in Baldwin and Capstick, 2007, p 4), leading to a perspective which marginalised the person living with the diagnosis. With his alternative theory he showed that there are more aspects of life that influence dementia and the person with dementia, including the social environment and the individual's own biography. He argued that: 'It is absurdly reductionistic to suggest, as some have done, that "everything in the end comes down to what is going on in individual brain cells"' (Kitwood, 1997a, p 41). Dementia is not only a problem that should be diagnosed and managed through medical skills; along with neurological dimensions, dementia should also be seen as a process with personal and social aspects, which makes its course unique, depending on the individual and the relevant context (Kitwood, 1988, 1993). Accounting for the person's individual experience of the condition can provide a different picture than the original idea of dementia as a process of inevitable deterioration, showing that people with dementia can maintain personhood and wellbeing (Kitwood and Bredin, 1992).

Currently, the most prevalent view of dementia in the general public is still far from accepting the personhood perspective of dementia. Although Kitwood saw positive changes in the culture of care for people with dementia (Kitwood, 1997b), the public discourse continues to present dementia as a terrifying condition. Killick and Allan (2001) suggest that many people are frightened when they encounter other people who seem to be fundamentally different from themselves, people they do not understand and with whom they cannot communicate. People different from ourselves represents a threat to societies' established patterns and order. A terrible, yet widespread, response to this fear is to treat the diagnosed as if they are no longer people – at best ignoring them; at worst locking them away (Killick and Allan, 2001).

According to Kitwood, such conduct towards people with dementia undermines their personhood, even if unintended, and has negative effects on their wellbeing and abilities; this causes the individual to experience 'excess disability', unwarranted and avoidable disability due to the behaviour of others, beyond the disability experienced as a consequence of neurological processes (Sabat, 2001). Kitwood termed this behaviour of others *malignant social psychology* (Kitwood, 1997a, p: 45-9). An example of this behaviour is *ignoring*, where people carry on a conversation or do things in the presence of the person with dementia, as if he or she were not present. A second example is *outpacing*: actions or activities, or questions asked, are carried out at a pace that causes the individual to be left out of activities or conversations. A third example is *disempowerment*: tasks are done for the person with dementia, even though he or she could do these tasks on his or her own (Sabat, 2001). Kitwood made a list of 17 items of malignant social psychology, which led to the development of an alternative approach. While social contexts can have a negative effect, as discussed, they should also be able to work the other way around – improving wellbeing through positive interaction, or what Kitwood termed, *'positive person work'*. Examples of this include *negotiation*, where people with dementia are consulted about what they want or need, and *holding*, where safety and warmth are provided for people with dementia. In caring for people with dementia, the primary goal should be maintaining personhood, which can be achieved by meeting the personal needs of the person with dementia. Kitwood defines five overlapping needs: comfort, attachment, inclusion, occupation and identity, all coming together in the central need for love. When these needs are met, the likelihood is that wellbeing will be improved and personhood maintained (Kitwood, 1997a; Brooker, 2007).

Following the above, Kitwood suggests that the problem is not so much about how to change the person with dementia or how to 'treat' their behaviour, but has everything to do with how those around them deal with their *own* fears and defences. It may be helpful for people to become aware of the fact that the ways in which they behave towards people with dementia may reflect their own anxieties about becoming demented. Acknowledging this may mean that people can start to address the root of their concerns about the condition. Due to the fact that a significant proportion of people with dementia will find themselves – at least for some period of time – in a formal care setting, Kitwood wanted to initiate change at the level of organisations and their culture of care, taking the individual approach into the larger level of organisational structures (Kitwood, 1995). The reason for including the organisation level in Kitwood's approach is that the malignant social psychology appeared to be condoned, or even triggered, by the institutional and organisational context. Changing organisations and cultures of care was, therefore, regarded as a crucial step in changing society in a more positive direction, resulting in a different view and culture of dementia (Kitwood, 1997a).

Subsequent to his initial work in this field, Kitwood felt that by the late-1990s greater openness could be found towards dementia, and he suggested that the stigma was fading (Kitwood, 1997a). Yet a decade or more of evidence following his work suggests that negative attitudes – on the part of the public and professionals alike – are still apparent. Dementia is still predominantly a subject preferably not discussed, and the stigma still appears to be strong. George and Whitehouse (2010, p: 343) have suggested that: 'Losing one's mind to dementia is, for many, the worst imaginable illness.' It seems evident that dementia is still what many people fear the most (George and Whitehouse, 2010; Sabat, 2010). And yet, subjective experiences of people with dementia are still rarely taken seriously. Although beginnings of change have been noted, the immensity of the culture change Kitwood sought has yet to be achieved.

Beyond Kitwood

Although Kitwood's work has been significant in considering personal experiences of those with dementia and working towards social inclusion and cultural change, it also has some limitations. Three in particular have been identified and will be addressed in the following discussion: the lack of empirical support for his approach, personhood and citizenship as underdeveloped concepts, and the transformation of organisational culture.

First, an important limitation of Kitwood's work was that it was not supported by empirical data and tested methodologies (Flicker, 1999; Epp, 2003; Baldwin and Capstick, 2007). Kitwood began with relatively new and unexplored ideas wherein there was no existent methodology or empirical data to support his ideas. His main intention in publishing his ideas was to provoke new approaches and to trigger new research formats that could further develop and support his perspective. However, the methodological considerations that he contributed did not contain clear guidelines of how to apply his theory in practice (Epp, 2003; Dewing, 2008). Therefore, although his work undoubtedly enhanced care of older people with dementia, more research must be carried out to ensure the validity of his ideas and methods (Adams, 1996).

Second, it is clear that important aspects of his work on personhood are underdeveloped, especially with regards to connections between personhood and citizenship. Kitwood's concept of personhood, for example, has particular limitations in the broader social context. Stein (2004) observes that Kitwood does not focus on the influence of broader socio-political factors, that is, why people are treated as they are within the context of age-based discrimination and social inequalities. Kitwood's objective is less towards analysis of the broader cultural context and more towards small-scale reform (Stein, 2004); therefore, it could be said that Kitwood focuses on the individual in his/her micro environment and has limited attention for macro-level issues. A related point is the tendency to understand his concept of personhood in terms of passivity and dependence (Nolan et al, 2002). His concept perceives personhood as something that is conferred on somebody, which does not promote the vision of an active social agent; it focuses on maintaining status, rather than stimulating opportunities for growth and development (Baldwin and Capstick, 2007; Bartlett and O'Connor, 2010). This static focus on personhood fails to challenge the biomedical model and associated legal procedures, thus keeping the concept of personhood dependent on an intact mental capacity (Behuniak, 2010).

Third, Kitwood's idea of organisational culture, and its possible transformation, also requires further elaboration. His neglect of the influence of socio-political factors in his conceptualisation of personhood creates a tendency to overestimate the potential for organisational change. Kitwood seems to idealise his conception of a culture of care and its possibilities, favouring his proposed reform over standard practices (Stein, 2004). However, there are many different factors that influence the care culture, such as the influence of broader socio-political factors on the ways people with dementia are treated within a given society (Baldwin and Capstick, 2007; Bartlett and O'Connor, 2010; Sabat, 2010). For instance, governments decide on the amount of money reserved for supporting care facilities and, in many countries, budgets have experienced major constraints – notably with the economic recession following the banking crisis of 2008. This has caused the delivery of good quality care to come under severe pressure and, therefore, not always succeed in the delivery of anticipated outcomes. Furthermore, changing the organisational care culture does not mean that the dominant opinions about institutionalised care and people with dementia will also change. In this regard, Kitwood overlooks the person living with dementia as an active autonomous participant in the caring relationship and the role each person can play in culture change (Nolan et al, 2002).

Following the above, there are several unresolved themes in Kitwood's work, and an overestimated potential for change. Despite these limitations, however, his work is still considered by many as an important source of inspiration and innovation (Goldsmith, 1996; Barnett, 2000; Wilkinson, 2002; Baldwin and Capstick, 2007). The next section of this chapter reviews developments applying and refining the approach put forward by Kitwood.

Beyond cultural neglect: dementia and citizenship

The psycho-social or humanistic approach centred on the person with dementia appears to be an important step forward in comparison with a biomedical understanding focused solely on neurological dimensions. However, as Bartlett and O'Connor state: 'The picture needs to broaden and continue to evolve once again' (2010, p 4). This would require including the experiences and actions of people with dementia and recognising them as full members of society. However, people with dementia continue to be stigmatised in societal, organisational and institutional practices (Bond et al, 2004; Innes, 2009). As Bartlett and O'Connor (2010, p 98) argue:

> Societal attitudes towards people with dementia remain extremely stigmatizing and discriminatory. Those affected by dementia are still often seen as "tragic", weak and completely incapable, and the popular media, in particular, continue to represent "dementia" as a catastrophe and death sentence. This does not help the people with dementia to move forward....

Making progress and helping people with dementia to move forward, however, calls for a continuing process of raising awareness with regards to their lives and experiences. In this respect, it is helpful to have a closer look at the many organisations working in the field of Alzheimer's around the world. While they are all committed to raising awareness on dementia and to support people who suffer from this condition, their objectives, approaches and strategies vary considerably. The Alzheimer's Association in the US, for example, has its first goal as eliminating Alzheimer's disease through the advancement of research; they envision a world without Alzheimer's. It is only later in their strategic plan that they mention the importance of more attention for personal needs and encouragement for those with dementia to speak up about the illness (see www.alz.org). The Dutch Alzheimer Association also claims the 'fight against dementia' as their objective, but mentions the need to strive for a better life for people with dementia and their close relatives. Goals include raising the level of awareness of dementia, being an advocate for the interests of people with dementia and those who live with them, and financing scientific research. All these goals are aiming at a better future, ultimately without dementia (www.alzheimer-nederland.nl). The British Alzheimer's Society wants to help people with dementia to live well today and to find a cure for tomorrow. They envision a radically improved world for people with dementia, a world in which they have their rights recognised, where they can fully contribute to family and community life and where they can live with dignity, free from discrimination. But again, ultimately they strive for a world without dementia (www.alzheimers. org.uk). The objectives of the German Alzheimer Society are to raise awareness that people with dementia belong to society and should not be forgotten. They advocate a better allocation of funds available for dementia, with more attention and consideration for what those diagnosed with dementia really need to improve the quality of their life (www.deutsche-alzheimer.de) This last point appears to come close to Kitwood's intentions of letting the person with dementia come before the diagnosis of the disease.

Generally, the Alzheimer associations of different countries want to raise awareness to make dementia a global health priority in order to receive funding for research on prevention, cure and treatment; in trying to achieve these aims they point to the exploding costs of dementia (Alzheimer's Disease International, 2009, 2010). At the same time, however, the pharmaceutical industries are lobbying to have the costs of drugs or services covered by health insurance (Ballenger, 2006; Sabat, 2010). Belgian research has shown that in this context a strongly negative story about dementia and its epidemic dangers is seen as, at minimum, strategically necessary to get funding for scientific research (van Gorp and Vercruysse, 2011). The latter two points are clear examples of the types of perspectives that still need to be overcome in order for the goal of valuing people with dementia as human beings, having their voices heard, improving their status and including them in societal structures to prevail (Kitwood, 1997a; Bond et al, 2004; Ballenger, 2006; Bartlett and O'Connor, 2010).

Recently there have been major initiatives to improve the quality of life and wellbeing of people with dementia by encouraging them to take a more active part in social life, illustrated by projects that are working towards dementia-friendly communities. With these examples, the focus is on redesigning the living environments of people – creating a dementia-friendly physical and social environment that would support the social participation of people with dementia (Davis et al, 2009). Much attention is devoted to exploring the perceptions, experiences and use of the outdoor environment by people with dementia, so that the safety of their living spaces and neighbourhoods can be improved. These initiatives are often still in a research context, from which designers are just beginning to be advised on how to develop urban areas for people with dementia (Mitchell and Burton, 2006, 2010). Unfortunately, the medical model, with its established claims on the institutional contexts, still has a dominant position and more balanced social models of care; thus, there have been difficulties in influencing researchers to open up these projects to the personal views and experiences of the people concerned (Davis et al, 2009; Lichtenberg, 2009). One of the central challenges in developing dementia-friendly communities is to encourage people with dementia to actively participate in everyday life so that they can have meaningful relationships in a safe and warm environment, being both valued and seen as adding something of value to the community (Vollmar et al,

2011). However, if the voices of people with dementia are not heard, there is a risk that all these well-intended initiatives are simply becoming another way of managing people with dementia, rather than truly working to improve their lives (Baldwin and Capstick, 2007).

Bartlett and O'Connor (2010) have made an important contribution in correcting some of the tendencies discussed above. They have articulated the idea of social citizenship, which is intended to broaden the usual legalistic perception of citizenship, focusing on rights and responsibilities. To claim these rights and responsibilities one must be cognitively able; thus, people with dementia tend to be excluded from society (Graham, 2004). Most legislation, which intends to promote citizenship for people with dementia, offers little support and has limited capacity for facilitating their full citizenship status (Boyle, 2008). Bartlett and O'Connor state that it is time for the role of social citizenship for people with dementia (2010). This is being defined as:

> ... a relationship, practice or status, in which a person with dementia is entitled to experience freedom from discrimination, and to have opportunities to grow and participate in life to the fullest extent possible. It involves justice, recognition of social positions and the upholding of personhood, rights and a fluid degree of responsibility for shaping events at a personal and societal level. (Bartlett and O'Connor, 2010, p 37)

In this approach, people create their own statuses as citizens through the dynamics of everyday talk and actions, including the experiences of people with dementia in a broader societal framework. A citizenship model of dementia thus needs developing through integrating active personhood and citizenship. To empower people with dementia, the personal and political need to be linked (Baldwin, 2008), placing the experiences of dementia in a broader context of interrelating subjective experiences, the interactional social surroundings and the broader social and cultural context. The starting point to this is for people with dementia to themselves have influence: they need to be seen as active social agents.

If this role of social citizenship is to be realised and strongly based in society, it is crucial to change the negative stereotyping and cultural representation of dementia (Bond et al, 2004). In this respect, Kitwood's primary goal, to recognise the people behind the diagnosis, remains important. This approach might assuage the collective fear of dementia that is behind the exclusion of people with dementia, one of the most dreaded terms of our time (George and Whitehouse, 2010; Sabat, 2010; van Gorp and Vercruysse, 2011). These negative ideas are understandable considering the standard biomedical paradigm and negative stereotyping that comes with it, but they practically dehumanise people who suffer from dementia, neglecting their personhood and excluding them from society (Bond et al, 2004; Gilmour and Brannelly, 2010).

To change these persistent structures of social exclusion, it is necessary to confront these structures with the personal stories and experiences of people with dementia, in particular, to raise awareness that there is more to the experience of dementia than that associated with medical and related support. The public view of dementia needs a wider lens that includes personhood, autonomy and citizenship, as well as the complexities of human experience (Bond et al, 2004; Bartlett and O'Connor, 2007). Letting the person come first, as Kitwood stated, not just in care situations but also in everyday life, and hearing the subjective experiences of people with dementia, are priorities that continually need to be voiced in public debate. These practices might make a change toward acquiring a broader, more complete picture of dementia; the stories from people with dementia need more attention. Respecting citizenship involves challenging stigma and exclusion (Gilmour and Brannelly, 2010), and recognising people with dementia as dignified human beings who are, at the same time, very different as individuals, accepting people with dementia as people who have something to say and who can interact in meaningful ways (Kontos, 2004). In these respects, radical changes are needed in society and the ways in which it is organised (Cantley and Bowes, 2004).

Even sociological and psychological research on dementia is struggling with the idea that people with dementia might be worth listening to, that they might have something to say and a voice of their own. They believe that letting the story of people with dementia be heard is not the way to get attention, or even more important, funding (Cheston and Bender, 1999). This is demonstrated by the scarcity of data available concerning the experiences and perspectives of people with dementia. Few studies include their views, and if they do, they tend to be mainly small-scale studies (van Baalen et al, 2011). Most dementia research is based on observations and judgements by others (that is, caregivers), and using people with dementia as informants in scientific research is still exceptional. However: ' ... the notion that all people with dementia lack the capacity to report reliably on what they find important for their quality of life seems to have been taken at face value and is lacking empirical support...' (van Baalen et al, 2011, p 115). To improve the situation that faces people with dementia, it is crucial that they remain recognised as dignified human beings and citizens, listening to their stories and accepting their actions as meaningful interactions (Kontos, 2004), not just in care or research, but also in social life, society and its broader structures.

Conclusion

The ideas of Tom Kitwood have played an important role in changing views on dementia in the past 25 years; instead of seeing dementia only as a biomedical condition, he placed the *person* before the disease. Although much work has to be done to achieve more person-centred care, his work has limitations in one-sidedly focusing on care settings and care approaches rather than on society at large. The public stigma of dementia is still very strong; it is not a subject that is discussed by the general population and it continues to be what most people fear most about ageing (George and Whitehouse, 2010). Confronted with this problematic situation, Bartlett and O'Connor (2010) state that it is time to broaden the dementia debate to include people with dementia, as well as grant them the status of social citizenship. People with dementia should have the right to act as active social agents; to fulfil this aim, however, Kitwood's idea to see and hear the person behind the disease remains crucial. Although the medical deficiency model may be supplemented with an attention for quality of life, personal feelings and experiences, people with dementia will still not be taken seriously as human beings of equal dignity. They remain widely ignored by society and put away in formal care settings, often (literally) behind closed doors. Unfortunately, the subjective experience of the diagnosed is still very rarely heard; changes in society would require a large shift both within and, especially, outside of formal care-setting walls. Recognising the *person* with dementia is still far away. Even if dementia was given the highest priority in the distribution of societal resources, resulting in more funding, the big question would still be how this money would be spent. Would it be spent, for example, in an attempt to arrive at a world without Alzheimer's? Or are we, at least in the meantime, going to listen to the people with dementia, to find out what they need, as the German Alzheimer Society suggests? Making their voices heard is an important subject that needs to be addressed. There are plenty of narratives from relatives, care workers and researchers, but the narratives of those who actually live with the disease are usually overlooked in most care settings, and certainly in society. However, where Kitwood's work did not go far enough to reach society and its structures, the advocates of social citizenship are stepping into the societal debate too soon. To get people with dementia recognised in their full humanity and accepted as social citizens, with the dignity and respect they deserve, it is their voices that must be heard.

References

Adams, T. (1996) 'Kitwood's approach to dementia and dementia care: a critical but appreciative review', *Journal of Advanced Nursing*, vol 23, pp 948-53.

Alzheimer's Disease International (2009) *World Alzheimer report 2009. Executive Summary*, London: Alzheimer's Disease International.

Alzheimer's Disease International (2010) *World Alzheimer report 2010. The global economic impact of dementia*, London: Alzheimer's Disease International. Baldwin, C. (2008) 'Narrative, citizenship and dementia: the personal and the political', *Journal of Aging Studies*, vol 22, no 3, pp 222-8.

Baldwin, C. and Capstick, A. (eds) (2007) *Tom Kitwood on dementia: A reader and critical commentary*, Maidenhead: McGraw-Hill/Open University Press.

Ballenger, J.F. (2006) *Self, senility and Alzheimer's disease in modern America: A history*, Baltimore, MD: The Johns Hopkins University Press.

Barnett, E. (2000) *Including the person with dementia in designing and delivering care: 'I need to be me!'*, London: Jessica Kingsley Publishers.

Bartlett, R. and O'Connor, D. (2007) 'From personhood to citizenship: broadening the lens for dementia practice and research', *Journal of Aging Studies*, vol 21, no 2, pp 107-18.

Bartlett, R. and O'Connor, D. (2010) *Broadening the dementia debate: Towards social citizenship*, Bristol: The Policy Press.

Behuniak, S.M. (2010) 'Toward a political model of dementia: power as compassionate care', *Journal of Aging Studies*, vol 24, no 4, pp 231-40.

Berchtold, N.C. and Cotman, C.W. (1998) 'Evolution in the conceptualization of dementia and Alzheimer's disease: Greco-Roman period to the 1960s', *Neurobiology of Aging*, vol 19, no 3, pp 173-89.

Boiler, F. and Forbes, M.M. (1998) 'History of dementia and dementia in history: an overview', *Journal of the Neurological Sciences*, vol 158, no 2, pp 125-33.

Bond, J., Corner, L. and Graham, R. (2004) 'Social science theory on dementia research: normal ageing, cultural representation and social exclusion', in A. Innes, C. Archibald and C. Murphy (eds) *Dementia and social inclusion: Marginalised groups and marginalised areas of dementia research, care and practice*, London and Philadelphia: Jessica Kingsley Publishers, pp 220-36.

Boyle, G. (2008) 'The Mental Capacity Act 2005: promoting the citizenship of people with dementia?', *Health & Social Care in the Community*, vol 16, pp 529-37.

Brooker, D. (2007) *Person-centred dementia care: Making services better*, London and Philadelphia: Jessica Kingsley Publishers.

Cantley, C. and Bowes, A. (2004) 'Dementia and social inclusion: the way forward', in A. Innes, C. Archibald and C. Murphy (eds) *Dementia and social inclusion: Marginalised groups and marginalised areas of dementia research, care and practice*, London and Philadelphia: Jessica Kingsley Publishers, pp 255-71.

Cheston, R. and Bender, M. (1999) *Understanding dementia: The man with the worried eyes*, London: Jessica Kingsley Publishers.

Clare, L., Baddeley, A., Moniz-Cook, E. and Woods, R. (2003) 'A quiet revolution', *The Psychologist*, vol 16, pp 250-4.

Davis, S., Byers, S., Nay, R. and Koch, S. (2009) 'Guiding design of dementia friendly environments in residential care settings: considering the living experiences', *Dementia: The international Journal of Social Research and Practice*, vol 8, no 2, pp 185-203.

Dewing, J. (2008) 'Personhood and dementia: revisiting Tom Kitwood's ideas', *International Journal of Older People Nursing*, vol 3, pp 3-13.

Epp, T.D. (2003) 'Person-centred dementia care: a vision to be refined', *The Canadian Alzheimer Disease Review, April 2003, p 14-18.*

Flicker, L. (1999) 'Dementia reconsidered: the person comes first', *British Medical Journal*, vol 318, no 7187, p 880.

George, D. and Whitehouse, P. (2010) 'Dementia and mild cognitive impairment in social and cultural context', in D. Dannefer and C. Phillipson (eds) *The Sage handbook of social gerontology*, Los Angeles, CA and London: Sage Publications, pp 343-56.

Gilmour, J.A. and Brannelly, T. (2010) 'Representations of people with dementia – subaltern, person, citizen', *Nursing Inquiry*, 17, pp 240-7.

Goldsmith, M. (1996) *Hearing the voice of people with dementia: Opportunities and obstacles*, London and Philadelphia: Jessica Kingsley Publishers.

Graham, R. (2004) 'Cognitive citizenship: access to hip surgery for people with dementia', *Health*, vol 8, no 3, pp 295-310.

Innes, A. (2009) *Dementia studies*, London: Sage Publications.

Killick, J. and Allan, K. (2001) *Communication and the care of people with dementia*, Buckingham and Philadelphia: Open University Press.

Kitwood, T. (1988) 'The contribution of psychology to the understanding of senile dementia'. Reprinted in: C. Baldwin, and A. Capstick, (eds) (2007) *Tom Kitwood on dementia: A reader and critical commentary*, Maidenhead: McGraw-Hill/Open University Press, p.108 – 18.

Kitwood, T. (1990a) 'The dialectics of dementia: with particular reference to Alzheimer's disease', *Ageing & Society*, vol 10, pp 177-96.

Kitwood, T. (1990b) 'Understanding senile dementia: a psychobiographical approach', *Free Associations*, vol 19, pp 60-76.

Kitwood, T. (1993) 'Person and process in dementia', *International Journal of Geriatric Psychiatry*, vol 8, no 7, pp 541-6.

Kitwood, T. (1995) 'Cultures of care: tradition and change'. Reprinted in: C. Baldwin, and A. Capstick, (eds) (2007) *Tom Kitwood on dementia: A reader and critical commentary*, Maidenhead: McGraw-Hill/Open University Press, p.306-13.

Kitwood, T. (1997a) *Dementia reconsidered: The person comes first*, Buckingham: Open University Press.

Kitwood, T. (1997b) 'Personhood, dementia and dementia care', in S. Hunter (ed) *Research highlights in social work*, London: Jessica Kingsley Publishers.

Kitwood, T. and Bredin, K. (1992) 'Towards a theory of dementia care: personhood and well-being', *Ageing & Society*, vol 12, no 3, pp 269-87.

Kontos, P.C. (2004) 'Ethnographic reflections on selfhood, embodiment and Alzheimer's disease', *Ageing & Society*, vol 24, no 6, pp 829-49.

Lichtenberg, P. (2009) 'Controversy and caring: an update on current issues in dementia', *Generations*, vol 33, no 1, pp 5-10.

Mitchell, L. and Burton, E. (2006) 'Neighbourhoods for life: designing dementia-friendly outdoor environments', *Quality in Ageing and Older Adults*, vol 7, no 1, pp 26-33.

Mitchell, L. and Burton, E. (2010) 'Designing dementia-friendly neighbourhoods: helping people with dementia to get out and about', *Journal of Integrated Care*, vol 18, no 6, pp 11-18.

Nolan, M., Ryan, T., Enderby, P. and Reid, D. (2002) 'Towards a more inclusive vision of dementia care practice and research', *Dementia: International Journal of Research and Practice*, vol 1, no 2, pp 193-211.

Sabat, S.R. (2001) *The experience of Alzheimer's disease: Life through a tangled veil*, Oxford/Malden: Blackwell Publishers.

Sabat, S.R. (2010) 'Prepositioning, malignant positioning, and the disempowering loss of privileges endured by people with Alzheimer's disease', in F. Moghaddam and R. Harré (eds) *Words of conflict, words of war: How the language we use in political processes sparks fighting*, Oxford: Praeger, pp 89-104.

Stein, P. (2004) 'Social life under the evacuation of culture: Lost minds, demented selves and social solidarities', Unpublished: Submitted in partial fulfilment of the requirements for the Degree Doctor of Philosophy, Rochester, New York: University of Rochester.

Stokes, G. (2000) *Challenging behaviour in dementia: A person-centred approach*, Bicester: Speechmark Publishing.

Taylor, R. (2007) *Alzheimer's from the inside out*, Baltimore, MD, London and Sydney: Health Professions Press.

van Baalen, A., Vingerhoets, A., Sixma J. and de Lange, J. (2011) 'How to evaluate quality of care from the perspective of people with dementia: an overview of the literature', *Dementia: The International Journal of Social Research and Practice*, vol 10, no 1, pp 112-37.

van Gorp, B. and Vercruysse, T. (2011) *Framing en reframing: Anders communiceren over dementie*, Brussels: Koning Boudewijnstichting.

Vollmar, H. C., Buscher, I., Goluchowicz, K., Dönitz, E., Wilm, S., Beckert, B. and Bartholomeyczik, S. (2011) *Health care of people with dementia in Germany in 2030 – A multidisciplinary scenario process* (www. uni-wh.de).

Whitehouse, P. and George, D. (2008) *The myth of Alzheimer's: What you aren't being told about today's most dreaded diagnosis*, New York: St Martin's Griffin.

Wilkinson, H. (2002) *The perspectives of people with dementia: Research methods and motivations*, London and Philadelphia: Jessica Kingsley Publishers.

SIX

Self-realisation and ageing: a spiritual perspective

Hanne Laceulle

Introduction

This chapter looks at the relevance of perspectives on spirituality and ageing in relation to self-realisation in later life. First, it outlines individualisation processes, the corresponding rise of individual self-realisation as a cultural and moral ideal, and the implications of these developments for ageing individuals. Second, the ethical–philosophical concept of self-realisation and views about the nature of the self are discussed. Third, the chapter examines how perspectives on spirituality and ageing can contribute to our understanding of the subject of self-realisation in late modernity. The argument developed here holds that spiritual perspectives within gerontology, such as those advanced by Thomas Cole (1992), Lars Tornstam (2005) and Robert Atchley (2009), raise important issues about self-realisation in later life.

Individualisation, self-realisation and ageing in late modernity

Giddens (1991) has argued that the contemporary condition is most accurately described as 'late' or 'reflexive' modernity. These terms suggest that modernity is not so much 'over' (as the term 'postmodern' would imply), but has developed into a specific form that is to be distinguished from the common or 'massive' modernity that characterised the previous era (Baars, 2006a). Late modernity represents a post-traditional order that is full of uncertainties and insecurities. People are confronted with endless and multiple options and possibilities that require constant and reflexive choice. Reflexivity, in this respect, points to the fact that almost all aspects of people's lives are susceptible to revision in the light of new information or knowledge. Individuals are forced to continuously negotiate their own lifestyle among these choice options, and thereby create and structure their self-identity. This process takes place against the backdrop of the pervasive social and institutional structures of modernity that influence processes of identity building (Giddens, 1991).

Individualisation can be seen as one of the tendencies most intimately connected to modernisation processes in general. For Beck and Beck-Gernsheim (2002), individualisation brings together two interrelated dimensions. First, the disintegration of previously existing, traditional social forms: old modes of life that were ordained by religion, tradition or the state are breaking down and people are no longer defined by traditional social categories such as class, gender or age. However, the new modes of life replacing the traditional ones are not necessarily less constraining for the late modern individual. This points to the second aspect of individualisation identified by Beck and Beck-Gernsheim, namely, that new and pressing demands are placed on the individual, most notably the requirement to lead a 'life of their own' (Beck and Beck-Gernsheim, 2002). Bauman's (2001) interpretation focuses on how the supposedly greater modern 'freedom' to create your own identity coincides with the pressuring task of 'becoming who you are' and fulfilling your individual possibilities. Giddens (1991) stresses the reflexive inclination of late modern identity formation. Both authors underscore the fact that individuals have to confront these challenges without the comforting presence of self-evident social, cultural, religious and moral frameworks to rely on. The late modern socio-cultural outlook is one of facing existential anxieties and fading securities – all on your own. And being the architect of your own lifecourse is far from an easy, carefree job (Giddens, 1991; Bauman, 2001).

Following the above, the individualisation of the lifecourse, characteristic of modernity, implies for inhabitants of late modern society the challenge of constituting their own individual lifestyle, in which they shape themselves and their lives in accordance to their individual possibilities and to what is meaningful to them. Although we may argue that not everyone is offered the same chances or social position to realise themselves in this respect (cf Walker, 2007), the dominance of individual self-realisation as a cultural ideal nevertheless presents itself with great force.

It is important to emphasise that this ideal represents an explicitly *moral* stake. Self-realisation is not conceived as an optional extra, the 'icing on the cake' of late modern existence, but is supposed to supply a fundamental guiding framework to individuals for a 'good life'. At the same time, due to the fundamental insecurities that characterise the late modern outlook, this guiding framework is fragile and requires constant revision. Several critiques have analysed the views of Giddens and Beck as over-optimistic when it comes to their estimation of the possibilities of human agency, necessary for exercising self-realisation. Dannefer (2008) argues that in general there is a tendency to overestimate the scope of human agency, given the ways human beings are embedded within and influenced by social contexts. While it is very important to underscore the intrinsic aspect of agency that is fundamental to human activity, it is crucial to appreciate that this agency can only function against a determining background of social interaction and social structure. Since this relationship is necessarily asymmetrical, Dannefer and Kelley-Moore (2009) use the term 'agentic asymmetry'. This is an important observation, given the moral weight that is placed on the reflexive constitution of one's own identity and biography under late modern conditions.

According to Baars (2006a), the problems surrounding the specific late modern, reflexive appearance of individualisation analysed by Beck and Beck-Gernsheim (2002) can best be interpreted as problems of moral uprooting, due to the disintegration of traditional frameworks shaping morality. Questions about what represents a good life or a morally responsible course of action must be answered without being able to rely on pre-given roles or respected moral authorities. Baars (2006a) points to a problem inherent in Beck and Beck-Gernsheim's (2002) view of individualisation, namely, that the moral dimension of individualisation becomes intermingled with an empirical interpretation, as though the latter automatically follows from the former. The moral appeal to shape your individual existence according to your own independent choices does *not*, however, automatically imply that individuals are indeed capable of doing so, or that the circumstances they are living under permit them to exercise the supposedly self-evident freedom to decide (Baars, 2006a). This is an important critique that calls for caution when it comes to drawing conclusions regarding the actual practices aiming at self-realisation in the daily life of late modern individuals.

The link between individualisation and self-realisation is highly complex. Honneth (2004), for example, argues that individualisation has been subjected to diverse interpretations, some of which are contradictory or represent underlying paradoxes. He agrees that self-realisation, the demand placed on individuals to present themselves as authentic and autonomous designers of their own, unique lives, is inseparable from the complex and multi-interpretable processes of individualisation. However, his appreciation of these developments and their consequences for individuals within society is far from optimistic. Importantly, Honneth is concerned with the fact that self-realisation, as a cultural ideal arising from diverse processes of individualisation, is used by late modern consumer capitalism to strengthen its own purposes at the expense of the possibilities for the individual to acquire real freedom and autonomy. The result is that instead of truly developing their own authentic lives, individuals are subjected to standardisation processes and the compulsive demand to experiment with lifestyles that are, in fact, largely prescribed by the dynamics of an economic system characterised by deregulation. This produces heteronomy rather than autonomy, and what on the surface seems to be an authentic existence is in fact only a shallow appearance camouflaging a deep dependency on the system. According to Honneth (2004), this leads to experiences of inner emptiness and instability for the individual.

Although Honneth's warning about the lack of a positive, meaningful and directive content for the ideal of self-realisation has to be taken seriously, his overall view seems excessively gloomy, and fails to appreciate the positive chances for individual growth and development offered by the ideal of individual self-realisation, thereby also neglecting the moral importance of it. Honneth also seems to underestimate the individual possibilities for resistance to the dynamics of the societal systems, and the way social structures are themselves partially constituted by the actions of individuals. Against this, Dannefer argues that: 'individual agency and social forces continuously shape each other in a reconstitutive, dialectical process' (2008, p 7), and this dialectical process might allow for a larger scope for individual agency than Honneth would be willing to admit. Despite the problems he recognises, Honneth does agree that the dominant cultural and moral ideal of late modernity may be described most accurately in terms of the realisation and fulfilment of one's own unique self, within the complex order of late modern, post-traditional society. The self concerned here, however, is not a stable entity, but dynamic and in constant need of redefinition, as discussed further below.

Although the analyses by Giddens, Bauman and Beck pay little attention to the consequences of different life stages of the obligation to shape your own identity, we may safely assume that the individualisation of the lifecourse also has implications for ageing individuals. As Baars (2006b) suggests, ageing in late modern conditions differs in fundamental ways from what it was in earlier times. To start with, the population of elderly individuals, at least in the Western world, shows substantial numerical growth as a result of the drastic increase in life expectancy, thanks to huge scientific improvements, for instance, in medical care and hygienic conditions. At the same time, the phase in which people are considered to be 'old' or 'growing older' has spectacularly extended in length and now – on average – contains multiple decades. This is caused not only by the increased life expectancy, but also in particular by the fact that society is labelling people as 'older' at an ever-younger age. Of course, this labelling has far-reaching consequences and may very well influence older people's possibilities for measuring up to the demands of self-realisation sketched above as a dominant cultural ideal.

Societal arrangements and socio-cultural images concerning ageing individuals determine to a large extent how this long span of their lifetime may – or may not – be filled. There are, however, no more self-evident frameworks that help people to shape their lifecourse and old age. This contributes to a great amount of variation in ageing trajectories open to individuals or social groups. Hendricks (2010) explains how the social and societal changes accompanying modern processes of globalisation will deeply influence the self-experience of ageing individuals and the way they are perceived by others. Hendricks also points out the resulting differentiation among ageing individuals related to these changes: 'There is an increasing fluidity, even fracturing of the life course, as society becomes progressively pluralistic so that ageing itself follows multiple trajectories as it is affected by social change' (2010, p 255).

In short, there seems to be an intrinsic tension between: (a) the late modern demand for shaping and realising yourself in your own old age; and (b) the restrictions placed on the freedom to fulfil this task, by the societal arrangements and scripts surrounding the life stage, and by the lack of cultural resources for a meaningful old age. As a result, ageing populations in late modern societies increasingly consist of a pluralistic collection of individuals searching for their own, meaningful ways of shaping their later life phase, facing the challenges of ageing in late modern society with limited external help.

Self-realisation and the self

Philosophically and historically speaking, the concept of self-realisation has deep roots, reaching back to the Socratic ideal of 'knowing yourself', the Aristotelian concept of self-fulfilment, the Romantic quest for self-expression and the Nietzschean requirement of 'becoming who you are' (cf Taylor, 1989). The classic interpretation of self-realisation is defined by Gewirth (1998, p 3) as 'a bringing of oneself to flourishing completion, an unfolding of what is strongest or best in oneself, so that it represents the successful culmination of one's aspirations or potentialities.' The self concerned here is, in the words of Gewirth (1998, p 13), 'a continuing or enduring embodied entity that is aware of itself as a distinct person, that can anticipate a future for itself, and that has desires on which it can reflect.'

Although some concrete historical and cultural expressions of self-realisation may be accused of deteriorating into a form of narcissism (Taylor, 1991), the concept has mostly been conceived as a *moral* task aimed at a 'life well lived', that is to say, a life in accordance with the best of one's capacities, striving towards self-chosen aims. Influential ethical theories throughout history have located this highest level of human capacities in the sphere of rationality and autonomy and based their ethical principles on the human inclination to strive for self-realisation (cf Gewirth, 1998; Gerhardt, 1999). A possible problematic aspect arises from the conceptualisation of autonomy or agency that these ethical perspectives employ, which emphasises negative freedom and individual rational choice. Holstein (2010) rightly argues that a viable moral perspective on ageing requires an alternative conception of autonomy that is able to integrate experiences of loss and dependency inherent in ageing, while at the same time recognising the potential for self-realisation. She states: 'we must enrich our understanding of autonomy so that it accounts for the kinds of selves we are, or are struggling to be, when loss impedes what might otherwise be taken for granted' (2010, p 256).

To be of relevance in the context of late modern identity formation, we need a view of self-realisation that is able to address the existing differentiation between people in terms of social position, gender, education, 'race' and – most important for our present purposes, age or stage in life. The individual or moral subject cannot be taken as a largely abstract entity, as is sometimes the case in the above-mentioned perspectives on self-realisation. While both Gerhardt (1999) and Gewirth (1998) acknowledge the fact that the self-realising individual exists within a social context that influences individual goals, the question is whether the universalistic claims of their moral philosophies allow enough space for differentiation. Walker (2007) emphasises how the way we conceive our lifecourse, and the potential for choice we experience in shaping our lives, is deeply influenced by our placing within networks of differentiating parameters such as class, gender, age and 'race'. Naturally, our position within these networks also influences our possibilities to exercise the 'best capacities' (like autonomy and rationality) supposedly inherent to our humanness that are conditional for self-realisation in the above-mentioned views.

Underlying some interpretations of self-realisation is a conception of the self in which it is considered to be a distinct, autonomous whole, containing a collection of aspirations to be fulfilled and capacities to be realised. Such a concept of a stable 'core' self, however, poorly matches the late modern situation of individualisation in which the self is viewed more like a dynamic, reflexive project, involved in constant transformation processes (cf Giddens, 1991). The 'self' to be realised as viewed by the late modern discourse on identity and the lifecourse, instead of a 'pure' core self, is seen as socially constructed and deeply influenced by cultural factors. It may be fragmented or divided within itself (cf Gergen, 1991; Elliot, 2001). Its realisation is therefore necessarily a tentative, searching process, in which many obstacles may have to be overcome. The outcome is insecure and depends on many factors the individual does not control. In this respect, the interpretations of self-realisation mentioned above seem to fall short of addressing the situatedness of late modern self-identity formation in a satisfactory manner.

However, despite the fragmented, socially defined and often unstable nature of late modern 'selves', there appears to be a deep-rooted need in people for a sense of coherence and integration of one's identity. The quest for self-development throughout the lifecourse and the constant narrative creation of identity through telling stories about one's life, reconciling seemingly contradictory story lines, clearly speaks of this need for some sort of 'unity'. This presents self-realisation as an ideal that is still relevant, even urgent, for late modern individuals, although we need to incorporate current insights about selfhood in our understanding of the concept.

A viable concept of self-realisation also needs to acknowledge the social influences active in constituting our identity. Honneth (2001) underscores important conditions in terms of recognition that have to be met in order to be able to speak about a successful process of self-realisation. First, there has to be a certain amount of self-confidence, rooted in primary relationships; second, there has to be a legally enshrined recognition of individual autonomy; and third, there has to be 'solidarity', that is, the social recognition of a person's ability to choose his/her own way of life, or, in other words, his/her ability for self-realisation, defined by Honneth as 'the unforced pursuit of freely chosen aims in life' (2001, p 50). Honneth also makes a fundamental connection between the goal of self-realisation and ethics, but his view has the advantage that it recognises ethics to be a historically constituted and therefore variable factor, rather than a formal, timeless concept. That gives us the opportunity to differentiate among groups of (ageing) people in the possibilities they have for self-realisation, due to the varying degrees of the necessary forms of recognition late modern society has to offer them.

In sum, we need to look for perspectives on self-realisation and development that are able to integrate the insights and influencing factors regarding identity development that are typical for the late modern condition. A possibly promising road to such new perspectives is offered by research on spiritual development. Developments in the domain of spirituality show both the individualising tendencies and the 'searching' character of identity characteristic for late modernity. At the same time, research on spiritual development and ageing points towards an alternative understanding of self-realisation that enriches our understanding of the moral and existential value of the concept.

Sprituality and self-realisation in later life

Traditionally, religious and spiritual traditions were among the most important suppliers of guidelines and inspiring frameworks on how to lead a meaningful life – including how to grow older (Sapp, 2010). For all major religious traditions, the theme of ageing is inextricably intertwined with the search for acceptation of human mortality. In some form, all religious traditions offer a perspective on the transient nature of human existence that makes it possible to provide death – and the ageing process inevitably leading up to it – with a context of meaningfulness by connecting human existence to a dimension of transcendence (Sapp, 2010).

As a consequence of modernisation and individualisation, the self-evident validity of these traditional perspectives has been eroded. Consequently, the ways in which religion and spirituality may guide people's lifecourse has also undergone fundamental changes. Taylor (2007) dismantles the one-sided view that the rise of the (natural) sciences and the corresponding imageries has produced the general demise of religion in society, a process commonly known as 'secularisation'. Taylor offers a richer and differentiated view of secularisation. He argues that secularisation does *not* mean the general decline of religious and spiritual institutions and their influence within society in favour of more scientific ones. Rather, it points to the process in which a variety of different and often conflicting spiritual views becomes available to people, none of which can claim the natural validity and authority comparable to the position these views had in earlier (pre-modern) times. The spiritual or religious views people adhere to no longer offer the self-evident stability and security they used to have. Modern people are destined to live within a universe of spiritual views that are fundamentally insecure, temporary and replaceable. While there are still many people who find their spiritual 'home' within the traditional religious institutions and views, there is no authority to provide the status of unquestionable truth to any one of them. This leaves individuals with the task of constantly searching for their own paths within this differentiated universe of religious and spiritual views. The modern world has been transformed to a domain where searching and uncertainty have become *structural* features of our spiritual lives. Of course, it is not hard to see the similarities between Taylor's analysis of the spiritual outlook of the 'secular age' and Giddens and Beck's views of late modernity in terms of reflexivity and fundamental insecurities discussed above.

Coleman (2010) suggests that older people face an even more complicated task in adequately responding to the changing spiritual outlook of late modernity. Current generations of older people form a 'transitional' group, educated in the religious traditions of their ancestors but also prone to the individualising tendencies in spirituality common for younger generations. While these younger generations feel that the language of (post-traditional) spirituality suits the pluralistic and fragmented reality of their lives much better than any tradition could, older people experience more of a conflict. This impedes the possibility for intergenerational communication about matters of religion, spirituality and meaning. As Coleman (2010, p 172) argues: 'the old may feel that loyalty and witness to their own religious faith is no longer relevant or appreciated by the young. But if spirituality is understood as essentially about the task of affirmation and integration of what is of ultimate meaning in life, older people should have much to contribute to the young from their life experience.'

Wuthnow (1998) provides important insights regarding the consequences of the individualisation of the lifecourse and the resulting task of continuous identity formation for the spiritual outlook people choose or experience in their lives. He draws a distinction between a 'spirituality of dwelling', in which people find their spiritual 'homes' within the comforting havens of traditional religious institutions or spiritual communities, and a 'spirituality of seeking', in which individuals have lost their self-evident faith in the metaphysical truths these places of dwelling have to offer and are destined to a constant search for their own parcels of spiritual truth and wisdom, to provide their life with much-needed direction.

The late modern individual, involved in a reflexive process of continuous redefinition of identity, typically employs a spirituality of seeking, which is much more person-centred. Wuthnow articulates the alternative conception of the self that goes with a spirituality of seeking, as follows:

> In the older view, identity was manifested by the holding of predefined social positions within institutions.[...] In the newer view [...] because their roles are not predefined, individuals have to worry about who they are, who they want to be, and how they want other people to perceive them. Self-definition is not necessarily more problematic, but it is understood to be more a matter of personal choice, more the result of an active process of searching, and more contingent on one's own thoughts and feelings than on the statuses that institutions confer. (Wuthnow, 1998, p 10)

Of course, one might argue that underlying all major religious traditions are the original spiritual experiences of their founding fathers. Their inner spiritual experience is, in that case, perceived as fundamental, while the religious institutions present the derivative form that mediates this original experience for the community. Atchley (2009) points to the fact that the individual spiritual journeys characteristic of late modernity might be interpreted as a quest for experiencing an authentic spirituality comparable to those 'founding' spiritual experiences, but unmediated by religious authority.

In sum, perspectives on the place of spirituality under late modern conditions draw our attention to the transformation of a society wherein religious institutions offered stable, unquestioned spiritual views, towards a society wherein a 'spirituality of seeking' seems to have obtained a structural status. This means we have to deal with the – seemingly paradoxical – situation of a 'structuralisation' of individual spiritualities.

Ageing and spiritual development

Having delineated some general changes regarding spirituality in late modern society, the connection between ageing and spiritual development can now be examined. For a considerable period, the subject of spirituality was somewhat undervalued in gerontological research. Most attention was given to the salutary role religious or spiritual belief appeared to play in maintaining health and wellbeing in later life. This, it might be argued, represented a one-sided focus on the extrinsic, instrumental benefits of spirituality for later life, rather than on the intrinsic meaning of religious or spiritual belief (Coleman, 2010). Lately, however, a renewed interest seems to have developed, as illustrated in Atchley's (2009) *Spirituality and aging*. While most research on ageing and spirituality so far has been done from a religion–centred angle, Atchley (2009) calls for a new perspective. This is needed, he argues, because in late modern circumstances, the population of older people increasingly consists of individuals perceiving themselves as people on a spiritual journey towards inner growth and higher forms of consciousness and development. Atchley presents empirical evidence from longitudinal studies, both quantitative and qualitative, that suggests that spiritual experience and spiritual development obtain an increasing importance for middle-aged and older people. Questions regarding the meaning of their own existence and of life in general, as well as reflections on their place in the succession of generations, their connection to other people and their relation to a universal, 'cosmic' reality, come to the fore. For many people, spiritual insights and experiences are an important resource in coping with (both positive and unwelcome) changes occurring as a result of ageing (see also Coleman, 2010).

Atchley (2009) provides an encompassing conceptual and theoretical picture of spirituality. Much earlier research on ageing and spirituality, he suggests, lacks sufficient depth in its presentation of the concept. For example, often spirituality is equated with religious affiliation, but especially in late modern circumstances people tend to disconnect these two themes, and place them in separate, possibly but not necessarily, linked realms. Many people loosely or not at all connected to traditional religious institutions may nevertheless picture themselves as spiritual beings and actively engage in spiritual journeys. Of course, religious traditions and institutions still may have an important role to play in the spiritual experiences of many people. Yet even within those institutions the trend seems to be that people are increasingly looking for their own individual appropriation of traditional spiritual resources. So, alongside the more traditional religious forms of spirituality, there seems to be a growing variety of 'secular' and individual spiritualities these days. Atchley therefore explicitly avoids using language that would restrict spirituality to experiences within traditional religious settings, to create a broader scope. Attempting to do justice to the variety of appearances, he chooses to understand spirituality as a 'sensitising concept': unlike denotative concepts it does not describe a specific or concretely observable part of reality, but instead tries to create a sensitivity about the special qualities of experience that may occur within a broadly defined region of interest, namely, the field of spirituality. This field is roughly delineated by concepts such as an experience of 'pure being', consciousness, connectedness or transcendence. In any case, spirituality in Atchley's view represents an inner, subjective experience.

Atchley covers a broad range of topics, such as the nature and quality of spiritual experience; the relation between spirituality and self or identity; the notion of spiritual development; the possible contribution 'sages' or 'spiritual elders' may have in society, organisations and communities; spiritual experience and its relation to time; and the possible role of spirituality and spiritual growth in coping with existential questions and experiences regarding age-related losses, or finitude and death. While Atchley's conceptual endeavours regarding the topic of spirituality are important and bring us a theoretical clarity, the most valuable and illuminating theme of his book is the connection between spiritual growth or development and later life. Just like Tornstam in his gerotranscendence theory (Tornstam, 2005), Atchley pictures later adulthood and old age as stages of life with a special potential for spiritual *development*. Since the notion of self-realisation entails not only the capacity to shape your life according to freely chosen aims but also the striving towards a future self that represents these goals in a higher or fuller way, the notion of development is interwoven with the ideal of self-realisation. Therefore, it is important to elaborate a little more about this topic.

Developmental psychologists and theorists such as Jean Piaget, Lawrence Kohlberg or Erik Erikson have traditionally envisioned development in general in terms of 'stages'. Many of these classical theories consider human development completed after adolescence, with the exception of Erikson whose model covers the entire lifespan. The stage model was also used for spiritual and religious development, notably by Fowler (1981), in his faith development theory. There are, however, several objections to a vision of development using stage-based models.

First, stage models suggest a biologically grounded predictability of development that becomes increasingly problematic as people age, since individual differences tend to accumulate when people are growing older. Not surprising, developmental theories that cover the whole life span, such as Erikson's psycho-social development theory, are rather vague in their description of the later stages. Also, social and cultural factors influencing people's development tend to be ignored or downplayed by the ontogenetic reductionist claims of such models. Dannefer (1999) rightly warns us about the 'fallacy of naturalisation' in developmental theory, meaning the tendency to treat certain phenomena as if they were an inescapable trait of the natural human condition, whereas they are in fact deeply influenced by social interaction and human activity.

Second, stage models imply a growing complexity with age to be a self-evident feature of human development. Passing through the earlier stages of development is supposed to be conditional for reaching the later, 'higher' stages of development. However, it is questionable whether earlier and later stages are comparable like that. It might just as well be argued that each stage of life has its own complexity and therefore its own developmental goals, not necessarily arising from earlier stages.

Atchley interprets human development along the lines of his own 'continuity theory' (cf Atchley, 1999). This theory assumes an evolutionary developmental process, oriented towards adaptation to change, while simultaneously preserving a sense of continuity necessary for maintaining a subjective, coherent experience of character. This applies to the role of spirituality in people's character as well, although spiritual experience might also be abrupt and radically altering the self-system of the individual, for instance, in the case of a religious conversion. In his own view of spiritual development, he further outlines a 'stage model' comprising 'awakening interest', 'inquiry', 'endeavour', 'integration' and 'intention' (towards a new spiritual direction). However, he seems to escape some of the objections to such models mentioned above. First, he does not pair these stages of spiritual development with a certain chronological time course or age, although he does maintain the view that ageing and the capacity for spiritual development coincide. Second, Atchley stresses the cyclical character of his stage model, thereby creating more flexibility to acknowledge the growing individual differences with age, and avoiding the pitfalls of more traditional, linear stage models of (spiritual) development.

For Atchley, spirituality represents a capacity that continues to develop and grow throughout people's lives, regardless of what happens to them in their later lives. Ageing and the inevitable losses accompanying processes of senescing might even be seen as a vehicle for stimulating spiritual growth and self-discovery. This may be clarified by a distinction Mowat (2010) draws between three discourses regarding ageing. The first discourse presents a rather pessimistic view, stating that ageing is a biological 'problem', to be solved eventually by scientific progress and medical interventions. The second discourse is much more optimistic and sees ageing as a period that brings wisdom and satisfaction, the only problem being the fact that these joys of old age are poorly recognised by society. This may appear attractive but it tends to downplay the fact that growing older also increases human vulnerability and may therefore lead to suffering and loss. The third discourse does not deny the fact that people are senescing and that losses are inevitably associated with that process, but it transcends these losses by stating that ageing is also a spiritual journey and a medium for spiritual self-realisation and/or self-transcendence (Mowat, 2010). People develop a new and different perspective on life that stimulates reformulating their identity in a spiritual way.

This matches with gerotranscendence theory, in which Tornstam (1997, 2005) also elaborates on developmental spiritual changes that are supposed to be specific for ageing individuals. Gerotranscendence is defined as 'a shift in metaperspective, from a materialistic and pragmatic view of the world to a more cosmic and transcendent one, normally accompanied by an increase in life satisfaction' (Tornstam, 1997, p 143). The concept is divided into three dimensions, a cosmic dimension, a self dimension and a relational dimension, covering roughly the same existential questions and concerns from Atchley's empirical studies mentioned before. Tornstam's primary objective is to offer a new positive developmental perspective on ageing, but in formulating his theory he also offers important critical feedback on the often-negative way ageing is presented, both by mainstream gerontology and in society at large. He wants to transcend the 'misery perspective' surrounding the process of ageing, and emphasises how a recognition of the spiritual developmental potential of later life might lead to more appreciation of the resources old age has to offer, both to individuals and to society (Tornstam, 2005).

Cole made the same point in *The journey of life: A cultural history of aging in America* (1992). Departing from a historical point of view, Cole is able to show how certain aspects of ageing, notably existential and spiritual ones, have virtually disappeared from the cultural and societal discourses regarding ageing. While the focus of much of gerontological research on senescing processes that can be controlled or even overcome has undoubtedly been of great importance, Cole warns us about the dangers of one-sidedness looming here:

> Obviously, certain problems of ageing – poverty, isolation, treatable disease – can and should be alleviated. Yet others – the gradual decline of physical vitality, the eventual path to death – are intractable. Our culture's ability to infuse these existential mysteries with vital meaning has been profoundly weakened over the last two centuries. Our ability to see the spiritual possibilities of ageing has been equally impaired. (Cole, 1992, p xxv)

So again, according to Cole, to avoid losing valuable and much needed cultural narratives on the existential value of later life, we should revalue spiritual perspectives on ageing. A small critical remark seems in order, however, regarding Cole's conception of the 'existential' dimension of ageing. He seems to link this almost exclusively to aspects of growing older that emphasise vulnerability, unavoidable limitations and the confrontation with human finitude, while I would like to propose that enriching experiences of deepening individual uniqueness (cf Baars, 2006b), wisdom, life acceptance, intergenerational connectedness, gerotranscendence and so on that are also potentially part of the process of growing older also carry an existential meaning. This clearly follows from the descriptions of spiritual developmental processes Atchley (2009) provides from his empirical research. His respondents testify to the richness and depth their lives are infused with as a result of their spiritual experiences. In the process of their spiritual development, confrontations with existential vulnerability are often transformed into experiences of meaning, resulting in attitudes of wisdom and acceptance.

Discussion: the merits of the spiritual perspective in relation to self-realisation

The discourse of spiritual development and ageing explored by researchers such as Atchley, Cole, Coleman and Tornstam opens up discussion on some interesting considerations when connected with the discourse of self-realisation characteristic for late modernity. First, regarding ageing, we may wonder about the implications of vulnerability and dependency related to the experience of senescing for the goals of self-realisation. It is exactly when confronted with such experiences that existential questions concerning the process of ageing, as mentioned by Cole, come to the fore. Taking into account the fundamental moral stake that underlies the ideal of self-realisation, it seems unsatisfactory to restrict the purpose of self-realisation to the phase of later life in which people are still relatively healthy and vital. Although some authors tend to connect the goal of self-realisation specifically to the 'third age' (cf Laslett, 1989; Weiss and Bass, 2002; Moen and Spencer, 2006), the argument of this chapter is that a satisfactory conception of self-realisation must be able to apply to the more vulnerable 'fourth age' as well (see further Chapter Four, this volume). However, when self-realisation is conceptualised in terms of the flourishing and bringing to completion of one's best capacities, what happens when these capacities are diminishing or even vanishing completely? The discourse on ageing and spirituality suggests a way out of this seeming paradox: age-related vulnerability and loss are not the enemy of developmental capacities and further self-realisation, as long as self-realisation is modified into a concept which integrates and transforms these so-called 'losses' into a new perspective that transcends the common language of decline and opens up new possibilities for meaning. In this respect, developing a spiritual perspective can support ageing individuals in their search for a personal, meaningful connection with the inevitabilities of their ageing process, as Atchley, Tornstam and Cole emphasise. A quote from one of Atchley's respondents, an 85-year-old male who found a spiritual way of coping with his hearing impairment, might serve as an example:

> 'When I first began to lose my hearing, I was frustrated that I could no longer effortlessly participate in things. [...] I tried reading lips but never really got the hang of it. Then I began trying to simply "be" with the people – to merely be there with them, to look gently into their eyes, to sense their energy. It was an amazingly pleasant experience.' (quoted in Atchley, 2009, p 21)

The question arises, of course, whether the access to such a spiritual perspective depends solely on an already existing spiritual interest flowing from someone's life history, or whether the development of such a perspective could be actively stimulated by policies aimed at a better quality of life for the frail elderly. This question cannot be answered here although sensitivity regarding the possibilities of a spiritual perspective for caretakers and policy makers concerned with older people can help open up valuable new ways of thinking about ageing and vulnerability.

Second, regarding the conception of 'self', the spiritual views in some respects conflict with the considerations regarding late modern selfhood mentioned above. Although the 'searching' nature of spiritual self-development processes seems to accord very well with late modern circumstances, the spiritual perspectives as described above fail to incorporate another important point of late modern critique regarding certain perspectives on selfhood. Atchley's holistic concept of the self allows for, maybe even presupposes, the existence of a 'core' self that seems to be at odds with the characteristics of late modern selfhood observed by theorists. The goal of spiritual development in the views Atchley sketches ultimately boils down to regaining our 'pure', 'true' or 'deeper' selves and attaining, through strategies of transcendence, a sense of 'wholeness' and 'integration'. This idea of wholeness is at odds with the fragmented and socially constructed forms of integration to which late modern selfhood – and thus late modern self-realisation – seems to be restricted. In this respect, Atchley's perspective should be complemented by a situated conception of integration or 'unity' that is more suitable for late modern conditions. Margaret Walker, for instance, offers such a conception, emphasising both the local, temporary and flexible configuration of experiences of coherence or integration and the importance of connecting our individual selves to a larger context that transcends us. For Walker (1999), it is this sense of connectedness with people, things or situations, that is specific for certain periods in our lives and may undergo many changes along the way, that provides us with an experience of integration. Her interpretation of this integration also underlines the importance of a spiritual perspective, but defies some potentially problematic implications of Atchley's vision of wholeness and thereby offers a valuable addition.

Third, we must not forget that self-realisation, even conceptualised in the way suggested above, does not take place in a vacuum. Both the process of (spiritual) self-realisation itself and the opportunities for individuals to shape this process are deeply influenced by the socio-cultural context in which people live and by structural societal arrangements. We have argued how, in late modern circumstances, the context conditioning the way people age is determined by two seemingly contradictory trends: the demand to shape your own identity and to design your own unique, individual way of living into old age, and the many ways society can facilitate and stimulate, but also manipulate, constrain or impede the opportunities to realise this task. One of the merits of Atchley's study is the tentative, yet vivacious sketch of the spiritual potential of later life and its possible contribution to society, communities and organisations. It is, however, a limitation that his work fails to consider on a more profound level the consequences of the 'structuralisation' of individual spiritualities under late modern circumstances, and that the possible impeding influence of structural factors fails to receive attention in his argument. Nevertheless, Atchley's work does stimulate important critical feedback on our society, because the latter fails to recognise the existential value a spiritually developed old age may have, not only for the individuals concerned but also for society and culture at large. Important questions are thereby raised, concerning how our society, and the position of elderly people within it, might look like, were there to be a greater appreciation and recognition of the spiritual potential of later life. Consider, for example, the many ways in which spiritual awareness motivates people to pay their services to the community, be it in volunteering, caretaking or mentoring the next generation. Atchley's respondents report that the undertaking of these activities in the context of spiritual development deepens their experience and adds meaning and connectedness to their daily lives, as this middle-aged woman testifies:

> 'When I first started doing this [volunteer work in a homeless shelter] I found it difficult to be around that much suffering all in one place. The discomfort I felt made me want to close down, to harden my heart. But I knew somehow that I needed to do just the opposite, to summon all the reserves of love I could find and stand there with a heart open to the suffering. Through this I was able to gently connect spiritually with the people being served and realise that we are all being served.' (quoted in Atchley, 2009, p 17)

These forms of community service, of which many middle-aged and older people perform more than their share, obviously have great potential in meeting many needs Western welfare states are struggling to deal with. Yet the appreciation of this invaluable contribution to society made by ageing individuals and the status these forms of service are endowed with often seems to be quite low. Many critical gerontological perspectives point out that our society is unable to provide elderly people with meaningful social roles, and that they are often confronted with ageism, neglect and contempt. The spiritual perspectives that infuse these 'modest' forms of community service by older people with meaning could offer interesting new roads to (re)value social roles taken by older people, conceived as strategies of self-realisation. At the same time, the spiritual perspectives can generate criticism about the structural disregard and downplaying of these contributions to society.

So, viewed from a critical perspective, one of the merits of the spiritual perspectives discussed in this contribution is that they try to do justice to the particular quality of spiritual experience and its supposed affinity with later life, while at the same time offering the opportunity of critical reflection on certain structural tendencies and images of ageing in our society. A spiritual perspective could even be useful for critical gerontology investigating in a new manner the background motivations of the commitment to changing older people's lives within society.

A potential disadvantage of speaking about spirituality in general seems to be that the language evoked by the subject itself tends to suggest that spirituality is something that occurs in a separate, mystical domain concerned with a cosmic, transcendent dimension, free from the restricting bonds with 'trivial' worldly matters. To be of use from a critical gerontological perspective, spirituality cannot be envisioned like that, but has to be taken as a phenomenon embedded in a specific context that influences its experience and interpretation. Only from that angle can we fruitfully address the arising critical questions about ageing in our society described above. It seems to me that of the authors discussed here, Cole (1992) in particular is trying to overcome such dualism between spiritual and worldly concerns, by underlining the interdependence of both, and the way the spiritually developing (ageing) individual or self is embedded in a cultural, historical and societal context that may stimulate but also impede its realisation.

Fourth, attention should be drawn to the connection between self-realisation, spirituality and morality, in the context of late modern ageing. Implicit in the ideal of self-realisation is the idea that one should be able to live life in a relatively self-determined way, in accordance with the self-chosen values ones cherishes most. At the same time, the possibilities and the space to realise a 'good life' and a 'good old age' for oneself depend deeply on the opportunities and restrictions offered by the structural societal arrangements regarding ageing, over which individuals have very limited power of control. Self-realisation as a moral goal requires the development of a relationship with oneself in which there is a balance between the active appropriation of one's own life and one's authentic self-development, and the mindful awareness of those aspects in life that cannot be controlled and therefore require an attitude of acceptance and acquiescence. Spiritual perspectives tend to favour the latter attitude, but paradoxically, this attitude, if successfully developed, may offer a transformational potential favourable to a 'good life' in the moral sense, that extends itself beyond the individual existence towards the realm of social relations and societal structures.

Conclusion

In sum, perspectives on ageing and spirituality offer promising new roads to study how ageing individuals are searching for self-development and self-realisation under the complex societal circumstances of late modernity. Although self-realisation can be argued to be one of the most fundamental moral ideals of late modernity, representing the path through which one is supposed to create one's own 'good', meaningful life, it is also potentially a deeply problematic ideal. There is a tension between the idea of integration and wholeness implicit in the notion of self underlying the ideal and the fragmented self-experience characteristic of late modernity. Moreover, opportunities to perform the necessary processes of choice and valuation are profoundly influenced by structural factors impeding chances of self-realisation. Moreover, these chances are often argued to be unevenly distributed, so that people living in less favourable conditions (for example, due to their socio-economic position, but a poor health condition and the related vulnerability and frailty may also be important) are severely hindered in their self-realisation. The value of the spiritual perspectives discussed in this chapter lies in the fact that an alternative perspective on self-realisation is offered which connects this ideal with processes of spiritual development. Such a perspective, if further developed, may be able to offer a different view on questions around the late modern self and its problems of identity and integration, to transcend existing prejudices and ageist views by showing the opportunities for meaning and development possible even in conditions of vulnerable later life existence, and to offer critical reflection on the structural-societal processes framing the life experience and status of older individuals.

References

Atchley, R.C. (1999) *Continuity and adaptation in aging: Creating positive experiences*, Baltimore, MD: The Johns Hopkins University Press.

Atchley, R.C. (2009) *Spirituality and aging*, Baltimore, MD: The Johns Hopkins University Press.

Baars, J. (2006a) 'Beyond neomodernism, antimodernism, and postmodernism: Basic categories for contemporary critical gerontology', in J. Baars, D. Dannefer, C. Phillipson and A. Walker (eds) *Aging, globalization and inequality: The new critical gerontology*, Amityville, NY: Baywood Publishing, pp 17-42.

Baars, J. (2006b) *Het nieuwe ouder worden. Paradoxen en perspectieven van leven in de tijd* (2nd edn) [*The new ageing. Paradoxes and perspectives of living in time*], Amsterdam: SWP.

Bauman, Z. (2001) *The individualised society*, Cambridge: Polity Press.

Beck, U. and Beck-Gernsheim, E. (2002) *Individualization*, London: Sage Publications.

Cole, T.R. (1992) *The journey of life: A cultural history of aging in America*, New York: Cambridge University Press.

Coleman, P.G. (2010) 'Religion and age', in D. Dannefer and C. Phillipson (eds) *The Sage handbook of social gerontology*, London: Sage Publications, pp 164-76.

Dannefer, D. (1999) 'Neoteny, naturalization and other constituents of human development', in C.D. Ryff and V.W. Marshall (eds) *The self and society in aging processes*, New York: Springer Publishing Company Inc, pp 67-93.

Dannefer, D. (2008) 'The waters we swim: Everyday social processes, macrostructural realities, and human aging', in K.W. Schaie and R.P. Abeles (eds) *Social structures and aging individuals: Continuing challenges*, New York: Springer Publishing Company, pp 3-22.

Dannefer, D. and Kelley-Moore, J.A. (2009) 'Theorizing the life course: New twists in the paths', in V.L. Bengtson, D. Gans, N.M. Putney and M. Silverstein (eds) *Handbook of theories of aging* (2nd edn), New York: Springer Publishing Company, pp 389-411.

Elliot, A. (2001) *Concepts of the self*, Cambridge: Polity Press.

Fowler, J.W. (1981) *Stages of faith: The psychology of human development and the quest for meaning*, San Francisco, CA: Harper & Row Publishers.

Gergen, K.J. (1991) *The saturated self: Dilemmas of identity in contemporary life*, New York: Basic Books.

Gerhardt, V. (1999) *Selbstbestimmung. Das Prinzip der Individualität [Self-determination: The principle of individuality]*, Stuttgart: Phillipp Reclam jun.

Gewirth, A. (1998) *Self-fulfillment*, Princeton, NJ: Princeton University Press.

Giddens, A. (1991) *Modernity and self-identity: Self and society in the late modern age*, Cambridge: Polity Press.

Honneth, A. (2001) 'Recognition or redistribution? Changing perspectives of the moral order of society', *Theory, Culture & Society*, vol 18, nos 2/3, pp 43-55.

Honneth, A. (2004) 'Organized self-realization: Some paradoxes of individualization', *European Journal of Social Theory*, vol 7, no 4, pp 463-78.

Hendricks, J. (2010) 'Age, self and identity in the global century', in D. Dannefer and C. Phillipson (eds) *The Sage handbook of social gerontology*, London: Sage Publications, pp 251-64.

Holstein, M.B. (2010) 'Ethics and aging, retrospectively and prospectively', in T.R. Cole, R.E. Ray and R. Kastenbaum (eds) *A guide to humanistic studies in aging*, Baltimore, MD: The Johns Hopkins University Press, pp 244-70.

Laslett, P. (1989) *A fresh map of life. The emergence of the third age*, London: Weidenfeld & Nicholson.

Moen, P. and Spencer, D. (2006) 'Converging divergences in age, gender, health and well-being: Strategic selection in the third age', in R.H. Binstock and L.K. George (eds) *Handbook of aging and the social sciences* (6th edn), Burlington, MA: Academic Press, pp 129-45.

Mowat, H. (2010) 'Ageing, health care and the spiritual imperative. A view from Scotland', in J. Bouwer (ed) *Successful ageing, spirituality and meaning: Multidisciplinary perspectives*, Leuven: Peeters, pp 109-20.

Sapp, S. (2010) 'Aging in world religions: an overview', in T.R. Cole, R.E. Ray and R. Kastenbaum (eds) *A guide to humanistic studies in aging*, Baltimore, MD: The Johns Hopkins University Press, pp 121-38.

Taylor, C. (1989) *Sources of the self: The making of the modern identity*, Cambridge: Cambridge University Press.

Taylor, C. (1991) *The ethics of authenticity*, Cambridge, MA: Harvard University Press.

Taylor, C. (2007) *A secular age*, Cambridge, MA: Belknap Press of Harvard University Press.

Tornstam, L. (1997) 'Gerotranscendence: The contemplative dimension of aging', *Journal of Aging Studies*, vol 11, no 2, pp 143-54.

Tornstam, L. (2005) *Gerotranscendence: A developmental theory of positive aging*, New York: Springer Publishing Company.

Walker, M.U. (1999) 'Getting out of line. Alternatives to life as a career', in M.U. Walker (ed) *Mother time: Women, aging and ethics*, Oxford: Rowman & Littlefield Publishers, Inc, pp 97-111.

Walker, M.U. (2007) *Moral understandings: A feminist study in ethics* (2nd edn), Oxford: Oxford University Press.

Weiss, R.S. and Bass, S.A. (2002) *Challenges of the third age. Meaning and purpose in later life*, Oxford: Oxford University Press.

Wuthnow, R. (1998) *After heaven: Spirituality in America since the 1950s*, Berkeley, CA: University of California Press.

SEVEN

Social ability or social frailty? The balance between autonomy and connectedness in the lives of older people

Anja Machielse and Roelof Hortulanus

Introduction

Social relationships constitute an important resource in daily life. For this reason people who are embedded in a network of meaningful personal relationships generally enjoy a higher level of wellbeing than those without such a network. This applies in particular to primary relationships with spouses and family, but social relationships in a broader sense also have a positive influence on feelings of wellbeing. Yet the ability to maintain such relationships may be affected by broader changes affecting society. These may drastically alter the structure of daily life, granting more freedom in some areas while at the same time increasing the demands placed on individuals. The more personal competencies people have, the more capable they are to be of shaping their lives in the way they want. They are also more likely to succeed in maintaining meaningful and supportive networks and taking advantage of these when necessary. Wellbeing is greatest when people succeed at finding a balance between individual autonomy and independence on the one hand, and connectedness with others on the other. Such balance enables people to fully enjoy the individual freedom of late modernity but at the same time feel safe in the face of limitations and adversity. It is also crucial for dealing with problematic situations and circumstances with which people are confronted, and which tend to happen more often as people age.

This chapter examines the extent to which involvement in a meaningful social network has enriching consequences both for individuals in general and for their chances of ageing *well*. The chapter first considers why meaningful relationships have a positive effect on personal wellbeing and quality of life. Second, the social environment of late modern society is reviewed along with the possibilities for social integration under these new social conditions. Third, the personal networks of Dutch older adults are described, the changes that are occurring in these networks, the role of major life events and the importance of social competencies when dealing with such events. Fourth, the chapter examines the role of personal competences and social networks. Finally, a concluding section draws together a number of remarks about ageing well in contemporary society.

The empirical data in this chapter is derived from the study *Social isolation in modern society* (Hortulanus et al, 2006).[1] The goal of this research project was to map out the nature and scope of social isolation in the Netherlands, and to offer insight into the background, causes and consequences of the phenomenon. The study was carried out in the form of an oral survey, gathering data in two phases. In the first phase of the study, nearly 2,500 respondents (aged 18 years and over) were interviewed in a face-to-face setting on the basis of a very extensive list of topics. An important part of this first survey concerns a series of questions to map out the personal networks of the respondents. This was done using the exchange approach devised by Fischer (1982), which attempts to find the people with whom respondents (regularly) undertake concrete activities and/or from whom they expect support. The quality of these social contacts in terms of loneliness was determined with a validated loneliness scale (de Jong Gierveld and Kamphuis, 1984). In the second phase, six months later, a number of respondents ($n = 460$) were interviewed for a second time. These interviews explored in greater detail a number of personal topics (such as life events, life attitude and socialisation). The questionnaire also contained questions about the support people found after important life events and the consequences of these for their social network. The arguments in the sections on life events and personal competences are based on data from these in-depth interviews.

Meaning of personal relationships

Many researchers have confirmed a positive link between a meaningful personal network and a person's level of wellbeing (Berkman and Glass, 2000; Heller and Rook, 2001; Sarason et al, 2001; Pescosolido and Levy, 2002). This association is connected with the fact that social relationships provide several preconditions for 'social existence' (Weiss, 1974; Thoits, 1985). These are expressed in three main functions of social relationships: first, they are important for the development and maintenance of *identity and self-respect*, in particular through the recognition and appreciation of significant others (Myers, 1999). Members of social networks also offer possibilities for determining social roles and social comparisons, and support for personal aspirations (Heller and Rook, 2001).

Second, social relationships contribute to *social integration*, allowing people to feel they are part of a social group in which they experience personal involvement, intimacy and friendship. Contacts within this group provide a *social* identity and a frame of reference that influences the values and norms that individuals develop as well as their choices and plans (Myers, 1999). Belonging to a group or category of people that they regard as worthy also contributes to the maintenance of self-esteem (Baumeister and Vohs, 2005). Third, social relationships are important because of the *social support* that they are able to provide. The *potential* support of personal relationships has a positive effect on wellbeing with the expectation that, when needed, people can count on others for help and support (Pescosolido and Levy, 2002). Several types of support have been identified:

- *Instrumental* support refers to material or practical help that meets the immediate need of the person involved (for example, money, food, clothing, household help, information)
- *Emotional* or affective support offers people the feeling that others care about them, that there is attention for their experiences and feelings, and that they can talk about personal problems
- *Companionship* support takes on the form of social companionship: the joint undertaking of social activities, such as shopping, going to the cinema together, going out for coffee or spending the evening playing cards (van der Poel, 1993; Machielse, 2006c).

Social relationships contribute substantially to a person's wellbeing at all phases of the lifecourse, but social integration and social support seem to be especially important for older adults. As people age, the possibilities of participating in some areas of social life may decrease, for instance, because of deteriorating health or limited mobility. The individual's need for help and support from others may increase as a result. However, these issues cannot be viewed separately from the self-image and the self-respect that people have built up over the course of their lives. It is precisely in a life phase in which people are confronted more often with radical life changes (such as experiences of loss or illness) that self-confidence and self-respect are important competencies when finding a new balance.

Social relationships in a late modern society

While meaningful relationships with relatives, neighbours, friends and acquaintances are important resources for personal functioning and wellbeing, such relationships have become less self-evident in late modern society. Three transition points have had fundamental consequences for the social relationships that people have with each other in daily life. First, personal networks have been affected by a process of 'de-traditionalisation' or individualisation (Giddens, 1990; Beck, 1992). Both terms refer to a transformation in a number of the institutions that underpin social relationships. These were structured and constrained by prescribed norms and behaviours. In late modern society individuals are much less guided by tradition. The traditional sources of collective identity and meaning (national state, class, work, church, family) no longer offer the necessary and self-evident personal security or social integration. Individuals themselves have to steer their lives and make choices from among the possibilities and strategies that are available (Giddens, 1990). This does not mean that personal relationships are no longer affected by structural constraints. On the contrary, it presumes that people deliberately integrate into networks that are relevant for realising their ambitions. Arising from this, the personal relationships that people maintain with each other are viewed as having become more instrumental and functional (Beck and Beck-Gernsheim, 2002; see further Chapter Two, this volume).

Second, economic changes underpinning individualisation have had significant consequences for social relationships. Under the influence of market-oriented thinking, more emphasis has come to lie on performance, competition and 'being better than others' (Bauman, 2001). Post-industrial capitalism plays constantly into this pattern by offering people possibilities to realise their individual uniqueness, autonomy and identity. This development has a major influence on the creation of relationships in the private domain, where contrasting groups are formed on the basis of shared preferences or lifestyles (Giddens, 1991). Relationships within such groups do not have a very lasting character. They are constantly re-examined in the light of other choice possibilities or changed individual preferences. The consequence is less authenticity and more the commercialisation and commodification of relationships (Kunneman, 2005).

Third, the rise of information and computer technology has transformed many features of the social environment. New communication possibilities have led to a fundamental change in social space, social relationships are less bound to geographic limitations and social contacts can take shape over increasingly large time-space contexts (Giddens, 1984). Such developments summon positive expectations in terms of possibilities for participation and integration. At the same time, the danger looms that impersonal forms of communication will increasingly replace *face-to-face* interactions.

These broader societal developments have major consequences for relationships in the private sphere as well as the public domain. In this context, Giddens (1994) speaks of 'a transformation of intimacy' in areas such as family life. Personal relationships are less obligatory and rigid and more flexible and voluntary than in previous times. This does not mean, however, that there are no longer structural constraints that affect the formation of networks. For example, work and income still condition the opportunities to find and maintain relationships (van Tilburg and Thomese, 2010). In late modern society the association between social positions and network structure becomes more complex than before. Equally, emancipation processes transform traditional male and female roles. The result is an increased labour participation of women, which has far-reaching consequences for family life; whereas women used to be responsible for family relationships, they are building their own life beyond traditional family contexts. Their former role of *socialiser* has come under pressure (Putnam, 2000; Beck and Beck-Gernsheim, 2002). In this way many personalised contradictions are also articulated in family and other personal relationships (van Tilburg and Thomese, 2010).

In late modern society family ties are based less on traditional rules of belonging, on 'natural' feelings of duty and obligation. By contrast, the significance of friendship and other informal relationships has increased (Allan, 2008). These relationships, based on mutual affinity, love and affection, have taken over any of the roles previously performed exclusively by the family. Friendships arise out of motivations that emanate from a person's own needs and not from given realities or social obligations. They are based on shared interests and values, on mutual affection and reciprocity options (Friedman, 1989). Such voluntary interdependence implies a general reciprocity in terms of, for example, mutual help, respect and support. Although in their friendships people strive towards a mutual exchange of support, respect and love, they will also try to maintain the equality if they are (temporarily) in an unequal situation (Pahl, 1998). In this way, friendship networks can offer the continuity and security that are so important for personal wellbeing.

Loneliness, social isolation and social exclusion

Fundamental societal transitions have influenced (and are still influencing) social life in general, and mutual relationships that people maintain with each other in daily life in particular. The importance of self-chosen or personal relationships has increased. As a consequence network structures in late modern society have become both more diffuse and less certain. Liberation from traditional and self-evident bonds is accompanied by the emergence of other types of social bonds that are often more abstract and less visible but at the same time imply new dependencies (Beck and Beck-Gernsheim, 2002). The degree to which people can participate in these networks is crucial for their possibilities to independently mould their own identity and life. This new social environment offers many new challenges, but also brings uncertainty and risks along, because individuals are required – more than before – to shape their own social world autonomously (Beck, 1992).

Modernisation and individualisation processes may well have produced more freedom, but at the same time higher demands may be made on individuals. Under the conditions of late modern society ample social competencies and skills are necessary to participate in social and societal life. Not everyone is equally capable of developing a solid identity and participating in relevant social bonds in society. For some, the new social conditions entail a widening of their field of action: they have enough competencies to react actively to the social changes and know how to fully take advantage of the increased freedom. They find possibilities to express their autonomy and independence and are capable of participating in meaningful networks that are relevant in order to realise their ambitions and goals. Others experience the freedom rather as a burden, and feel uprooted (Ehrenberg, 1995; Bauman, 2001). They miss the capacities that are needed to develop an active personality and choose (consciously or otherwise) the more passive strategy of adjustment and docility (Côté and Levine, 2002). This passivity is often accompanied by avoidance behaviour, in which people gradually retreat from social and societal life (Machielse, 2006a).

When people participate less in social bonds and appear incapable of building meaningful personal relationships, the quality of life will inevitably suffer. The absence of personal contacts, or the feeling that existing contacts do not meet the demands set, form a serious threat to individual wellbeing. Perlman and Peplau (1982) describe a number of important manifestations of *loneliness*: feeling symptoms (such as depression, stress, boredom), motivational symptoms (increased activities or apathy), cognitive symptoms (such as a low self-image or a strong self-orientedness), behavioural symptoms (abnormal patterns of self-revelation) and physical complaints (sleeplessness, headaches, alcoholism). Social isolation, social exclusion or marginalisation may also follow where older people retreat from society: *Social isolation* refers to the inability to maintain meaningful and supportive personal relationships. *Social exclusion* refers to a situation where people no longer have the feeling of being part of a meaningful cultural and normative world that is shared with others. *Marginalisation* or institutional exclusion occurs where people become detached from key social institutions such as the welfare state. (Machielse, 2011)

A network with meaningful, supportive relationships may be viewed as indispensable to personal functioning. At the same time we have seen that social conditions in contemporary society have fundamentally changed. Whereas younger generations experience these modern situations as natural, older generations have experienced the consequences personally – in the relationships with their spouses and children, in the wider family network, in their circle of friends and acquaintances and in their living environment (Victor et al, 2009). The question now is what makes older adults sufficiently able to handle things in this new social environment, in general and in dealing with major life events. What does social ability mean in the later life phases in which independence and the ability to cope on one's own often decrease due to deteriorating health or limited mobility, and in which ever more people keep dropping out of the network? And what is the meaning of personal relationships when dealing with such setbacks?

Social networks of older adults

To describe the social networks of older adults this chapter makes use of the social contacts typology developed by Hortulanus, Machielse and Meeuwesen (2006), which takes account of two dimensions of social networks: first, the scope of the social support network; and second, the presence or absence of feelings of loneliness. Each is related to a different aspect of the social network. People with a large network may feel lonely because the existing contacts do not meet their needs. By contrast, someone with a small network can be satisfied because the contacts are sufficiently supportive.

The typology for social contacts consists of four categories:

- The *socially competent* have many contacts, their social network functions satisfactorily and they do not feel lonely.

- The *socially inhibited* have only a few contacts, but they appear to be sufficient and meet their social needs.
- The *lonely* have many contacts yet nonetheless feel lonely because the existing contacts do not meet their wishes.
- The *socially isolated* are worst-off – they have few or no meaningful contacts, and feel lonely and unhappy.

Using this typology we can affirm that two thirds of Dutch adults (aged 18 and above) (64 per cent) have a meaningful social network that meets their needs and desires. For the rest, the social network looks less attractive. About 6 per cent of Dutch adults live in actual social isolation; they have few or no supportive contacts, and deal with strong feelings of loneliness. The socially inhibited and the lonely make up respectively 8 per cent and 22 per cent of the Dutch population; they are vulnerable because of a limited size or limited quality of their network, and are at an increased risk of social isolation (Hortulanus et al, 2006) (see Table 7.1 for a summary).

Table 7.1: Typology of contacts in the Netherlands, per age category (%)

Age	Socially competent	Lonely	Socially inhibited	Socially isolated
18-30	67	22	7	4
31-40	67	19	8	5
41-50	69	21	5	5
51-60	62	24	7	7
61-70	62	20	11	6
71-80	49	29	8	14
≥81	38	26	20	20
Average	64	22	8	6

Source: Data file on social isolation in the Netherlands (Hortulanus et al, 2006)

Table 7.1 demonstrates how the network appears less favourable as people age. The share of socially competent people is far below average in the oldest categories. In the group aged ≥81 we find nearly three times as many socially inhibited people (20 per cent) and even five times as many socially isolated individuals (20 per cent) than in the youngest age category. Although the *socially inhibited* are satisfied with the quality of their existing contacts, they are vulnerable. They depend on only a few others: if one or more people drops out from that network, this implies a risk of isolation. Both the *lonely* and the *socially isolated* deal with feelings of loneliness. They admit to being familiar with 'experiencing a sense of emptiness', 'not having enough people to fall back on', 'missing companionship', 'missing people around them' and 'having no friends to call on when in need' (Hortulanus et al, 2006, p 45). In all age categories, divorced and widowed people have twice as much chance to get socially inhibited or socially isolated. This is even more so for people in urban areas – the chance of becoming socially inhibited or socially isolated in cities is considerably higher than in rural areas (10 versus 3 per cent).

Changes in the network

Over the lifecourse, social networks change in composition, size and quality. This process can be understood from a variety of perspectives: social and personal transitions in later life, and the changes in the expected returns from relationships within the network and alterations in an individual's motivation that are associated with the limited time horizon of older adults (Carstensen et al, 2006; van Tilburg and Thomese, 2010). The research reported here found that alterations to personal networks are linked to major changes or events in life that have consequences for existing relationship patterns. Major events may cause networks to increase or decrease in size or quality. Some events lead to an *expansion* of the network, such as having children or getting married. There are also events that affect the network *negatively*, in the sense that they have a detrimental effect on the size or quality of the social network. These are experiences that imply some degree of loss, with older adults generally confronted with these more frequently than younger people. Events or circumstances that decrease the social contacts of older adults are losing one's partner or death of a loved one. Other reasons are mentioned that can be understood from a lifecourse perspective, such as issues that are more process-like and that do their work gradually, such as senescing and a deteriorating health condition.

The decrease in the number of contacts does not happen to the same degree for all older adults. It is striking that a decrease is observed most often among lonely and isolated older adults. It is thus precisely those who are already unhappy about the *quality* of their network who see it become gradually smaller; for them, the decrease of the network size is not the result of *selective shrinking* due to changed emotional engagement (Carstensen et al, 2006). It is particularly the consequence of a lack of personal competencies that are necessary to maintain meaningful relationships that meet their needs and desires. Factors interrelated to the lifecourse, such as senescing and deteriorating health, have a negative influence on their network. The actual loss of one or several network members often marks a turning point in the negative sense.

Among *socially competent* older adults the opposite seems to be happening. Satisfaction about the quality of the existing network appears to make it easier to maintain contacts or even expand the network. Senescing and deteriorating health have hardly any influence on their social networks. Their quality and size are sufficient to compensate for these changes and to maintain a good quality of life. Here we see the 'Matthew effect' in operation: those who already have a meaningful network are generally able to hold on to that network, whereas those whose network functions less well see it further disintegrate. A decrease in the number of social contacts tends to lead to a loss of quality of life, especially for the lonely and the isolated, a group who were not happy with their social life in the first place.

Life events

Important life events can have prolonged effects in the lives of people. An event that took place many years previously can still have an enormous impact on someone's present life. The most significant *positive events* that keep having an influence at an older age are related to the individual's personal life such as a good marriage and having children. The importance of a happy youth is the most salient. Three out of four older adults indicated that this was a determinant, in a positive sense, for their later life: a contented childhood and loving parents seem to form a solid buffer against negative events later in the lifecourse (Hortulanus et al, 2006).

The most important *negative* events that keep influencing a person's life are those of a personal nature, such as lack of attention and love during one's youth, the loss of someone close, a serious illness (of oneself or an important other), problematic relationships or the inability to find a suitable partner, and carrying a secret. There are also circumstances or events related to the societal roles people fulfil. The most important ones are not having an education, problems at work, incapacity for work and retirement. All these aspects tend to have a negative influence on quality of life up to an advanced age.

The number of negative events that still play a role in older adults' lives varies strongly for the four contact groups. Whereas the number of positive and negative events is fairly balanced among *socially competent* older adults, the *lonely* mention twice as many negative as positive events, and the *socially isolated* three times as many. Failure to form intimate ties in one's youth is much more common among the two high-risk groups and the socially isolated than among the socially able. The same applies for disappointments due to unrealised goals and for carrying a secret. In addition to negative events that more or less belong to the normal course of life, the two high-risk groups and the socially isolated have been hit more often in their lives by traumatic events which keep influencing their lives negatively, even at an advanced age.

Social support assists people in processing and managing negative events. This is mainly about the *emotional* support of a spouse, friends, family, friends and neighbours, sometimes supplemented by professional support from organisations or institutions. *Practical* support and information can also be important for processing things that happen. In some cases an appeal is made only to professional support, which mostly involves psychiatric help or help from social workers. When someone can mobilise the necessary help and support, he or she is more capable of limiting or alleviating the negative consequences of an event. People with a meaningful network are therefore more capable of facing adversity and problems. However, there are large differences in the social support that people can expect after a dramatic event. Although such support is self-evident for the socially competent, the same does not apply for the lonely, the socially inhibited or the socially isolated. The last group is especially worse off in this respect. After a drastic event they must do without the help or support of others, even though they need it. In many cases there may not be anyone in their environment who can offer help. They are also less adept at reaching professional organisations. All of this causes major life events to keep influencing their lives negatively. The socially able are better equipped to process negative events because their social networks offer more protection and support.

Personal competencies

The negative consequences of major life changes can be limited when people get the right help and support. This requires solution-oriented action from the person involved. Mobilising support in one's own network or seeking professional guidance and support appeals to individuals' personal competencies and the capacity for self-management. Coping strategies play an important role here (Hortulanus et al, 2006; Machielse, 2006a).

In general, two types of reactions to life events can be found in terms of general coping strategies: an *active* form of coping, which is aimed at a positive transformation, and a *passive* form of coping, which leads to a negative transformation (Lazarus, 1966). In an *active* strategy a person tries to find a place for the negative emotions that accompany negative experiences. The person looks for ways to undo the negative situation, for example, by an active process of revising or reappraising an event (see, for example, Taylor, 1983). An active strategy presumes open communication with members of the social network, the ability to share emotions, mutual involvement and trust. A *passive* coping strategy, by contrast, manifests itself in emotional denial, withdrawal and avoidance behaviour. The involved person is confronted with strong feelings of fear and shame, and the feeling of losing a foothold in all aspects of life. There is no open communication with others, which keeps away adequate help. The strategy that someone chooses (deliberately or otherwise) depends on personal competencies such as self-confidence and social skills. The fewer personal competencies a person has, the greater the chances of a passive coping strategy (Côté and Levine, 2002).

Personal competencies and an active coping strategy are thus important when processing negative events. When someone is more competent – has more self-respect, is capable of overcoming feelings of fear, guilt and shame, and dares show others his/her vulnerability – more adequate help can be offered. This can help people resume the thread of their lives in the course of time. For people with fewer competencies, negative events form a turning point in the negative sense. They run the risk of losing control over their lives and get into a downward spiral in which various problems keep piling up in the course of time. Personal competencies thus form an essential aspect of communicative self-management; the ability to take the initiative, to bring about a situation that is perceived as meaningful and to search for alternatives if the situation does not satisfy (Cornelis, 1997). It is the steering competencies that are necessary in contemporary society when striving for independence and autonomy.

The basis for the development of such steering competencies is laid down during one's younger years (Taylor, 1989). We have already noted that a happy and loving youth can constitute a protective factor for problems and adversity. The trust that exists between children and parents/carers under normal circumstances forms the basis for personal identity as well as the emotional and cognitive orientation towards the world and others. It also underlies the feeling of *ontological* safety that people normally develop (Giddens, 1991, p 38). This safety system can be seen as a sort of emotional protection against existential fear and against future threats and dangers. It is the protective cocoon that normally ensures that someone can deal with changes and uncertain or difficult circumstances later in life. These early life experiences are also of essential importance for *becoming social* (Giddens, 1991, pp 39-40). The development of competencies continues during a person's entire life cycle, via interactions in diverse social circles such as the neighbourhood, the school, work and friendship circles. The versatility of these social circles illustrates the complex interactions between the individual circumstances and the societal context in which individuals find themselves. The more a person is involved in social contexts, the more his or her competencies will be adequate and conducive towards meaningful relationships. By contrast, people who have few interactions with others have less developed and thus less adequate competencies. This may produce a passive coping strategy that may perpetuate or even enhance social isolation (Côté and Levine, 2002; Machielse, 2006a).

Social ability and personal competencies of older adults

As people age, they have to deal more often with major life changes in various areas of life; some life changes are connected with the process of senescing, such as the death of dear ones, limited mobility or a deteriorating health condition. Other life changes emanate from societal norms that allocate certain roles to people, such as work or retirement. Personal competencies, the capacity for self-management and the quality of the social network are determinant for the possibilities that older adults have to deal with such changes. The more personal competencies they have, the more possibilities they enjoy for communicative self-management in the sense that they are more capable of shaping their lives in the way they want. They also succeed more in maintaining supportive networks and taking advantage of them in coping with fundamental changes in personal life. The degree to which people are capable of finding a good balance between individual autonomy or independence and connectedness with meaningful others is crucial; ageing well means attaining such a balance. In this context it is interesting to look at the personal competencies in the four contact groups (see Table 7.2).

Socially competent individuals with *many* personal competencies are people in balance. They know how to find the proper balance between autonomy and connectedness. Socially competent individuals with *limited* personal competencies can also be classified as able because they have a network that can offer effective support when needed. This network can compensate for the limited personal competencies: they feel safe, even when their ability to cope on their own comes under attack. In case of drastic events they are able to optimally take

Table 7.2: Subgroup typification of the social contact typology by degree of personal competencies

	Socially competent	Lonely	Socially inhibited	Socially isolated
Many personal competencies	Balanced people	Misunderstood	Ambitious	Problem concealers
Limited personal competencies	Sheltered	Disappointed	Socially unskilled	Defeated

Source: Hortulanus et al (2006, p 221)

advantage of the existing network and face the problems. Both groups enjoy a good balance between connectedness and independence. The combination of personal input and input of the social network is in both cases such that striving for self-development and autonomy can continue, even in the presence of adversity and problems.

The *socially inhibited* with major personal competencies appear to deploy them mainly to satisfy their ambitions. They renounce – albeit temporarily – tight social relationships, compensating the lack thereof with activities that fill their time and sometimes also give them some degree of status. When socially inhibited people have minimal personal competencies, their limited social skills become more noticeable. They are dependent on a small social network that provides only a limited degree of connectedness.

For the *lonely*, the balance between independence and connectedness is disturbed in a different manner. Although they are connected to a large number of people, they feel misunderstood or disappointed. Lonely people with major personal competencies feel misunderstood because they have suffered experiences of emotional loss. Lonely people with limited personal competencies are very disappointed in others, because they cannot reduce their feelings of dependence and limited connectedness.

The *socially isolated* with major personal competencies experience a strong discrepancy. They can do a lot and can even handle themselves in more or less functional social environments. This allows them to hide well the problems they have with establishing and maintaining closer personal relationships. The socially isolated with limited competencies have little more than that if they are to keep up appearances. They are not connected with the people around them, and feel defeated. This makes them the opposite of the socially able with major social competencies (Hortulanus et al, 2006).

Ageing well

From the discussion thus far it has become clear that the chances of ageing well are unevenly distributed. People who have had a protective and happy youth that helped them develop good personal competencies are more successful later in life when it comes to building and maintaining a network that is meaningful and supportive, and can contribute to feelings of wellbeing. Those who are less lucky and who have grown up in a situation that had few possibilities for developing good personal competencies tend to also be at a disadvantage in their adult lives. Hence in many cases ageing well is the result of having a good youth. The disadvantages often have a persistent character, which has serious consequences.

Older adults with good social competencies have the resilience that is necessary to deal with setbacks and problematic life changes. Active coping strategies have become a natural part of their actions, enabling them to better deal with new societal conditions and with more personal problems that can arise in the course of life. They are also capable of building a meaningful network that can offer adequate support during negative events and circumstances. The ideal situation is that of *socially competent* older adults with major personal competencies, but the socially competent with limited personal competencies also do well. Although they have less self-confidence, social skills and problem-solving abilities, they feel safe in a network that offers support and contributes to their feeling of wellbeing. The quality of their network is sufficiently good to catch changes related to ageing and to maintain a good quality of life.

We have also seen that good personal competencies do not necessarily have to lead to good networks. Personal competencies tend to be deployed chiefly in specific life domains such as work situations or other formal contexts. We see this, for example, with the *socially inhibited* who have good social competencies. They are ambitious and attach great value to social success and a social position. It is only when the socially inhibited lose this role because they lose their job or because they can no longer participate in society due to deteriorating health or limited mobility that the lack of a supportive network becomes manifest.

The worst-off are the *socially isolated*. They do not have a supportive network, and miss the competencies to actively react to life events by themselves. A lack of direction and self-management makes them lean on others, burdening the existing contacts and making it much more difficult to maintain them. They usually follow passive strategies, experience little support from their social network, or do not know how to take advantage of the existing support. Those with major social competencies are often still capable of managing by themselves in practical terms. Their problems, then, remain hidden.

Socially isolated people with limited personal competencies are often cut off from every aspect of regular life. In addition, they are no longer able to find their way to facilities of the welfare state and are mainly busy trying to 'survive'. Their incapacity to be part of relevant networks is often accompanied by a lack of meaning. The social conditions of contemporary society make their lives even more harrowing; their passivity and withdrawal behaviour ensure that they literally become 'invisible'.

Conclusion

In recent decades our society has greatly changed under the influence of processes of individualisation and modernisation. These processes have drastically altered the social structure of daily life, and the personal relationships people are involved in. The liberation from traditional and self-evident bonds implies that people can give shape autonomously to their own social world. This may have brought along more freedom, but at the same time sets higher demands from individuals. People are less able to fall back on 'given' bonds such as family or neighbourhood relationships. Good personal competencies are necessary to function well in this new social environment and to make meaningful contacts. Such competencies are important in two ways: they enable people to function autonomously, and they should also make it possible to build a meaningful network and use it when necessary. The latter means that people can show their vulnerability and know how to ask for help in times of adversity. It also means they are able to build a certain degree of credit for moments in which the relationship is temporarily out of balance.

Although the social networks of older adults are not essentially that different from those of younger age categories, distinctions can be identified in the binding patterns of generations. The current older generation grew up in a time when family bonds were more or less taken for granted and could serve as a buffer against problems and misfortune. In this fast-changing society this is not so self-evident. Children live further away from their parents, women's participation in the labour market has increased sharply, and the significance of the neighbourhood has become less. The problems that ageing people encounter in making meaningful relationships are not the result of biological senescense, but situated within a particular societal constellation of the late modern society in which social competencies are more important than before.

New generations have to work actively at building a network with family and friends that offers safety and protection, and is supportive of their personal and societal participation. The situation in which people grow up is important for their opportunities to build up meaningful and supportive relationships in later life. Ageing well does not mean that people are not confronted with circumstances that make them vulnerable; it means that they belong to a network that makes it possible to cope with that vulnerability. Finding a good balance between independence and connectedness is crucial; ageing well means that someone can fully utilise the freedom of modern life and at the same time is feeling safe and protected in coping with problems and failures. For future generations of older adults, a good balance between independence and connectedness is crucial: only then can they fully enjoy the freedom, and at the same time feel safe and protected in the face of limitations and adversity.

Note
[1] Additional information about the study and research methods used can be found in Chapter Three of the *Social isolation in modern society* (Hortulanus et al, 2006).

References

Allan, G. (2008) 'Flexibility, friendship, and family', *Personal Relationships*, vol 15, no 1, pp 1-16.

Bauman, Z. (2001) *The individualized society*, Oxford: Blackwell.

Baumeister, R.F. and Vohs, K.D. (2005) 'The pursuit of meaningfulness in life', in C.R. Snyder and S.J. Lopez (eds) *Handbook of positive psychology*, Oxford: Oxford University Press, pp 608-18.

Beck, U. (1992) *Risk society: Towards a modern society*, London: Sage Publications.

Beck, U. and Beck-Gernsheim, E. (2002) *Individualization: Institutionalized individualism and its social and political consequences*, London: Sage Publications.

Berkman, L.F. and Glass, T. (2000) 'Social integration, social networks, social support and health', in L.F. Berkman and I. Kawachi (eds) *Social epidemiology*, New York: Oxford University Press, pp 137-73.

Carstensen, L., Mikels, J.A. and Mather, A. (2006) 'Aging and the intersection of cognition, motivation and emotion', in J.E. Birren (ed) *Handbook of the psychology of aging* (6th edn), Amsterdam: Elsevier, pp 343-60.

Cornelis, A. (1997) *Logica van het gevoel: Filosofie van de stabiliteitslagen in de cultuur als nesteling der emoties [The logic of feeling: philosophy of cultural stability and emotions]*, Amsterdam: Stichting Essence.

Côté, J.E. and Levine, C.G. (2002) *Identity formation, agency, and culture: A social psychological synthesis*, Mahwah, NJ: Lawrence Erlbaum Associates.

de Jong Gierveld, J. and Kamphuis, F. (1985) 'The development of a Rasch-type loneliness scale', *Applied Psychological Measurement*, vol 9, no 3, pp 289-99.

Ehrenberg, A. (1995) *L'individu incertain [The uncertain self]*, Paris: Calmann-Lévy.

Fischer, C. (1982) *To dwell among friends: Personal networks in town and city*, Chicago, IL: University of Chicago Press.

Friedman, M. (1989) 'Feminism and modern friendship: dislocating the community', *Ethics,* vol 99, no 2, pp 275-90.

Giddens, A. (1984) *The constitution of society*, Cambridge: The Polity Press.

Giddens, A. (1990) *The consequences of modernity*, Cambridge: Polity Press.

Giddens, A. (1991) *Modernity and self-identity: Self and society in the late modern age*, Cambridge: Polity Press.

Giddens, A. (1994) 'Living in an post-traditional society', in U. Beck, A. Giddens and S. Lash (eds) *Reflexive modernization: Politics, tradition and aesthetics in the modern social order*, Cambridge: Polity Press, pp 56-109.

Heller, K. and Rook, K.S. (2001) 'Distinguishing the theoretical functions of social ties: implications for support interventions', in B. Sarason and S. Duck (eds) *Personal relationships: Implications for clinical and community psychology*, New York: John Wiley, pp 119-39.

Hortulanus, R., Machielse, A. and Meeuwesen, L. (2006) *Social isolation in modern society*, London: Routledge.

Kunneman, H. (2005) *Voorbij het dikke ik: Bouwstenen voor een kritisch humanisme [Beyond the thick-I: Building blocks for a critical humanism]*, Amsterdam: SWP/Humanistics University Press.

Lazarus, R.S. (1966) *Psychological stress and the coping process*, New York: McGraw-Hill.

Machielse, A. (2006a) *Onkundig en onaangepast: Een theoretisch perspectief op sociaal isolement [Incompetent and maladjusted: A theoretical perspective on social isolation]*, Utrecht: Van Arkel.

Machielse, A. (2006b) 'Theories on social contacts and social isolation', in R. Hortulanus, A. Machielse and L. Meeuwesen (eds) *Social isolation in modern society*, London: Routledge, pp 13-36.

Machielse, A. (2006c) 'Social isolation: formal and informal support', in R. Hortulanus, A. Machielse and L. Meeuwesen (eds) *Social isolation in modern society*, London: Routledge, pp 115-36.

Machielse, A (2011) 'Social isolation among older people: a typology as guide for effective interventions', *Journal of Social Intervention: Theory and Practice*, vol 20, no 40, pp 40-61.

Myers, D.G. (1999) *Social psychology* (6th edn), New York: McGraw-Hill College.

Pahl, R. (1998) 'Friendship: The social glue of contemporary society?', in J. Franklin (ed) *The politics of risk society*, Cambridge/Oxford: Polity Press, pp 99-119.

Perlman, D. and Peplau, L.A. (1982) 'Theoretical approaches to loneliness', in L.A. Peplau and D. Perlman (eds) *Loneliness: A sourcebook of current theory: Research and therapy*, New York: Wiley, pp 123-34.

Pescosolido, B.A. and Levy, J.A. (2002) 'The role of social networks in health, illness, disease and healing: the accepting present, the forgotten past, and the dangerous potential for a complacent future', in J.A. Levy and B.A. Pescosolido (eds) *Social networks and health*, Amsterdam: JAI/Elsevier Science, pp 3-25.

Putnam, R.D. (2000) *Bowling alone: The collapse and revival of American community*, New York: Simon & Schuster.

Sarason, B.R., Sarason, I.G. and Gurung, R.A.R. (2001) 'Close personal relationships and health outcomes: a key to the role of social support', in B. Sarason and S. Duck (eds) *Personal relationships: Implications for clinical and community psychology*, New York: John Wiley, pp 15-41.

Taylor, S.E. (1983) 'Adjustment to threatening events: a theory of cognitive adaptation', *American Psychologist*, vol 38, pp 1161-73.

Taylor, C. (1989) *Sources of the self*, Cambridge: Cambridge University Press.

Thoits, P.A. (1985) 'Social support and well-being: theoretical possibilities', in I.G. Sarason and B.R. Sarason (eds) *Social support: Theory, research, and application*, New York: Wiley, pp 51-72.

van der Poel, M. (1993) *Personal networks: A rational choice explanation of their size and composition*, Lisse: Swets & Zeitlinger.

van Tilburg, T. and Thomese, F. (2010) 'Societal dynamics in personal networks', in D. Dannefer (ed) *The Sage handbook of social gerontology*, London: Sage Publications, pp 215-25.

Victor, A., Scambler, S. and Bond, J. (2009) *The social world of older people: Understanding loneliness and social isolation in later life*, New York: McGraw-Hill/Open University Press.

Weiss, R.S. (1974) 'Loneliness: the provision of social relationships', in Z. Rubin (ed) *Doing unto others*, Englewood Cliffs, NJ: Prentice-Hall, pp 17-36.

EIGHT

Critical perspectives on social work with older people

Mo Ray

Introduction

Using social work with older people as a case study, this chapter argues that the marginalisation of social work with older people in the UK effectively holds a mirror to the wider exclusion of those within this age group who use social work and personal social care services – in effect, older people with high support needs. The chapter draws on a critical perspective to highlight the complexities that are involved in contemporary, professional social work practice with older people, and points to future directions in the development of a professional social work role into the future. It examines first challenges facing social work practice with older people; second, trends in service provision; and third, developments in critical perspectives on social work with older people.

Challenges in contemporary social work practice with older people

In the UK, the role and purpose of social work with older people has always been contested and perceived as an under-valued area of practice when compared with other areas of social work practice, such as with children and families (Richards, 2000). While there is now some variation in the extent to which social work represents a visible contribution to the social care agenda with older people among the devolved nations of the UK, it has long been viewed as an area of work with limited occupational potential (Lymbery, 2005). The fragile and uncertain basis for social work with older people in the UK (shared with many other European countries) has been further eroded by the consequences of neoliberal policies in welfare services over the 1990s and 2000s. These have had a profound impact on the visibility, role and purpose of social work with older people. In respect of England, there has been a decline in demand for qualified social workers with adults

(CFWI, 2012), reinforced by budget cuts and a view that professional social work is less relevant in the current climate of reform (Beresford, 2012). Increasingly, a narrative about the role and purpose of social work with older people is notable by its absence or rendered invisible by the emphasis on the wider 'social care' agenda.

Traditionally, social policy and practice has shaped and reinforced pervasive beliefs about ageing and the ways in which the 'problems' of old age should be addressed, with particular emphasis on theories of ageing as a period of decline and deficit, accompanied by increased disengagement (Cumming and Henry, 1961) and passivity. While such theories have been robustly critiqued, they have perhaps had a pervasive impact on the low priority given to older people in the personal social services and the attendant low priority given to the development of professional gerontological social work. This is evidenced by interventions for older people, drawn from a limited range of options that have reinforced the low expectations about older people who use services. The dominance of bio-medical models of ageing served to reinforce the construction of old age in terms of dysfunction as well as to view the ageing process as a personal problem. 'The elderly' were constructed as a homogeneous and undifferentiated group, reinforced by a standardisation of the lifecourse and effectively separating older people from the rest of the lifecourse (Estes and Binney, 1989). During the 1970s and 1980s, long-standing cultures of belief focusing on the 'problem' of ageing continued to influence policy and practice which stultified the growth of community services and continued to rely on the traditional emphasis of the spatial separation of older people needing 'care'. Personal social services for older people were, therefore, characterised by a limited range of 'off the peg' services and a reluctance to develop services in the community (Means and Smith, 1998). State funding of residential care via social security payments provided a powerful disincentive to local authorities to make any sustained investment in community care resources and provisions. The dominance of residential care for older people deemed in need of care did little to unsettle the very long tradition of institutional care for older people constructed as dependent or in need of care.

One of the consequences of what amounts to at best a pessimistic view of ageing was that older people in need of personal social services were not seen as people whose life circumstances or presenting needs called for much professional social work services. Personal social services tended to focus on service-driven, limited, practical interventions aimed at managing or responding to deteriorations in activities of daily living. Moreover, the notion of ageing as an individual problem avoided any systematic recognition or action addressing the impact of lifecourse inequalities, age-based structural disadvantage and ageism. While it was recognised that transitions, for example, were a key factor in ageing experiences, there was little attempt to bring a more nuanced understanding of the experience into practice. It is unsurprising, therefore, that as other areas of social work were beginning to gather pace in terms of developing practice, supported by an appropriate knowledge base and raising critical questions about their effectiveness, social work with older people continued to lean towards an administratively oriented practice. The emphasis of social work practice was geared more towards liaison with care providers and coordination of care services (Lymbery, 2005) than consciously seeking, for example, to integrate gerontological research and emerging critical perspectives in gerontology into the knowledge and skill base of social work with older people.

The subsequent development of community care policy was influenced by a number of factors including a downturn in the economy, and fuelled by a neoliberal commitment to the marketisation of welfare services. In the UK, public sector services were criticised as monolithic, fragmented and slow to respond to calls for the deinstitutionalisation of services (Griffiths, 1987). The rhetoric surrounding community care policy merged a number of critical discourses underpinned by a focus on the economic burden of an ageing society (Estes et al, 2003; Vincent, 2003) and the importance of informal care to support the expansion of the elderly population. This set the scene in the UK for the allocation of personal social services resources to move from a consensual position towards the control and distribution of finite resources. The impact of managerialisation on the organisation of personal social services as a trend in many countries moved towards an administrative welfare model, characterised by standardisation and formalisation of procedures to allocate finite resources with associated implications for cost containment (see, for example, Blomberg and Petersson, 2010).

Current trends in service provision

In a UK context, eligibility for care services was defined by an assessment of need with the expectation that services would be delivered to those people deemed most 'in need'. Social workers were largely redefined as care managers, and were required, as the operational arm of community care, to identify people via assessment who were eligible (and, therefore, those too who were ineligible) to receive services and to broker those services in a cost-effective and efficient manner. The Labour administration in the late-1990s and early-2000s continued the commitment to market mechanisms and competition as fundamental principles in their aspiration to 'modernise' health and social services (see, for example, DH, 1998; Scourfield, 2007). A sustained critique of public sector social services underpinned the modernisation agenda. Response to problems and failures in the delivery of personal social services led to a 'reformed' managerialism that placed greater emphasis on accountability and quality evidenced through standard setting and performance management (Waine and Henderson, 2003).

The underpinning assumption was careful attention to performance as defined by targets. Standard setting and benchmarks, it was argued, would develop modern social services by creating clearer accountability, efficiency savings and effective and streamlined management of service. Systems of inspection, regulation and monitoring were introduced as vital elements of the modernisation agenda. Policies such as the 'duty of best value' (DH, 2002 highlighted the imperative to deliver 'quality' services as defined by national government and to clear standards by the most effective, economic and efficient means available. For example, the nationally defined eligibility criteria as a means of targeting and rationing services to people deemed most 'in need' is now an established feature of social care and personal social services. *Fair access to care services* (DH, 2002) was dominated by a focus on risk with an emphasis on the notion of individual risk. This diverted attention away from the possibility of considering other forms and processes of risk influenced by, for example, structural location, lifecourse inequalities and iatrogenic risk. As resources retract and there is a requirement to determine eligibility along ever more acute criteria, fewer older men and women are defined as eligible to receive services (CSCI, 2008; Tanner, 2010). Thus need is conflated with risk and focuses on danger to life and limb or the need for protection. The King's Fund (Humphries, 2011) report that the number of older people using publicly funded social care services between 2005-11 fell by over 7 per cent, reflecting the trend towards responding to fewer older people with the most complex needs.

From an already fragile and poorly developed position of professional possibility for social work with older people, the dye was cast in terms of an administrative focus with increased imperatives to bureaucratic requirements, geared towards managing resources and procedures focusing on routinised practice, so that '... practice with older people has become suffocated by the straitjacket of care management and therefore offers even less occupational potential than before' (Lymbery,

2005, p 131). By implication, older people who use personal social services have been subjected to bureaucratic procedures and assessments that have increasingly focused on what they cannot do or achieve in order to identify their eligibility for services. These kinds of assessment processes have contributed to the construction of older people using services in a language of dysfunction and problem states, focusing on physical tasks and activities. Opportunities for narrative approaches have declined, with increased attention on eligibility and the narrowing of service eligibility to declining numbers of older people.

The consequence of the above trends is that social workers are increasingly reported to struggle to articulate (and use) appropriate theoretical frameworks and knowledge bases. Instead, the managerialisation of personal social services requires that practitioners rely more on pre-determined systems and procedures (McDonald et al, 2007) which are rarely adequate in addressing the diversity of complex situations a social worker is likely to encounter in practice. Similar findings were echoed in the review of the role and tasks of social work (Social Work Taskforce, 2009) that commented that a range of factors were holding back the profession, including organisational culture and expectations of social work burdened by bureaucratic procedures – and at the end of those procedures are older people. While there is a relative paucity of research examining what older people value about social workers and their relationships with them, it is clear that older people are critical of social work practitioners who over-focus on administrative requirements at the expense of a more person-centred approach. Manthorpe et al (2007, p 9) conclude from their research with older people who had received social work services that: 'Negative statements about social workers included references to unhelpful attitudes, guarding the council's money and rationing services, and being too slow to respond to requests for help or to undertake social care assessments, or in some cases, not responding at all.'

The findings of the Munro report for social work with children and families (Munro, 2011, p 17) resonates with the research relating to social work with adults in which practice had:

> ... evolved too far into a top-down, compliance-driven organisation. This stifled creativity and distorted priorities, with more attention given to the completion of bureaucratic tasks to specified timescales as the measure of success, than the appraisal of the quality of help received by children and their families.

This trend has a number of implications for older people who require support from social services. First, eligibility criteria imply that older people with high support needs, characterised by uncertainty, transition and change, are most likely to receive services. Paradoxically, these situations call for the highest levels of practice ability and professional judgement and autonomy, rather than practice dominated by procedures, extensive regulation and scrutiny with a concomitant emphasis on certainty. In the context of managerialised welfare, a bifurcation between a *narrative of social care* and the *narrative of older people* who use services is likely. Social care policy makers focus on a narrative of economic challenge in the procurement and funding of 'care', and in this sense, care is constructed overwhelmingly as a financial commodity (Lloyd, 2010). In responding to the administrative demands of their role, some practitioners may be discouraged from assessment practice that engages fully with an older person's narrative and embraces a co-produced assessment. This kind of assessment practice would include an analysis of need and circumstances, supported by appropriate biographical information, and an awareness of the actual and potential strengths of the older person. Assessment practice underpinned by a commitment to critical perspectives would also be alert to evidence of structural inequality and age-based discrimination. Instead, assessment formats were likely to be devised as 'tools' that ultimately determine 'severity' of need, eligibility and cost of care. As a result, priority is given to a narrative of dysfunction, focused at the level of the individual 'at risk' and characterised by a language of pessimism along with limited attention to the impact of structural forces on older people.. Moreover, opportunities to work directly with individuals have become effectively replaced by resource finding within a market economy (McDonald et al, 2007, p 7), which may ultimately have little to do with the expressed needs and aspirations of older people and their circumstances.

The potential for service users to access cash to make and purchase their own care arrangements has been legally possible in England, Wales and Northern Ireland since 1995. The idea of self-directed support has its roots in the disabled people's movement that argued that traditional community care provision emphasised an inappropriate individualised (and medicalised) approach to impairment. That is, community care services have focused on disabled people's individual 'problems' or 'needs' rather than their rights as citizens (see, for example, Oliver et al, 2012). The disabled people's lobby for self-directed support fitted with the Labour government's aspirations for ongoing modernisation and a move towards an increase in self-responsibility of service users to procure and manage their own support services. Thus the narrative of the disabled people's movement was incorporated into policy development and critiqued traditional approaches to social care provision. Services, they argued, focused on meeting 'care' needs rather than on enabling people to make individual decisions about their support requirements and to have a choice about how they were achieved (Scourfield, 2007). It was certainly true that the continued emphasis on eligibility for services with a focus on procedural practice in order to manage finite resources could hardly be said to have created flexible, individualised personal social services.

This narrative of independence, underpinned by an ideological commitment to productive or active citizenship, has continued to chime with the aspirations of the present Coalition government, with their emphasis on building community capacity to promote the maintenance of independence and prevention of dependency. Similar criticisms of the present arrangements for social care support have emanated from the present government. By contrast, it is argued that access to self-directed support via cash payments will respond to a wider range of outcomes (for example, support requirements to ensure that disabled people can work, access education and make personal lifestyle choices) rather than simply meeting personal care needs. The aspiration of the present Coalition government is to increase the use of direct payments as far as possible by 2013 with the goal that when 'people develop care and support needs, our first priority should be to restore an individual's independence and autonomy' (DH, 2010 p 9). This policy orientation appears to be reflected in trends about the resources committed in social care services to different groups of people with an apparent decline in the spend on older people. Humphries (2011, p 6), for example, has commented, 'whereas councils are clearly trying to respond to the rising number of working age people with social care needs, for older people the trend towards a decline in spending with fewer people receiving services defies demography.'

In addition, the current goals of policy strongly connect with the notion of active ageing (WHO, 2002). While definitions of 'active ageing' originally encompassed diversity and arguably sought to include older people regardless of their health, economic or social standing, it is increasingly recast and characterised in contemporary policy by a narrower definition which gives priority to instrumental and essentially, normative expectations about activity, independence and social purpose. Such an approach is unlikely to illuminate the impact of lifecourse inequality and the likelihood of a sharpening of inequalities as people move into older age (Grenier, 2012).

The risk with the move towards an increasingly functional and normative orientation about what is effectively deemed to be 'good' ageing is that policy narratives will combine to create an idea that social care, as defined by the personalisation agenda, is all about restoring people to their functions as citizens, defined in terms of activity, independence and self-responsibility. This may, of course, be a laudable and entirely appropriate aspiration for some people who use social services. However, as has been argued, this narrative speaks rather more to the 'third age' than it does to older people with high support needs who 'must rely on the discretion and benevolence of others to care for them' (Lloyd, 2010) instead of having clearly defined rights. There is no guarantee that a direct payment – the proposed care arrangement – will provide opportunities for empowerment in terms of altering an older person's ability to exercise power, or indeed, in terms of challenging the structural inequalities and oppressions that affect older people with complex needs. Evidence of care for older people with high support needs being based on a notion of discretionary benevolence and framed as a commodity is perhaps found in the persistent and steady progression of reports highlighting failures in care 'systems', institutional abuse and poor practice and undignified care focusing predominantly on older people with high support needs, complex situations and at the end of their lives (see, for example, Francis, 2010; EHRC, 2011; Health Service Commission for England: Ombudsman's Report, 2011; Commission on Improving Dignity in Care for Older People, 2012). The government paper which launched its aspirations for personal budgets (DH, 2010) was almost silent on the matter of practice with older people with complex and changeable needs, and highlights the reality that dependence across the lifecourse, as a factor of human life, remains largely unacknowledged (Lloyd, 2010).

The current emphasis on self-responsibility in securing care through cash payments means that older people with high support needs who may not wish to make use of direct payments are further cast as dependent, and, in the current government narrative, a 'failure' as an active citizen or, as Scourfield has argued, experience a 'subordinated citizenship, doubly underlined by failing to take up direct payments' (Scourfield, 2007, p 119). But, understanding that older people may not want to manage a personal budget, is '"… not the same as denying their right to be fully engaged in decisions affecting their care – rather, it is a practical response to people's lived reality' (Lymbery and Postle, 2010, p 2515). Ensuring that a person's needs are appropriately met in a manner that ensures the person's dignity and wellbeing is an ethical concern rather than a matter turning solely on notions of independence and choice (Lloyd, 2010).

Taking the narrative of independence further, government policy (DH, 2010) has also voiced a commitment to self-assessment, arguing that this will further enhance service users' rights to exercise choice and control. Self-assessment enables a person who has support needs to complete his or her own assessment either independently, or with assistance perhaps from a family member, supporter or voluntary agency. Social work assessments have been criticised for becoming a gatekeeping tool and as a means of establishing eligibility, and this has been used to add weight to the argument that self-assessment is a desirable and innovative development in the independence and choice agenda (see, for example, Lymbery and Postle, 2010).

However, an argument that self-assessment is inevitably desirable and will lead to better outcomes for a person who uses services must be treated with caution. In situations of complexity and uncertainty (which realistically characterise most referrals from or about older people to social services teams) it is difficult to envisage how, for example, an older person with high support needs will inevitably be able to best articulate, or indeed analyse, the nature of his or her difficulties as well has having the knowledge base required to negotiate and perform in a bureaucratic care context. An older person may be coping with memory and other cognitive impairments caused by dementia that may have an impact on his or her ability to cope with self-assessment as well as potentially having an impact on his or her understanding of why an assessment might be of benefit. Other circumstances such as a sudden change in the person's circumstances caused by the ill heath or death of a carer, or being at the end of his or her own life, will doubtless have an impact on a person's ability or motivation to self-assess. Moreover, older people may have needs and aspirations which are in conflict with family members who provide support, thus making self-assessment a potentially very difficult process, inevitably influenced by the dynamics of power inherent in family and social systems under pressure. There may be safeguarding or abuse to consider which people may need professional support to talk about or unravel. Finally, it is perhaps unlikely to expect that all older people who approach social services are willing or able to identify in a self-assessment the impact of structural inequality or age-based discrimination on their present circumstances.

Developing critical perspectives

This chapter argues that the consistent marginalisation of older people with high support needs is reflected in the marginalisation of social work with older people. The experiences of older people who use personal social services are influenced by the policies which have traditionally focused on the 'problem' of ageing, with an attendant lack of engagement with the complexities likely to face older people as they experience difficult and multiple transitions in older age. The resultant impact often focuses on services delivered to respond to a narrow perspective of an older person's need, focusing predominantly on the deterioration and dysfunction of the ageing body and its failure to perform in a way that continues to achieve the status bestowed by notions of independence. The current policy emphasis on self-directed care is underpinned by the concept of active citizenship, with concomitant prominence given to independence and self-responsibility in managing support needs and indeed, one's own risks.

Commentators have cautioned against social work being placed solely alongside the agenda of choice and independence at the expense of other social work activity (see, for example, Jordan, 2004; Lloyd, 2010) as it creates the potential for a construction of independence which results in another form of imposed homogeneity. That is, marginalised people are effectively forced to rely on their own resources, even if its results are isolation and the burden of managing alone or doing without. This potentially reflects the rhetoric of empowerment that, on the face of it, offers the promise of greater control, but in reality, is experienced as another form of disempowerment (Fook, 2002).

The question to consider here is: does social work with older people have a part to play in achieving a culture of practice which more appropriately addresses the concerns and lived experience of older people with high support needs? If we are to take seriously the expertise of people who use services, then a future direction for social work skills and knowledge is clear. The National User Network (Beresford, 2007, p 5) identified key skills that were highly valued in social workers by people who used services. They included: advice and advocacy; negotiating with other agencies; counselling and psychotherapeutic support; signposting; and practical guidance and help. Research with older people to explore their perceptions and experiences of social work is rarely available. However, the research which does exist confirms the value that participants place on '... the skills and qualities of social workers whom they considered were knowledgeable about specialist services, persistent, committed, reliable and accessible, supportive, sympathetic and prepared to listen' (Manthorpe et al, 2007, p 1142). Critically, the same research espoused the importance of social workers with older people being *more* rather than *less* knowledgeable.

It is argued that for social work to have a future, both in general and for older people, the profession must regain and take pride in its moral core (Bisman, 2004, p 120). The International Federation of Social Work (IFSW) definition of social work embraces activities that focus on 'social change, problem solving in human relationships and the empowerment and liberation of people.... Principles of human rights and social justice are fundamental to social work.' The definition goes on to explore the value base for social work, highlighting '... respect for equality, worth and dignity of all people ... human rights and social justice serve as the motivation and justification for social work action.... In solidarity with people who are disadvantaged, the profession strives to alleviate poverty and to liberate vulnerable and oppressed people in order to promote social inclusion' (IFSW, 2000). Indeed, it is the emphasis on social justice that makes a persuasive argument for social work, and in particular, social work with older people. Without it, Bisman (2004) argues that the case for social work cannot confidently be made as other skills traditionally championed as belonging to social work can, in reality, be claimed as appropriate professional territory by other groups. A critical perspective in practice with older people would reasonably place a greater emphasis on a human rights perspectives as a means to guide appropriate actions to challenge age-based discrimination and to promote the commitment that older people with high support needs have the right to personhood and citizenship being upheld, supported and defended.

To this end, social work should properly concern itself with promoting opportunities for empowerment that take account of the contexts of power and how it is exercised. Ultimately, social work should support opportunities to embrace the equality, worth and dignity of older people with high support needs and promoting pluralist understandings of the experience of older age and older people living with high support needs. This would mean developing a practice that understands that dependency is at various times part of all of our lives and thus emphasises the importance of interdependence, relationships and a more nuanced, socially situated understanding of independence and how it may be differently constructed and experienced, both across the lifecourse and between individuals. Such an approach offers the potential to contribute a more rounded understanding of care relationships beyond the contemporary emphasis on the economy of care. Moreover, developing stronger links between critical scholarship in social work with critical perspectives in the study of ageing would enrich the knowledge and skill base of this area of practice.

Qualitative research (McDonald, 2010) which explored social work practice with the Mental Capacity Act, 2005, especially in the assessment of decision-specific mental capacity and best interests decisions, identified that practitioners with a 'rights-based' orientation used the legal test of capacity and effectively advocated for older people to retain their chosen lifestyles. Rights-based practitioners were critical of proceduralised approaches to practice, which reinforced stereotypes of older people living with dementia. McDonald (2010, p 1240) comments that '... at the heart of this approach was an awareness of the social construction of dementia as an outcome of complex threats to identity rather than its acceptance as an objectively ascertainable medical category translated as a legal disability.' In the context of practice with people living with dementia, O'Connor (2010) reflects on the importance of a move away from rational, cognitively focused assessments (for example, of decision-making capacity) towards a relational lens which acknowledges that personhood is constructed through relationships with others, and as Grenier (2012) has argued, reflecting a much more complex and nuanced lived experience for older people than merely the acquisition of impairment. Such an approach calls for the integration of knowledge of both the structural and experiential issues that an older person may face.

The consequences for practice with older people include fostering strength and capacity by encouraging participation and creating an assessment experience which 'minimises trauma, maximises competence, and assures the well-being of the person being assessed' (O'Connor, 2010, p 25). By implication, social workers have a critical role to play in advocating for their own professional autonomy and judgement which includes understanding how best to offer professional assessment and intervention which appropriately contextualises a person's difficulties or his or her feelings and experience of being in transition, the person's strengths, aspirations and resources. The implications are clear for professional social work assessment where the social worker's knowledge and expertise are offered as a service (Lymbery and Postle, 2010), and supporting a narrative approach that enables people to tell their own story and reflect on their lived experience.

It is critical that older people who use social work services are not further discriminated because they do not want to make use of direct payments. It is imperative that the concern for autonomy and independence does not exclude other rights that are important for older people living with high support needs, uncertain futures or at the end of their lives. Other factors such as comfort and security, preserving attachments and reciprocal relationships, are also essential and must be included in social work practice with older people (Ray et al, 2009). Of course, making use of direct payments does not preclude these considerations, but they must be fundamentally part of any intervention. This raises ethical questions about care as well as serving as a reminder that public sector services emerged to support people who were 'necessarily dependent ... are treated with respect and dignity, to ensure a collectivised approach to risk, and to ensure that secure and reliable forms of support outside the market and family are available' (Scourfield, 2007, p 108).

Older people with high support needs are often less able to exercise power, and social workers with humanitarian values at its core are perhaps best placed to make visible, and intervene in addressing the structural inequalities and forms and processes of discrimination often experienced by older people. This means taking a critical approach to the diversity of experiences in ageing and challenging 'essentialist' perspectives that pervade assumptions or beliefs about the late lifecourse. The impact of poverty, age-based discrimination, racism and gender-based oppressions should be within the purview of a social work practitioner, especially in considering how they intersect with the experience of impairment and frailty. There are many examples that highlight the systematic inequalities older people experience, particularly as they enter very old age at the same time as experiencing complex and high support needs. For example, the Mental Health Foundation (2010) estimate that 10-15 per cent of older people living in the community show symptoms of depression, and this figure rises to approximately 40 per cent for older people living in care homes (Dening and Milne, 2009). Yet, detection, diagnosis and appropriate treatment and support remain sporadic and often unavailable. For older people living with dementia, especially those deemed to have so-called 'challenging behaviour', the over-use of antipsychotic medication constitutes a serious risk to wellbeing, and increased morbidity and mortality. Yet the evidence base on appropriate psychosocial support and interventions remains poorly developed and has experienced a history of under-investment (Alzheimer's Society, 2004). Specific groups of older people such as people ageing with a learning disability, or people from minority ethnic groups are likely to have experienced other forms of oppression and discrimination across the lifecourse which is likely to sharpen in later life. There is, for example, a lack of interest in research and scholarship in ageing with a learning disability that Read (2012) has highlighted as 'ageing with indifference'.

It is evident that to be able to effectively engage with a social work practice with older people that works with the complexities outlined here, an appropriate and gerontologically informed knowledge base is critically important. Appropriate empathy arises from the ability to theorise and utilise appropriate knowledge(s) in order to make sense of complex, multidimensional issues that people who use services face and experience (Pullen-Sansfaçon and Cowden, 2012). Social work education does not often adequately address the issue of ageing and critical perspectives on ageing in the context of the lifecourse. The result is that social work students may be ill-equipped and disinterested in grasping the complexities of the lived experience of older people as they develop complex, long-term impairment and illness which fundamentally changes their perceptions of self, continued engagement with their social networks, roles and responsibilities and their strategies and approaches to coping with such transitions (Grenier, 2012). The requirement of a gerontologically informed practice has implications for social work education and training, both in terms of developing capacity for teaching with a gerontological focus as well as developing the social work academy to foster the participation of social work in the gerontological research agenda and to use existing research to inform practice.

Conclusion

The marginalisation of older people with high support needs is an area of primary concern for professional social work. A critical gerontological perspective illuminates the potential for social work to develop in a way that addresses the complexities of ageing and the transitions and contexts that accompany late life. The vision for a transformed social care service as exemplified in contemporary policy is relatively silent on the needs and circumstances of older people with high support needs whose lived experience may be characterised by uncertainty, multiple transition and change. The same policies have also failed to grasp in a coherent way future directions for professional gerontological social work Critical perspectives offer the opportunity of providing a more nuanced and comprehensive understanding of the complexity of late life experiences as well as demonstrating the opportunity to reflect on what a professional gerontological social work might yet become.

References

Alzheimer's Society (2004) *Neuroleptic/antipsychotic drugs, policy position*, London: Alzheimer's Society.

Beresford, P. (2007) 'Service users do not want care navigators', *Community Care*, 12-18 April (www.communitycare.co.uk).

Beresford, P. (2012) '*Safeguarding* the future of social work with adults to ensure person-centred support/personalisation and co-production', Think Local Act Personal Social Care blog, 9 February (

Bisman, C. (2004) 'Social work values: the moral core of the profession', *British Journal of Social Work*, vol 34, no 1, pp 109-23.

Blomberg, S. and Petersson, J. (2010) 'The increasing importance of administrative practice in the shaping of the welfare state', *Social Work and Society: International Online Journal*, vol 8, no 1 (www.socwork.net/sws/article/view/24/67).

CFWI (Centre for Workforce Intelligence) (2012) *The future social worker workforce*, London: CFWI (www.cfwi.org.uk/publications/the-future-social-worker-workforce-an-analysis-of-risks-and-opportunities).

Commission on Improving Dignity in Care for Older People (2012) *Dignity in care for older people: Draft report and recommendations*, London: NHS Confederation (www.nhsconfed.org/priorities/Quality/Partnership-on-dignity/Pages/Draftreportrecommendations.aspx).

CSCI (Commission for Social Care Inspection) (2008) *The state of social care in England 2006/2007*, London: CSCI.

Cumming, E. and Henry, W. (1961) *Growing old: The process of disengagement*, New York: Basic Books.

Dening, T. and Milne, A. (2009) 'Depression and mental health in care homes for older people', *Quality in Ageing*, vol 10, no 1, pp 40-6.

DH (Department of Health) (1998) *Modernising social services*, London: DH.

DH (2002a) *Fair access to care services: Guidance on eligibility criteria for adult social care*, London: DH.

DH (2010) *A vision for adult social care: Capable communities and active citizens*, London: DH.

EHRC (Equality and Human Rights Commission) (2011) *Close to home: Older people and human rights in home care*, London: EHRC (www.equalityhumanrights.com/news/2011/november/home-care-often-fails-to-meet-older-peoples-basic-rights-says-inquiry/).

Estes, C. and Binney, E. (1989) 'The biomedicalization of aging: dangers and dilemmas', *The Gerontologist*, vol 29, no 5, pp 587-96.

Estes, C., Biggs, S. and Phillipson, C. (2003) *Social theory, social policy and ageing: A critical introduction*, Buckingham: Open University Press.

Fook, J. (2002) *Social work: Critical theory and practice*, London: Sage Publications.

Francis, R. (2010) *Independent inquiry into care provided by Mid-Staffordshire NHS Foundation Trust, January 2005-March 2009, Volume I*, London: The Stationery Office.

Grenier, A. (2012) *Transitions and the lifecourse: Challenging constructions of 'growing old'*, Bristol: The Policy Press.

Griffiths, R. (1987) *Community care: Agenda for action*, London: Department of Health.

Health Service Commission for England: Ombudsman's Report (2011) *Care and compassion? Report of the Health Service Ombudsman on ten investigations into NHS care of older people*, London: Parliamentary and Health Service Ombudsman.

Humphries, R. (2011) *Social care funding and the NHS – An impending crisis?*, London: The King's Fund.

International Federation of Social Work (2012) *Definitions of Social Work,* http://ifsw.org/policies/definition-of-social-work/

Jordan, B. (2004) 'Emancipatory social work? Opportunity or oxymoron', *British Journal of Social Work*, vol 34, no 1, pp 5-19.

Lloyd, L. (2010) 'The individual in social care: the ethics of care and the "personalisation agenda" in services for older people in England', *Ethics and Social Welfare*, vol 4, no 2, pp 188-200.

Lymbery, M. (2005) *Social work with older people*, London: Sage Publications.

Lymbery, M. and Postle, K. (2010) 'Social work in the context of adult social care in England and the resultant implications for social work education', *British Journal of Social Work*, vol 40, no 8, pp 2502-22.

McDonald, A. (2010) 'The impact of the 2005 Mental Capacity Act on social workers' decision making and approaches to the assessment of risk', *British Journal of Social Work*, vol 40, no 4, pp 1229-46.

McDonald, A., Postle, K. and Dawson, C. (2008) 'Barriers to retaining and using professional knowledge in local authority social work practice with adults in the UK', *British Journal of Social Work*, vol 38, no 7, pp 1370-87.

Manthorpe, J., Moriarty, J., Rapaport, J., Clough R., Cornes, M., Bright, L., Illiffe, S. and OPRSI (Older People Researching Social Issues) (2007) '"There are wonderful social workers but it's a lottery": older people's views about social workers', *British Journal of Social Work*, vol 38, no 6, pp 1132-50.

Means, R. and Smith, R. (1998) *From poor law to community care: The development of welfare services for elderly people*, Bristol: The Policy Press.

Mental Health Foundation (2010) *Depression and older people* (www.mentalhealth.org.uk/help-information/mental-health-a-z/O/older-people/).

Munro, E. (2011) *The Munro review of child protection: Interim report – The child's journey*, London: Department of Health.

O'Connor, D. (2010) 'Personhood and dementia: toward a relational framework for assessing decisional capacity', *The Journal of Mental Health Training and Practice*, vol 5, no 3, pp 22-30.

Oliver, M., Sapey, M. and Thomas, P. (2012) *Social work with disabled people*, Basingstoke: Palgrave Macmillan/British Association of Social Workers.

Pullen-Sansfaçon, A. and Cowden, S. (2012) *The ethical foundations of social work*, Harlow: Pearson.

Read, S. (2012) 'Ageing with indifference: Older people with learning disability', personal communication, 5 March.

Richards, S. (2000) `Bridging the divide: elders and the assessment process', *British Journal of Social Work*, 30, 1, pp. 37–49.

Scourfield, P. (2007) 'Social care and the modern citizen: client, consumer, service user, manager', *British Journal of Social Work*, vol 37, no 1, pp 107-22.

Social Work Taskforce (2009) *The final report of the Social Work Taskforce*, London: Department for Education and Skills.

Tanner, D. (2010) *Managing the ageing experience: Learning from older people*, Bristol: The Policy Press.

Ray, M., Bernard, M. and Phillips, J. (2009) *Critical issues in social work with older people*, Basingstoke: Palgrave Macmillan.

Vincent, J. (2003) *Old age: Key ideas*, London: Routledge.

Waine, B. and Henderson, J. (2003) 'Managers, managing and managerialism', in J. Henderson and D. Atkinson (eds) *Managing care in context*, London: Routledge/Open University, pp 49-74.

WHO (World Health Organization) (2002) *Active ageing: A policy framework*, Geneva: WHO.

NINE

Community-based participatory action research: opportunities and challenges for critical gerontology

Friederike Ziegler and Thomas Scharf

Introduction

Critical gerontology has evolved from a commitment by researchers to challenge and ultimately change the ways in which Western societies construct ageing and shape the lives of older people (Phillipson and Walker, 1987). This value-based approach is founded on critical gerontologists' ethical engagement with concerns of social justice and equity across the lifecourse and, particularly, as they relate to later life (Holstein and Minkler, 2003). In addition, researchers working within the critical tradition refer to the existence of a moral obligation to change the ways in which societies construct the cultural, economic and political parameters that frame the ageing of an increasingly diverse group of citizens (Phillipson and Walker, 1987; Martinson and Minkler, 2006). There are, of course, a variety of ways in which researchers can attempt to bring about social change. As a result, the targets of critical approaches in gerontology range from national and international policy making to those who live and work in local communities.

The value base associated with a critical approach influences not only the substantive themes of research in critical gerontology, but also helps to shape the methodological approaches adopted in empirical studies. In recent years, driven by a commitment to bring about social change, critical gerontologists have increasingly engaged with participatory or participative methods of doing research (Martinson and Minkler, 2006; Blair and Minkler, 2009). This represents part of a broader shift in Western societies to engage older people in the production and dissemination of gerontological knowledge and in the development of policy and practice (Godfrey et al, 2004; Hennessy and Walker, 2011).

Increasingly, older people have themselves been supported to develop their own expertise in research and thereby assume responsibility for the entire research process (Glanz and Neikrug, 1997; Clough et al, 2006; Cornes et al, 2008). In essence, proponents of a more participatory approach argue that older people's direct involvement in research processes can lead to the empowerment of otherwise marginalised or socially excluded groups. Rather than targeting structural change at the potentially remote level of national or international policy processes, participatory methods can lead to social change in ways that are more meaningful for ageing adults (Blair and Minkler, 2009). However, the 'participatory turn' has not occurred unchallenged. Several researchers have advised caution in employing participatory methods with older people, pointing out the many challenges and issues pertaining to the use of this research method (see, for example, Ray, 2007; Blair and Minkler, 2009; Jacobs, 2010).

In many ways, critical gerontology and participatory action as research approaches can be viewed as being complementary, sharing at least three common concerns. First, both approaches favour critical thinking in relation to issues around social justice, social inequality and marginalisation. Second, both share the goal of bringing about social change: participatory action research in terms of transformation primarily through community action (Kesby et al, 2007), critical gerontology mainly through policy-level change (see, for example, Phillipson and Scharf, 2004; Scharf et al, 2005; Walker, 2009). Third, critical gerontologists engage in reflection on their own roles in the production of knowledge relating to their research themes (Baars, 1991; Minkler and Holstein, 2008). The reflexive approach represents a vital part of the participatory action research tradition, with its challenges and limitations having been subject to wide debate among practitioners in development studies, geography and other disciplines (Pain, 2004; Nicholls, 2009; Smith et al, 2010).

In this chapter, we seek to reflect on the, at times, uncritical way in which participation has been employed in critical gerontology, potentially resulting in the furthering of policies and practices around ageing which continue to disadvantage certain population groups. By highlighting some of the conceptual and philosophical debates which have accompanied participatory research in other disciplines, including development studies and geography, our aim is to encourage critical gerontologists to reflect further on the underpinning assumptions of their research approach and practice and to consider the consequences of this for the social construction of knowledge around ageing. While the argument is underpinned by findings drawn from a range of participatory action research projects, particular attention is paid to our experience with a project conducted in low-income neighbourhoods in Manchester, England.

The chapter is organised into four main sections. First, we describe the CALL-ME research project (Community Action in Later Life – Manchester Engagement). Second, we discuss the politics of participation in the context of neoliberal policy developments around citizenship, empowerment and engagement. Here, we caution against the use of participatory methods outside of a critical framework as these may inadvertently further the marginalisation of the very older people whose lives are targeted by this approach. Third, and in order to gain a better understanding of the mechanisms of empowerment for social change, an approach that draws on Foucault's understandings of power relations is used to illustrate the workings of power and the formation of subjectivities. Fourth, we argue for more awareness among gerontologists of the technologies of knowledge production in academia and policy and their impact on the everyday lives of older people. The chapter concludes with a review of key messages arising from our argument. These are directed towards researchers working within both the critical gerontology and participatory action research traditions.

CALL-ME project

Our reflections and discussion are based on fieldwork carried out between 2008 and 2011 as part of a participatory action research project in four low-income neighbourhoods in Manchester, England. The Community Action in Later Life – Manchester Engagement (CALL-ME) project built on an earlier empirical study undertaken in similar neighbourhoods of three English cities, including Manchester, which highlighted a range of ways in which older residents were prone to forms of social exclusion (Scharf et al, 2002, 2005, 2007). CALL-ME was developed in close collaboration with Manchester City Council's Valuing Older People partnership, a strategic initiative aimed at improving life for older people in the city and involving a number of different services, organisations, agencies and, notably, older Manchester residents themselves (Manchester City Council, 2004, 2010; McGarry and Morris, 2011). Reflecting a finding of the earlier study that older people in disadvantaged communities displayed close attachments to their place of residence (Scharf et al, 2002), CALL-ME sought to enhance opportunities for social engagement for potentially isolated older people in their residential neighbourhoods.

For the duration of the project, the CALL-ME team worked with older residents in each of the four neighbourhoods to facilitate activities encompassing chair-based exercise, art and information technology (IT) classes, as well as community action, gardening and women's groups. Reflecting Manchester's diverse population, several groups included people belonging to the city's black and minority ethnic communities (Murray and Crummett, 2010; Middling et al, 2011). Researchers initially carried out visits to the neighbourhoods to learn about current opportunities for social participation for older people through meetings with residents and representatives of statutory, voluntary, community and religious organisations. Where residents identified a need for further opportunities and a willingness to engage in the research process, the team then collaborated with individuals or organisations to facilitate and support the group's development.

As noted above, the aim of the participatory action research project was to enhance opportunities for social participation for older people in their communities by making the groups sustainable beyond the lifetime of the research project. In spite of numerous challenges faced by participating individuals and groups and by the facilitating researchers involved, to be discussed below, this aim has been achieved for most groups (Murray and Crummett, 2010; Middling et al, 2011). Nine months after the formal end of CALL-ME, a review of the eight groups found that the chair-based exercise class continued to meet weekly, and the (four) gardening groups remained active in raising funds and working to enhance their living environments; some of these groups had gained public recognition for their activities, in some cases winning prizes for their efforts (McGarry and Morris, 2011). The art group continued its creative activities and had become more adventurous, engaging with a wider community to secure support and seek further publicity for their work.

These experiences highlight long-standing tensions that characterise debates within critical gerontology in relation to individuals' ability to shape their own ageing when faced by what may appear to be daunting structural constraints (for example, poverty and material deprivation, low socio-economic status across the lifecourse and a range of health and social care needs). The 'small victories' achieved by groups involved in CALL-ME should be viewed within the broader socio-political context of welfare state retrenchment and a politicisation of citizen engagement in participants' residential communities.

Politics of participation

In many Western nations, but especially in those with residualised welfare states with historically low levels of state-sponsored social provision, recent decades have been marked by a decisive reorientation of public policy (Scharf, 2010). In countries such as the UK this has seen increasing emphasis placed on an individualised and market-driven neoliberalism (Phillipson, 2012). At the same time, both politicians and researchers have noted a decline in civic engagement and a loss of 'community' (Putnam, 1995, 1996), giving rise in recent years to a range of efforts aimed at counteracting these developments. Whereas public discourse around ageing and older people was once almost uniquely associated with the rhetoric of 'burdens' arising from demographic change (Walker, 1990), such language increasingly co-exists with a parallel discourse that recognises older people as a 'resource' for their communities (DWP, 2009; Cox, 2011; WRVS, 2011). Although this can be seen as a positive development in principle, the new policies generate increasingly normative expectations of older people's social and civic participation in their communities (Holstein and Minkler, 2003). Involvement in political, community and civic organisations is increasingly viewed as a 'moral duty' (Reed et al, 2008) of older citizens who are otherwise considered to be 'unproductive' and 'burdensome'.

Neoliberal political discourse has taken up the notion of 'empowerment' through community participation and choice (DH, 2005; Means, 2007). Whereas participation and empowerment were once the distinctive cornerstones of radical political activism against dominant ideologies and forms of governance (see, for example, Freire, 1970), more recently these concepts have become 'mainstreamed', losing some of their critical edge for the emancipation of those experiencing forms of social disadvantage. Miraftab (2004), for instance, has suggested that the concepts of participation and empowerment became de-politicised through their adoption by governments outside the contexts of critical discussions around dominance. Rather than being employed for radical social change, the concepts were increasingly used by governments to justify the withdrawal of essential public resources from disadvantaged groups and communities. Seen in this light, participation becomes a normative expectation for 'good' older citizens rather than a tool for questioning structural sources of inequality and injustice that critical gerontology identifies as being key features associated with ageing in Western societies (see also Chapter Four, this volume).

If anything, the economic downturn arising from the global financial crisis of 2008 and its aftermath has re-politicised ideas around participation and empowerment in nations such as the UK. The adoption of empowerment and participation as a means of justifying neoliberal policies based on citizenship has become highly political. For instance, the 'Big Society' envisioned by the UK's Conservative-Liberal Democrat government since 2010 reflects assumptions that citizens, including older people, represent resources to be used for the benefit of their communities (Alcock, 2010; Cox, 2011). In emphasising individuals' responsibilities and obligations to society, this new form of citizenship conflicts with notions of social justice (Smith and Pangsapa, 2008; Kisby, 2010). Any assumption implying an automatic link between community participation and citizen empowerment through the freedom to change one's immediate living environments is open to critique. Neoliberal discourses base the process of empowerment through community participation on consumerist notions of individual choice and action. Where individuals and groups have been marginalised and subject to social injustices over a lifetime, or even over generations, a lack of personal and community resources may result in few choices remaining open for individuals or groups regarding their contributions to society. The empowerment of citizens through community participation, therefore, has to be carried out in the context of a critical and ethical perspective concerning issues of justice between social groups. Where such critical awareness is absent, particularly in times of economic scarcity, the individualised neoliberal approach to empowerment is likely to lead to a further widening of socio-spatial inequalities. Communities with abundant personal, financial and community resources and facilities will benefit much more than socially disadvantaged communities in need of long-term commitment and investment to generate equivalent community resources and individual capabilities. In the UK, this potential for widening inequalities is reflected in cuts in community development budgets and statutory service delivery implemented since 2010, and an ongoing shift from service *delivery* to the *commissioning* of services to be delivered either by voluntary sector organisations or community groups themselves (Alcock, 2010; Kisby, 2010).

The politics of participation are not solely an abstract matter of concern for academic researchers. They also have a direct impact on the lives of older people, especially those living in disadvantaged urban communities. As we experienced during the CALL-ME project, neoliberal approaches to citizen empowerment ignore the simple fact that relatively under-resourced communities have many more challenges to overcome if their residents are to become better engaged in community life. In CALL-ME, issues facing older residents included, for example, building up, formalising and maintaining a community group, negotiating a path through complex systems of funding support and provision, and sourcing community venues to host activities. In some study areas, the people with whom the researchers were seeking to build relationships had become almost entirely disengaged from their communities. In one neighbourhood, it took a member of the research team many weeks to establish face-to-face contact with older residents before they even considered joining a community group (Murray and Crummett, 2010). The researcher's regular and visible presence in the community was necessary to build trust, and to ensure that residents felt that she was indeed committed to supporting them in the longer term. In those neighbourhoods without a strong tradition of community action or group involvement it took months and, in some cases, well over a year for individuals to identify as members of a group with a common goal. The art group achieved this through their individual and collective pride in the output of their creative activities, and the recognition attained from the wider community at public displays of their artwork (Murray and Crummett, 2010).

The CALL-ME experience emphasises that the kind of capacity building necessary to enable groups to flourish in disadvantaged areas is extremely time-consuming and resource-intensive (Scourfield and Burch, 2010). We found that recent cuts in community funding had led to support services being either withdrawn entirely or reduced to such an extent that they had become practically worthless (see also Berner and Phillips, 2005). While attempts had been made in Manchester since 2000 to build capacity for community engagement and social participation through neighbourhood renewal and regeneration schemes, since 2010 investment in professional community development has largely been withdrawn and replaced by internet-based informational support. Information on funding opportunities for community groups, guidelines and support is now mostly available on websites or distributed through email lists. Such self-help from a distance renders inaccessible necessary support for most older residents of the neighbourhoods in which CALL-ME was active. While growing numbers of older people in the general population have internet access, the majority of CALL-ME participants did not have a personal computer or lacked sufficient IT skills to use the internet in their local library. Many had left school when they were 14 and had not come into contact with computers during their adult lives. Moreover, patterns of communication established during the lifecourse of these birth cohorts favoured personal and face-to-face relationships; some even regarded the telephone as a more recent development in communications (Ziegler, 2012).

In spite of such individual and structural obstacles, in one community the CALL-ME project succeeded in establishing an IT class with the help of a local volunteer instructor. After more than 12 months of weekly classes, the participating group used their newly acquired IT skills within the context of a collaborative project with the neighbouring arts group. Working together, the groups designed a photo calendar of their neighbourhood, and sold this to raise essential funds for both groups. In contrast, none of the members of the chair-based exercise class were confident in the use of computers. As a result, they were unable to apply for funding without substantial support from a member of the research team. Although this was the topic of regular discussion during the research period, no one in the group wished to develop their computer skills, with participants commenting instead that the group would somehow manage to get by without such knowledge.

These examples show that social participation and community engagement in disadvantaged areas may need substantial investment of time and resources before people acting alone and as groups are able to contribute independently to the development and enhancement of their communities. However, without such investment older citizens and their communities will fail to reap the potential benefits of the vision for a Big Society, thus reinforcing the widening gap between advantaged and disadvantaged people and communities (Lawless, 2011). In order to avoid contributing to widening inequalities, we would therefore argue that older citizens' responsibilities should be linked to a critical awareness of lifelong injustices through the development of engagement and participation processes drawing on the politics of everyday lived experience across the lifecourse (Hopkins and Pain, 2007). In this context, participatory action researchers aim to politicise everyday lived experience by uncovering the workings of power and domination in older people's lives and thus providing a grounding for meaningful citizen engagement and action. Based on feminist notions of citizenship, participatory action research considers personal experience to be political. In order to be meaningful for individuals or groups, community action has to evolve from critical awareness and the personal experience of injustices in everyday life. This personal experience of systemic injustices perpetrated against individuals on the basis of social identities (such as age, class or gender) provides a powerful motivator for developing and implementing social change.

In contrast, the adoption of participation as a neoliberal strategy for individual and community development leads to a de-radicalisation of participation as a tool for the critical analysis of the workings of power within society. As noted above, rather than aiming at radical social change and social justice, participation has become a moral duty (Reed et al, 2008) and is now expected of the older citizen. Such ideas also resonate strongly with recent work in critical gerontology. For example, concerns have been voiced regarding normative expectations, which leave older people with little choice to withdraw from society after a full and active life if they so wish (Minkler and Holstein, 2008). Minkler and Holstein (2008) argue that even as safety nets for older people and other vulnerable groups are withdrawn, the same groups are increasingly called on to engage in community participation. The role of civic and community engagement is increasingly one of plugging holes in public funding. In order to avoid creating normative expectations regarding participation or engagement in later life, Minkler and Holstein (2008) call for a critical awareness of the unintended consequences of discourses around active ageing and participation, which essentially further oppress individuals and groups and narrow older people's choices.

In CALL-ME, facilitators from the university-based research team often had to strike a balance between encouraging and enabling participants to contribute to the groups and projects, while also recognising and respecting participants' individual challenges that rendered their ongoing participation problematic. Alongside ill health, family commitments and caring responsibilities, individuals' priorities and motivations changed over the course of the project's duration. Facilitators sought to maintain an awareness of the actual and potential impact of involvement on participants' physical, mental and emotional wellbeing. Individuals in several groups had to limit their involvement in CALL-ME because of health concerns or family commitments, such as caring for a relative or grandchild. In some cases, this withdrawal was temporary or sporadic, but in other cases it became permanent. Groups and facilitators needed to be sufficiently flexible to allow for this withdrawal, while at the same time ensuring that individuals felt able to re-join the group or to continue their participation at a reduced level. Some authors have commented on the potential harm to older people arising from their involvement or participation, in particular when expectations are high or are not met, or when interpersonal relationships become frayed through conflict (Ray, 2007; Scourfield and Burch, 2010). Of course, these concerns do not apply exclusively to participatory research with older people. Expectations need to be carefully negotiated throughout the participatory action research process. However, conflict may have a disproportionately greater impact on older people's social relationships as their social networks tend to be smaller and more locally based (Cattell, 2001). Exclusion from one community group may have knock-on effects leading to withdrawal from other activities. As a result, participatory action research places demands on researchers to be sensitive to the minutiae of everyday interaction, and seek to create an atmosphere that enables all participants to give voice to their concerns (Minkler, 2004; Flicker et al, 2007). Within the context of a research project such as CALL-ME, participatory ethics therefore reaches beyond the usual 'no harm' premise of research by facilitating participants to determine their own goals and levels of involvement.

Ideally then, participatory work should, on the one hand, be responsive to individuals' own shifting capabilities of making a contribution to community change, while on the other hand, encouraging engagement with dominant ideologies which stereotype older people as being either 'frail and passive' or 'resourceful and active'. As will be discussed in more detail below, it is at this level that ageist stereotypes can potentially be challenged through the construction of knowledge around the heterogeneity and complexity of ageing by older people themselves.

Em-power-ment, the subject and space

The term 'empowerment' is frequently used by researchers, including those working in the critical gerontology tradition, who favour participatory or participative research methods. However, its meaning is seldom clearly defined or its mysterious workings elucidated. In order to arrive at an understanding of how empowerment works, it is helpful to address assumptions concerning the structuring of power relations within society.

Two main conceptualisations of 'power' are employed: traditionally, critical gerontology has tended to understand power as being the property of a sovereign force, such as governments and other institutions of the state (see, for example, Walker, 2009). Based on this interpretation, power is understood to be owned by some and not others, and thereby to be unequally distributed in society. This view of power as repressive tends to operate within a discourse of dualistic notions of powerful versus powerless or poor versus rich (Kapoor, 2002). Empowerment thus occurs when those in power give up some of their power to those who are power-less. Viewed uncritically through this lens, older people may be perceived as dependent on those in power to make changes *for* them in their lives and communities. By investing politicians with the power to make decisions over older people's lives, a case might even be made for critical gerontology having become complicit in perpetuating the very social inequalities that it seeks to eradicate. For example, attempts to highlight the experiences of older people prone to forms of 'social exclusion' (see, for example, Scharf et al, 2002, 2005) might simply mark out excluded individuals and groups for further marginalisation. Without sufficient attention given to the potential negative outcomes of this approach, there is a risk that a too-narrow focus on disadvantaged older adults will simply perpetuate subjectivities that are passive and dependent and in need of representation by others who are considered more powerful (for example, researchers or older people's organisations). In essence, concentrating uncritically on those who are most marginalised may reinforce a view of older citizens as people whose rights are granted by those *in power*. Viewed in this context, em-powerment becomes impersonal and de-contextualised because it is bestowed by those who tend to be far removed from, and may have little understanding of, the everyday reality of older people's lives.

In this respect, critical gerontology can be informed by debates that characterise community-based participatory action research. Participatory action researchers typically understand 'power' as permeating relationships on all levels and as producing specific outcomes that enable or condition possibilities in everyday life. This conceptualisation draws on Foucault's interpretation of power and considers power as inherently unstable, effects of which have to be continuously reproduced in everyday practice. It is, therefore, always contextualised in the daily lives of participants. In broad terms, participatory action researchers thus consider that power relations can be changed by rendering visible the ideas and practices which create inequalities and power-lessness. Their approach seeks to create subjectivities which are reflexive, critically thinking and active change agents who have the potential to empower *themselves* through learning and through representing their own lives as being meaningful and valued (Kesby et al, 2007. Kesby (2005) refers to empowerment in terms of a 'journey of self-discovery' and to empowered agency as being fluid and constantly changing. According to this approach, participatory action research aims to enable older citizens to own their rights and give expression to that ownership through making decisions about the way they wish to be. Empowerment arises in the political, geographic, economic and social context of each individual and group. By beginning with the promotion of self-efficacy and individual agency, empowerment can evolve into a collective effort focused on changing laws and institutional practices.

Some geographers have reflected on the spatial characteristics of empowerment, in particular within the context of aspects of its performativity, that is, those 'practices which produce and subvert discourse and knowledge, and which at the same time enable and discipline subjects and their performances' (Gregson and Rose, 2000, p 433). Kesby (2005) and Kesby et al (2007), for instance, point out that empowerment is an unstable effect of participatory action research and that it needs to be repeatedly performed in order to be maintained. While participatory action research through its practice often creates those 'safe spaces' where empowerment can be trialled and performed, its positive effect does not necessarily reach out to the actors' lives beyond that safe space. Nevertheless, participatory spaces can facilitate the enactment of non-hierarchical relational practices of governance whose existence in themselves may challenge and critique dominant societal structures and discourses. As we experienced in CALL-ME, the very act of older people organising and representing themselves may threaten the seemingly innocent but often patronising beneficence of those who consider representing older people's interests to be their principal raison d'être. Taking matters into their own hands, one group had to fight to be considered by managers sufficiently responsible and capable of improving the gardens around their sheltered housing complex.

Considering empowerment as an unstable effect of spatially situated relational practices opens up the question whether and how this effect can be transferred successfully to other spheres in participants' lives. Some researchers advise caution regarding expectations of the potential empowerment of participants (Kesby, 2005). Where researchers may consider empowerment desirable and beneficial to older people, the effects can still be unpredictable for individual or groups. As older people are often embedded in lifelong existing relationalities in their communities (Ziegler, 2012), it is necessary to support participants in projects such as CALL-ME to determine the spatial and temporal extent of their empowered practice.

In CALL-ME, as the community groups evolved, participants took their projects into the public domain through a series of showcasing and networking events. It was evident that such opportunities contributed greatly to the development of some individuals' self-confidence, not only in terms of making decisions for themselves, but also in relation to their abilities to take on responsibilities for their groups. In these cases, empowered performances beyond the usual and comfortable spaces, where participants gained recognition from those outside their immediate sphere, broadened the effectiveness of empowerment by giving participants a voice outside their own communities. For example, a comparative (and competitive) element of one CALL-ME event held in Manchester's town hall contributed to the development of pride in their groups' achievements. Participants presented their projects alongside their facilitators in front of an audience of representatives from statutory and voluntary agencies as well as local residents and visitors. Participants subsequently commented, for instance, that they had enjoyed the event because it gave them an opportunity to hear the experiences of, and learn from, other groups. Groups learned that they were facing similar challenges and obstacles (such as securing funding, locating suitable venues for activities or increasing group membership), which in turn gave participants the confidence to continue with their endeavours.

Critics of participatory action research have exposed the way in which participation seems to have become the 'new tyranny' (Cooke and Kothari, 2001). They suggest that participation is not neutral, but in itself also represents a form of power. Far from being benign and empowering, participatory action research methods may create conditions for the production of certain forms of knowledge, often based on a consensus which may obscure individual difference. Although founded on a premise of inclusivity, participatory action research consensus building may in effect exclude those who do not wish to be part of an unfolding process. While dealing with conflict by promoting consensus represents a key tenet of participatory action research, this is not always straightforward. It becomes especially challenging when group members have a history of difficult or hostile relationships. In one of the CALL-ME gardening groups, repeated conflicts arose between members because of contradictory priorities, petty jealousies and a clash of personalities. Even the skills of an experienced facilitator proved inadequate in dealing with such hostility and could not prevent the withdrawal of those who felt injured by other group members.

Critics of participatory action research have also suggested that even in resisting mainstream discourses researchers cannot operate outside existing power relations. Resistance to power is only another form of power. In fact, it has been argued that for many marginalised groups resistance is a privilege which they cannot afford as it may harm them further. But as power cannot be avoided, Kesby (2005) suggests that participatory action researchers need to mobilise and work with positive forms of power which are based on the reflexive governance of participants. In CALL-ME, we experienced some older women's reluctance to assume responsibility for their groups; although happy to collect the weekly contribution from members on an informal basis, it took more than 12 months for a member of the chair-based exercise class to volunteer to assume a formal role as treasurer and signatory on the group's bank account. Many female participants perceived themselves as being incapable of dealing with bureaucracy. Eventually, however, and with encouragement and support from the facilitators and the wider group in which they were involved, the women began to engage with funders and other organisations. This seemingly modest step ultimately gave these women the opportunity to make decisions and to take control of their project, thus helping them to overcome their own self-stereotype of being incapable of dealing with officialdom. Taking their own time over this reflexive learning process, group members had assumed control of a re-definition of their own and others' representational identity of 'older women' as passive and powerless. This process also included overcoming a pervasive fear of making mistakes and, as a consequence, of being shown up as being 'ignorant' in front of others. Supportive and humorous relationships within the exercise group led to one member being able to laugh about her 'ignorance' and allowed her jokingly to recount to others some of the mistakes she had made in processing the formalities associated with opening a bank account.

Reflexivity and the production of knowledge

In recent years, many critical gerontologists have emphasised the need for macro-level analysis in the face of globalisation (Estes et al, 2003; Phillipson, 2012). Researchers have argued that traditional local networks have become loosened in the face of global flows of people and information. In spite of increasing individualisation, critical gerontology researchers point out that ageing has become constructed as a *global problem*. Researchers thus need to take account of, for example, global migration and the growing role of intergovernmental agencies in social constructions of old age (Estes et al, 2003). On the other hand, some critical gerontologists have also acknowledged the importance of studying the intersections between the individual, community and societal influences on ageing (see, for example, Baars et al, 2005; Bernard and Scharf, 2007; Grenier, 2012).

Participatory action research has often been criticised for its focus on small-scale local change and inadequate acknowledgement of the influence of macro-level factors. Notwithstanding such a critique, it is its focus on local change that also represents a key strength of the participatory approach. In CALL-ME, for example, no two groups were identical, and participants often had to deal with highly differentiated local circumstances. Differences concerned such factors as individual personalities, the availability and quality of suitable venues, ethnic and cultural characteristics, gender dimensions, contrasting neighbourhood politics and variation in the support available from other organisations. For example, while some groups benefited considerably from good relationships with elected local councillors, in several communities councillors showed no interest in the groups despite the best efforts of participants to build links with their political representatives. Locating suitable venues for their activities became a particular concern for many groups, being associated with a wide range of obstacles. For example, a Somali women's group had to find an alternative venue for their planned cultural activities, because their original meeting space was felt to be insufficiently private from male intrusion. Many groups found it difficult to raise funds to meet a growing trend for community venues to charge for their use. They were thus reliant on locating venues which were not only convenient and accessible to members, but also free of charge. As a result of such difficulties, the exercise class met in a highly restrictive, windowless and dark room in a local club. This was felt to be far from ideal, since participant numbers had to be limited and visually impaired individuals could not easily become involved.

Facilitation processes had to be adapted to those local circumstances and local relationships and access constantly re-negotiated. As a result, not one of the eight groups established across the four Manchester communities operated in the same way. Moreover, few general rules could be applied to ensure a group's success. Some groups needed considerable encouragement and practical help in setting goals, negotiating venues, planning and applying for finance over a long period of time. Others quickly became independent and even exceeded their initial goals. For example, one of the gardening groups won prizes for their exhibits the first time they entered the city-wide 'In Bloom' competition (Middling et al, 2011). But in all cases, it was essentially the commitment and enthusiasm of the older participants which overcame the many frustrations and drove the groups' successes. In this context, it is possible to view change not as the outcome of changing laws, procedures or rules – the macro-level analysis typically associated with critical gerontology – but as the result of hard work and perseverance of *individuals* and groups in their communities. This individual and community engagement is based on a recognition of the heterogeneity of groups of older people where broader policies often fail to account for existing inequalities, differences and diversity. Therefore change on a local level cannot be replaced by – but could lead to and be supplemented by – cultural, political and structural transformation (Kesby et al, 2007). This aligns closely with work in the critical gerontology tradition that recognises the importance of including older people in discussions affecting them in order to avoid *grand narratives* and generalisations (Minkler and Holstein, 2008).

The discussion of differing scales of change between critical gerontology and participatory action research is linked to assumptions around the production of knowledge on ageing and the validity and generalisability of research evidence. While critical gerontology has made a significant contribution in raising awareness of social, political and economic forces which create and shape social inequalities in later life, researchers belonging to this tradition have often been relatively uncritical and unreflective regarding their own role in this process. One early exception is Baars' (1991) discussion of the production of gerontological knowledge. He argues that, 'especially in developed countries the social constitution of *gerontology* influences the social constitution of *aging*, because the results of gerontological work modify the interpretation and structuring of the aging process' (1991, p 229; original emphasis). In other words, and as discussed above, rather than sitting outside of society as observers and critics of society, gerontologists actually contribute to the way in which society as a whole and individuals within it can make sense of their own present and future ageing. More recently, Minkler and Holstein (2003) have advocated critical and feminist approaches which reflect on research methodologies. In their critique of 'successful ageing', they argue that gerontologists need to consider ageing in all its complexities. This can only be understood 'from the inside' through the adoption of a spatially and temporally contextualised *interactive* research process. The authors suggest that, through the voices of older people, participatory approaches can reveal the 'disharmony, ambiguity and uncertainty' (Minkler and Holstein, 2003, p 791) of old age. But even in this interactive process, we argue that the researcher needs to remain conscious of his or her own role in the production of knowledge.

Reflexivity represents an important tool in the participatory action research change process. However, the need for reflexivity pertains not only to participants but in particular to facilitators and/or researchers. Reflexivity is a tool for raising awareness of our own assumptions which underlie the kinds of questions we ask in research and those we do not ask. It aims to situate the production of knowledge within a certain discourse or paradigm and can help us to ascertain whether our research practice is in line with our stated participatory aims which consider older people as equal partners in the production of knowledge. Reflexivity also allows researchers to consider their own role in terms of power relations in the production of knowledge. As academic researchers engaged in the CALL-ME project, we undoubtedly had influence in the communities in which we worked. At times, this operated to our advantage; for instance, in working as intermediaries between local organisations, policy makers and planners and the older people's groups, with an aim to support their sustainability. At other times, as non-local researchers, we may have been considered interlopers on others' research or community development territory. However, it was difficult at times to remain sufficiently detached to reflect on our own roles in the often-complex research process which was situated within the context of local politics, local relationships and history. Rose (1997), for instance, highlights the potential dangers of this navel-gazing reflexivity as it may produce an inward-looking researcher who is nonetheless unable to get to the bottom of his or her positionality as he or she is too entangled within a 'messy' research process. In order to gain an understanding across difference, she suggests instead that knowledge production should 'resist the authority of the academic and recognise the knowledges of both researcher and researched' (Rose, 1993, p 315).

Reflections

In conclusion, we would like to offer some reflections on the opportunities and challenges of using participatory approaches in critical gerontology, while also drawing out lessons from critical approaches for participatory action research. We intend these not as set in stone, but as a starting point for further discussion and reflection on the theoretical assumptions of, and impact on, issues around social justice and social change.

Participatory methods can provide researchers with an often-rewarding opportunity of hands-on and positive change to make a visible difference in older people's lives. While critical gerontologists often express their commitment to critically evaluate and change societal conditions of ageing, the practical value and impact of this commitment is not always discernible. At a time when 'impact' has become a buzzword for research funders, especially in the UK, participatory methods may provide a pathway for demonstrating real change which is meaningful to those creating it. Participatory action research represents an opportunity to create differentiated knowledges *with* marginalised older people *in dialogue*, rather than knowledge *on* or *about* those very people whose lives are affected by it. This is not to say that participatory action research represents an easy option for making a difference or for providing an impact. Participatory research is a 'messy' and, at times, unpredictable process. It requires many skills on the part of the researcher, such as flexibility, reflexivity, time, patience and perseverance, most of which tend to be undervalued by funding agencies and academic structures and processes. Equally, participatory action researchers can benefit from insights drawn from critical gerontology. In particular, this involves the need to engage systematically with critical perspectives in their research practice.

Participatory methodologies also enable critical gerontologists to remain grounded in the heterogeneity and complexity of the lived experience of older people's lives and to gain an understanding of the workings of power within those everyday lives. In considering power as diffuse rather than hierarchical, critical gerontologists can facilitate older people to become active and reflexive agents of change in the communities in which they live.

Considering the everyday politics of participation and empowerment provides opportunities for gerontologists working within a critical tradition to strengthen theories around social inequality in old age. It reminds us that there are no permanently valid and/or generalisable truths; rather, it helps us to understand the specific temporal, economic, political and social–cultural conditions of old age. In this context, there can be several challenges for the researcher; while acknowledging the validity of each older person's experiences and opinions, it is worth bearing in mind that it is often older people themselves who voice and perpetuate ageist and stereotypical views internalised in their younger days in a society which valued its citizens largely through their economic contributions. Through the use of reflexive practice and participatory learning, critical gerontologists may raise awareness among older people of their own roles in maintaining such stereotypes among those people who are most affected by them.

This awareness of ageing discourses and power relations across the lifecourse may also serve to raise critical awareness among younger people of the impact of their own and society's current views and structures on their future potentialities for a just old age. In all this, it is vital that participatory action research and critical gerontology remain critical and radical in their approach to issues of justice and power rather than allowing a neoliberal agenda to hi-jack participation and empowerment for its own purposes.

A further challenge for those using participatory approaches in critical gerontology is in considering not just the mechanisms and processes, but also the desired scale of change or level of impact. How can we ensure that social change achieved through participatory approaches reaches beyond academia and the local community? There are many ways in which this may be achieved, from the involvement of stakeholders and policy makers to the use of the media and the internet to raise awareness and publicise findings. Of utmost importance, however, is that older people are themselves active agents in this representational process in order to avoid being relegated to the position of needy and passive recipients of knowledge and change.

Acknowledgements
This chapter draws on the CALL-ME project which was supported by the UK Research Councils' New Dynamics of Ageing programme between 2008 and 2011 (Grant No RES-352-25-0031). We wish to acknowledge the contributions of CALL-ME team members Michael Murray, Sian Maslin-Prothero, Roger Beech, Jan Bailey, Amanda Crummett and Sharon Middling to the work reported here. We are also indebted to our community partners in Manchester and, in particular, to residents of the four study areas who participated so ably in the CALL-ME project.

References
Alcock, P. (2010) 'Building the Big Society: a new policy environment for the third sector in England'. *Voluntary Sector Review*, vol. 1, no 3, pp. 379–389.

Baars, J. (1991) 'The challenge of critical gerontology: the problem of social constitution', *Journal of Aging Studies*, vol 5, no 3, pp 219-43.

Baars, J., Dannefer, D., Phillipson, C. and Walker, A. (eds) (2005) *Aging, globalisation and inequality: The new critical gerontology*, New York: Baywood Publishing.

Bernard, M. and Scharf, T. (eds) (2007) *Critical perspectives on ageing societies*, Bristol: The Policy Press.

Berner, E. and Phillips, B. (2005) 'Left to their own devices? Community self-help between alternative development and neo-liberalism', *Community Development Journal*, vol 40, no 1, pp 17-29.

Blair, T. and Minkler, M. (2009) 'Participatory action research with older adults: key principles in practice', *The Gerontologist*, vol 49, no 5, pp 651-62.

Cattell, V. (2001) 'Poor people, poor places, and poor health: the mediating role of social networks and social capital', *Social Science & Medicine*, vol 52, no 10, pp 1501-16.

Clough, R., Green, B., Hawkes, B., Raymond, G. and Bright, L. (2006) *Older people as researchers: Evaluating a participative project*, York: Joseph Rowntree Foundation.

Cooke, B. and Kothari, U. (2001) *Participation: The new tyranny?*, London: Zed Books.

Cornes, M., Peardon, J., Manthorpe, J. and The 3YO Project Team (2008) 'Wise owls and professors: the role of older researchers in the review of the National Service Framework for Older People', *Health Expectations*, vol 11, no 4, pp 409-17.

Cox, A. (2011) *Age of opportunity: Older people, volunteering and the Big Society*, London: ResPublica.

DH (Department of Health) (2005) *Independence, well-being and choice*, London: DH.

DWP (Department for Work and Pensions) (2009) *Building a society for all ages*, London: The Stationery Office.

Estes, C.L., Biggs, S. and Phillipson, C. (2003) *Social theory, social policy and ageing: A critical introduction*, Maidenhead: Open University Press.

Flicker, S., Travers, R., Guta, A., McDonald, S. and Meagher, A. (2007) 'Ethical dilemmas in community-based participatory research: recommendations for institutional review boards', *Journal of Urban Health*, vol 84, no 4, pp 478-93.

Freire, P. (1970) *Pedagogy of the oppressed*, New York: Continuum.

Glanz, D. and Neikrug, S. (1997) 'Seniors as researchers in the study of aging: learning and doing', *The Gerontologist*, vol 37, no 6, pp 823-6.

Godfrey, M., Townsend, J. and Denby, T. (2004) *Building a good life for older people in local communities*, York: Joseph Rowntree Foundation.

Gregson, N. and Rose, G. (2000) 'Taking Butler elsewhere: performativities, spatialities and subjectivities', *Environment and Planning D: Society and Space*, vol 18, no 4, pp 433-52.

Grenier, A. (2012) *Transitions and the lifecourse: Challenging the constructions of 'growing old'*, Bristol: The Policy Press.

Hennessy, C. and Walker, A. (2011) Promoting multi-disciplinary and inter-disciplinary ageing research in the United Kingdom. *Ageing & Society*, vol 31, no 1, pp 52-69.

Holstein, M. and Minkler, M. (2003) 'Self, society and the new gerontology', *The Gerontologist*, vol 46, no 6, pp 787-96.

Hopkins, P. and Pain, R. (2007) 'Geographies of age: Thinking relationally. *Area*, vol 39, no 3, pp 287-294.

Jacobs, G. (2010) 'Conflicting demands and the power of defensive routines in participatory action research', *Action Research*, vol 8, no 4, pp 367-86.

Kapoor, I. (2002) 'The devil's in the theory: a critical assessment of Robert Chambers' work on participatory development', *Third World Quarterly*, vol 23, no 1, pp 101-17.

Kesby, M. (2005) 'Retheorising empowerment-through-participation as a performance in space: beyond tyranny to transformation', *Signs*, vol 30, no 4, pp 2037-65.

Kesby, M., Kindon, S. and Pain, R. (2007) 'Participation as a form of power: retheorising empowerment and spatialising participatory action research', in S. Kindon, R. Pain and M. Kesby (eds) *Participatory action research approaches and methods: Connecting people, participation and place*, London: Routledge, pp 19-25.

Kisby, B. (2010) 'The Big Society: power to the people?', *The Political Quarterly*, vol 81, no 4, pp 484-91.

Lawless, P. (2011) 'Big Society and community: lessons from the 1998-2011 New Deal for Communities programme in England', *People, Place & Policy Online*, vol 5, no 2, pp 55-64.

McGarry, P. and Morris, J. (2011) 'A great place to grow older: a case study of how Manchester is developing an age-friendly city', *Working with Older People*, vol 15, no 1, pp 38-46.

Manchester City Council (2004) *Towards a quality of life strategy for Manchester's older people*, Manchester: Manchester City Council, Valuing Older People.

Manchester City Council (2011) *Manchester: A great place to grow older 2010-2020*, Manchester: Manchester City Council, Valuing Older People.

Martinson, M. and Minkler, M. (2006) 'Civic engagement and older adults: a critical perspective', *The Gerontologist*, vol 46, no 3, pp 318-24.

Means, R. (2007) 'The re-medicalisation of later life', in M. Bernard and T. Scharf (eds) *Critical perspectives on ageing societies*, Bristol: The Policy Press, pp 45-56.

Middling, S., Bailey, J., Maslin-Prothero, S. and Scharf, T. (2011) 'Gardening and the social engagement of older people', *Working with Older People*, vol 15, no 3, pp 112-22.

Minkler, M. (2004) 'Ethical challenges for the "outside" researcher in community-based participatory research', *Health Education Behavior*, vol 31, no 6, pp 684-97.

Minkler, M. and Holstein, M. (2008) 'From civic rights to … civic engagement? Concerns of two older critical gerontologists about a "new social movement" and what it portends', *Journal of Aging Studies*, vol 22, no 2, pp 196-204.

Miraftab, F. (2004) 'Making neo-liberal governance: the disempowering work of empowerment'. *International Planning Studies*, vol 9, no 4, pp 239-259.

Murray, M. and Crummett, A. (2010) '"I don't think they knew we could do these sorts of things": Social representations of community and participation in community arts by older people', *Journal of Health Psychology*, vol 15, no 5, 777-85.

Nicholls, R. (2009) 'Research and indigenous participation: critical reflexive methods', *International Journal of Social Research Methodology*, vol 12, no 2, pp 117-26.

Pain, R. (2004) 'Social geography: participatory research', *Progress in Human Geography*, vol 28, no 5, pp 652-63.

Phillipson, C. (2012) 'Globalisation, economic recession and social exclusion: policy challenges and responses', in T. Scharf and N. Keating (eds) *From exclusion to inclusion in old age: A global challenge*, Bristol: The Policy Press, pp 17-32.

Phillipson, C. and Scharf, T. (2004) 'The impact of government policy on social exclusion among older people'. London: Social Exclusion Unit, Office of the Deputy Prime Minister

Phillipson, C. and Walker, A. (1987) 'The case for a critical gerontology', in S. di Gregorio *Social gerontology: New directions*. London: Croom Helm.

Putnam, R.D. (1995) 'Bowling alone: America's declining social capital', *Journal of Democracy*, vol 6, no 1 pp 65-78.

Putnam, R.D. (1996) 'The strange disappearance of civic America', *American Prospect*, vol 7, no 24, pp 34-48.

Ray, M. (2007) 'Redressing the balance? The participation of older people in research', in M. Bernard and T. Scharf (eds) *Critical perspectives on ageing societies*, Bristol: The Policy Press, pp 73-88.

Reed, J., Cook, G., Bolter, V. and Douglas, B. (2008) 'Older people involved in policy and planning: factors which support engagement', *Journal of Aging Studies*, vol 22, no 3, pp 273-81.

Rose, G. (1993) *Feminism and geography: The limits of geographical knowledge*, Cambridge: Polity Press.

Rose, G. (1997) 'Situating knowledges: positionality, reflexivity and other tactics', *Progress in Human Geography*, vol 21, no 3, pp 305-20.

Scharf, T. (2010) 'Social policies for ageing societies: perspectives from Europe', in C. Phillipson and D. Dannefer (eds) *Handbook of social gerontology*, New York/London: Sage Publications, pp 497-512.

Scharf, T., Phillipson, C., Kingston, P. and Smith, A.E. (2002) *Growing older in socially deprived areas*, London: Help the Aged.

Scharf, T., Phillipson, C. and Smith, A.E. (2005) 'Social exclusion of older people in deprived urban communities of England', *European Journal of Ageing*, vol 2, no 2, pp 76-87

Scharf, T., Phillipson, C. and Smith, A.E. (2007) 'Aging in a difficult place: assessing the impact of urban deprivation on older people', in H.-W. Wahl, C. Tesch-Römer and A. Hoff (eds) *New dynamics in old age: individual, environmental and societal perspectives*, Amityville, NY: Baywood Publishing, pp 153-73

Scourfield, P. and Birch, S. (2010) 'Ethical considerations when involving older people in public service participation processes', *Ethics and Social Welfare*, vol 4, no 3, pp 236-53.

Smith, L., Bratini, L., Chambers, D., Jensen, R.V. and Romero, L. (2010) 'Between idealism and reality: meeting the challenges of participatory action research', *Action Research*, vol 8, no 4, pp 407-25.

Smith, M.J. and Pangsapa, P. (2008) *Environment and citizenship*, London: Zed Books.

Walker, A. (1990) 'The economic "burden" of ageing and the prospect of generational conflict', *Ageing & Society*, vol 10, no 4, pp 377-90.

Walker, A. (2009) 'Why is ageing so unequal?', in P. Cann and M. Dean (eds) *Unequal ageing*, Bristol: The Policy Press, pp 141-58.

WRVS (2011) *Gold age pensioners: Valuing the socio-economic contribution of older people in the UK*, London: WRVS.

Ziegler, F. (2012) '"You have to engage with life, or life will go away": an intersectional life course analysis of older women's social participation in a disadvantaged urban area', *Geoforum*, vol 43, no 6, pp 1296-1305.

TEN

Commentary: contingent ageing, naturalisation and some rays of intellectual hope

Dale Dannefer and Jielu Lin

Introduction

We begin this commentary by underscoring the usefulness of the distinction made by Jan Baars and Chris Phillipson in Chapter Two, between contingent and existential ageing. As they define these terms, *contingent* ageing refers to '… limitations that are neither inherent in human life nor inevitable in senescing …', while *existential* ageing refers to 'vulnerabilities that are inherent in human life and will manifest themselves inevitably as people live longer.' This important distinction resurfaces in a number of complex ways throughout the chapters of this volume, and we employ it as one of two organising themes for this commentary chapter. The enduring theme of the tension between theory and practice arises in fresh ways in several of the chapters, and we focus on this tension as a second organising theme for our comments. We serially adopt these two sets of tensions – between (a) contingent and existential ageing and (b) theory and practice – as the primary frameworks within which to organise our comments on this set of informative and provocative chapters.

Contingent and existential ageing

Before proceeding to a discussion of individual chapters with reference to the contingent/existential distinction, the distinction itself warrants some further clarification and elaboration. First, we note the contingent/existential distinction largely reflects a social science/humanities divide, especially if one begins from a critical social science orientation. Social science seeks to explicate the role of social and institutional forces in shaping both culture and individual lives, including individual ageing. It is thus inherent in the logic of this approach to interrogate not just individual outcomes and individual differences but also their sources, and to explore whether variation across individuals may be accounted for in the social contexts within which the individual in question is immersed. By contrast, humanities scholars often tend to focus most fundamentally on the character of the experience and explore its depths, dimensions, boundaries and possibilities on its own terms.

Second, as we understand these terms, neither contingent nor existential ageing need be seen as inherently limited to 'limitations' and 'vulnerabilities'. Age-related experiences that are enriching and enervating can also often be thought of as either contingent (for example, the continuing refinement of well-practised skills, whether as an artist, teacher or poet, which relies on available resources and the freedom to do so), while others are existential (for example, becoming a parent/grandparent, or profiting from the seasoned perspective afforded by the continued accumulation of experience). The diverse array of both talents and limitations found among older populations, and indeed 'oldest-old' populations, should make clear that age has the potential to bring both salutary and adverse outcomes.

A third point that warrants discussion is that contingent ageing encompasses at least two analytically distinct (although related) types of social processes, which may respectively be termed *structural* and *hermeneutic*. *Structural* contingencies refer to social dynamics that relate to the age-graded distribution of resources and their consequences, operating through such well-known factors as the socio-economic gradient and cumulative dis/advantage. *Hermeneutic* dynamics refer to the interpretive level, and hence to the host of socially constructed definitions ascribed to age and related phenomena. A prime example is the historical shift in 'age consciousness' or age awareness, which has transformed the meanings ascribed to age at the societal level. Of course, this shift was driven by the bureaucratising and standardising impulses of late 19th- and 20th-century modernity, illustrating the interplay of the structural and hermeneutic forces. Such hermeneutic contingencies often have ideological significance, because they define and interpret socially organised age-related phenomena as determined instead by individual-level factors, whether individual preferences or pre-determined, trait-like individual characteristics.

Indeed, *structurally* produced contingencies are continuously being obscured and legitimated by *hermeneutic* ones, in the form of naturalisation and similar processes. *Naturalisation* refers to the practice of assuming something that is socially contingent to be a matter of individual volition or of 'human nature' (such as retiring at a certain age or desiring to have children). Thereby, it may entail an erroneous redefinition of contingent factors as existential ones.

An example of such naturalisation of structural differences (treating them as existential) is provided by Baars and Phillipson's observation that 'When all limitations are seen as *existential* limitations, ageing people have to accept all circumstances, however dreadful. The mantra in response to any problem or limitations would be: "It's your age." For many important problems, this is too easy: often situations can be improved and people can be helped.'

This important caution constitutes a fulcrum of several of the points we wish to argue in the pages below. However, as Baars and Phillipson also note, it is problematic to adopt the view that all ageing is seen as *contingent*, and that all the issues that arise as part of existential ageing can or will be neutralised. They rightly insist that existential ageing is real, and we also offer some comments on existential ageing as it appears in this volume.

Contingent ageing: structural aspects

As defined by Baars and Phillipson, *contingent ageing* refers to issues '… that are neither inherent in human life nor inevitable in senescing, such as poor housing conditions, insufficient care, social isolation, starvation, or ageism' (Chapter Two, this volume; see also Baars, 2012). We begin by a general observation, which is that the problem of structural contingencies – or more specifically, the question of how the continuing presence of such structural contingencies should inform our understanding of ageing – remains a central problem of ageing that is relevant, yet quite unevenly developed across the chapters comprising this volume.

Thus, in Chapter Seven Anja Machielse and Roelof Hortulanus focus on what they see as an achievable balance that: '… enables people to fully enjoy the individual freedom of late modernity but at the same time feel safe in the face of limitations and adversity'; in Chapter Six Hanne Laceulle emphasises the emergence of autonomy and related problems of identity; in Chapter Three Joseph Dohmen notes the need to focus on 'one's own life' as a concomitant of late modernity. Dohmen, consistent with Giddens, proposes that recent decades have seen a shift from a 'politics of emancipation' to a 'politics of life'. He writes: 'Although emancipation battles still exist in certain contexts, a clear shift can be identified from a *struggle for emancipation* to a *life politics*.'

It is true that, over the past two centuries, world life expectancy has more than doubled (about 25 years, to about 65 for men and 70 for women; see Riley, 2001). Yet in 2004, 1.4 billion (25.7 per cent) of the world population were living in poverty, living on less than US$1.25 a day (UN, 2010). In the US, in 2011, nearly 50 million people are still living under the poverty line, and the group with the highest rate of poverty is women over the age of 65 living alone (US Census Bureau 2012). Given such circumstances and given the rapid ageing of populations in nearly every society, with huge proportions of the overall populations and the aged populations living in poverty, we cannot agree with Dohmen's characterisation that concerns with social justice and emancipation now only 'exist in certain contexts'. Indeed, we suggest that it would be more reasonable to argue the opposite, that the luxury of focusing on a 'politics of life' and the attendant identity concerns is only affordable to individuals who 'exist in certain contexts'. Yet in a globalised world, even that statement would be problematic, since it avoids dealing with the reality that the lifestyle preoccupations of late modern citizens – the obsession with a 'life politics' – presupposes a level of comfort and consumer choice that is only made possible by the exploitation of labour elsewhere on the planet (Dannefer, 2002).

Such problems of inequality and inclusiveness occur not only between societies but also within them. Within late modern societies, the power of social stratification and inequality to shape life chances remains robust. To be clear, Dohmen, Laceulle and several other authors in this volume do acknowledge some degree of social contingency. Nevertheless, across several of these chapters a thematic vision of the current state of healthy and successful ageing is that, in Dohmen's words, 'older people remain more vital and health for a longer time with deferring of those conditions associated with dependency.' While this is true for many people, we have learned not to generalise about the older population. If it is true 'on average', the average merely obscures the high levels of inequality in the older population resulting from processes of cumulative dis/advantage. Although such processes may be ameliorated by welfare state policies, they appear to operate very generally.

In the US, the compression of morbidity into very old age is empirically found to be much more probable for people with high socio-economic status (House et al, 2005). Indeed, one of the major conclusions from studies of health and ageing is that there are substantial individual differences in the pattern of age-based change in health (see, for example, Crimmins et al, 2009; Rowe and Kahn, 1987). These health differentials have been explicitly linked to inequalities in socio-economic factors and the socio-economic gradient (Marmot, 2004), and they have been shown to be both pervasive and causal (Link and

Phelan, 1995). People with lower levels of education, income and wealth are more likely to experience earlier onset of chronic diseases and subsequently, more rapid progression of the loss of functioning. The health decline appears to be accelerated by social disadvantage. A person in his or her forties who lives in or near poverty has a level of physiological dysregulation similar to that of a person aged about 60 in a better-off family (Crimmins et al, 2009). There is a five- to ten-year mortality difference between people with higher socio-economic status and those with lower status (Hayward et al, 2000).

Contingent ageing: hermeneutic and ideological aspects

A major theme of the sociology of age has been the discovery that many aspects of ageing that are conventionally thought of as 'existential' (that is, as natural and inevitable) are really 'contingent', or socially produced. As noted above, the practice of treating socially constituted phenomena as though they are universal and inevitable aspects of human development and social life has been called *naturalisation*. We offer some cautionary comments concerning the inclination of several of our fellow authors to embrace such naturalised concepts, either explicitly or implicitly reclassifying phenomena as existential when they may be contingent. We limit ourselves to three concepts – social relations, developmental stages and traits, and agency.

In their analysis of social relations, Machielse and Hortulanus argue that their data suggested the prevalence of disconnectedness among older adults, as 20 per cent of the respondents aged 81 and above were classified as socially isolated, whereas smaller proportions (4-14 per cent) of isolation were found in other age groups. However, it also needs to be noted that adults over the age of 80 manifest a range of variations with respect to social isolation. Indeed, a great majority (80 per cent) of adults aged 81 and over are *not* classified as socially isolated. To provide theoretical support for their argument, the authors rely on socio-emotional selectivity theory that, as suggested elsewhere (Dannefer and Lin, 2012), functions in social gerontology as a rehabilitated and nuanced version of disengagement theory. Such influential narratives of ageing-as-decline implicitly offer legitimation of age-graded stratification of service delivery that often disadvantages elders, such as Mo Ray describes in the case of social work in Chapter Eight, and as Margreet Bruens describes in the case of long-term care in Chapter Five. In these and other cases, the ideas of socio-emotional selectivity and disengagement can be seen as legitimating ageist social institutions and practices by allowing them to be viewed as accommodations to individual needs, when they actually may contribute to creating the unwelcome conditions they are supposed to ameliorate (Dannefer, 2008).

A number of other chapters also look to developmental stage or other organismically grounded frameworks to understand existential ageing, whether those of Fowler (Laceulle, Chapter Six), Jung (Dohmen, Chapter Three), or Baltes (Grenier and Phillipson, Chapter Four). The entire premise of stage theories or other modes of organismic theorising assumes that these approaches are dealing with 'existential' ageing. Nevertheless, the socially constituted and historically and culturally specific character of virtually all such frameworks has been clearly demonstrated (see, for example, Kett, 1977; Dannefer, 1984; Broughton, 1987; Elrod, 1992; Katz, 1996). It is now well established that when such 'life stages' appear, they often reflect the widespread reliance on age as a principle of social organisation that was a concomitant of 19th- and 20th-century bureaucratisation and statism. The historian Howard Chudacoff (1989) demonstrated that before the mid-19th century, 'age consciousness' was largely absent, and little attempt was made to create formal age categories or to segregate individuals according to their chronological age at school or in the workplace. The 'institutionalised lifecourse', with its emphasis on temporalisation, chronologisation and individualisation, is a product of this widespread historical transformation (Kohli, 1986, 2007). Ironically, this same historical process can be seen as largely responsible for the challenges facing geriatric social work identified by Mo Ray, for the problems she identifies reside in the fact that the profession of social work is itself age-graded in the way it organises social problems and service delivery.

In addition to the cultural production of age-graded stages and patterns, there is extensive evidence indicating that individual preferences and individual patterns of activity, response, coping strategies and so on are also socially organised, even within a given social and cultural environment. This leads us to offer a caution concerning the typology of 'personal competencies' proposed by Machielse and Hortulanus. Although at points their narrative suggests the role of social interaction in developing competencies and hence their dynamic nature, their analysis positions individual competencies as causal and predictive variables. If it can be agreed that the competencies themselves are contingent on social opportunities that facilitate their development, it would seem to follow that the *conditions that give rise to competencies* (for example, access to meaningful social interaction with others) might be at least equal in analytical importance to the competencies themselves. We believe it would add to our understanding to pursue such questions.

The social organisation of preferences also applies to the topic of agency. The discussions of individual agency offered by Amanda Grenier and Chris Phillipson, Joseph Dohmen and Hanne Laceulle offer a number of thoughtful points. One seemingly vexing issue that resurfaces a number of times in these discussions is the paradox that what Dohmen and Laceulle describe as the 'freedoms' of late modernity actually lead to a historical shift in increased conformity in life transitions and perhaps lifestyle.

The logical result of this paradoxical combination is to compel the assumption that conformity expression must reflect commonalities of human nature. Thus, as Grenier and Phillipson note in Chapter Four, it is an argument that reduces historically and socially produced inclinations to putatively 'natural' preferences that can now express themselves.

Of course, such a view ignores the long emphasis of the critical tradition on the role of the corporate-induced consumerism and the state more generally (both public and private sectors) in shaping individual consciousness (see, for example, Wexler, 1977; Schor, 2004). Other scholars have documented the power of corporate product promotion efforts to shape individual consciousness (see, e.g., Ewen, 1977; Schor, 2004). In the same vein, Laceulle reminds readers of Honneth's claim that 'self-realisation' as a cultural ideal is used by late modern consumer capitalism to strengthen its own purposes at the expense of the possibilities for the individual to acquire real freedom and autonomy. In societies that rely on age as a key organiser of everything, from developmental markers to medical diagnoses to marketing strategies, it is not surprising that individuals' lifestyle 'choices' may also be age-graded. Similarly, within-age variability is seen as freely expressed individuality instead of inequality. Such a tendency is evident by the excessive emphasis on choice, agency and freedom as a result of late modernity.

In the face of such realities, agency does indeed continue its operations; it is an irreducibly present dialectical moment of human consciousness (see, e.g., Dannefer, 1999). Agency operates, as Laceulle rightly notes, in the context of '… a determining background of social interaction and social structure', and is subject to what she calls the 'fallacy' of naturalisation. What warrants continuous self-reflection is the extent to which the human intentions that are expressed in agentic behaviour are shaped by corporate and state agendas, rather than the authentic interests of the agentic actor. Thus, the question of how much of its operation can rightly be considered the pursuit of freely and rationally chosen lines of action or 'politics of life', as advocated by Giddens and Dohmen, remains a matter requiring careful interrogation.

Existential ageing

We propose that a discussion of existential ageing requires as its foundation at least a tentative understanding of human needs and interests in general. For this, Laceulle draws on Honneth, who proposes that self-realisation requires (1) self-confidence, (2) autonomy and (3) solidarity, or social affirmation. Dohmen notes that Giddens similarly enumerates three similar dimensions as defining the problem areas of late modern 'life politics': (1) expertise (paralleling competence), (2) lifestyle choice (paralleling autonomy) and (3) social connection (paralleling solidarity).

It is noteworthy that these three-dimensional formulations also parallel the influential framework of self-determination theory, articulated by motivational psychologists Deci and Ryan (1985, 2008), who propose *competence*, *autonomy* and *relatedness* as the three irreducible and basic human needs. As noted elsewhere, that challenge of getting these needs met grows with age. The absence of means for meeting these basic needs maps closely onto what nursing home reformer Bill Thomas identified as the 'three *plagues* of life in nursing homes' – helplessness, boredom and loneliness (see Thomas, 1996; Shura et al, 2011). We are struck by the common identification of quite similar dimensions across these frameworks that span multiple disciplines. If these three dimensions may be taken as referring to basic needs, it is especially important to recognise that these needs have no age limit. There is no basis within any of these frameworks for assuming that they diminish or atrophy with age; there is no 'lifecourse trajectory' of such needs and interests, as disengagement-oriented approaches touched on by Machielse and Hortulanus might imply.

We note that these multiple but structurally similar frameworks (of Giddens, Honneth, Deci and Ryan, and Thomas) all imply a conceptual modification to the 'autonomy-connectedness' dimension put forward by Machielse and Hortulanus. In self-determination theory, for example, it is explicit that the three basic needs are analytically distinct and independent of each other, each comprising a separate dimension. It is entirely possible, and indeed important for wellbeing, to be 'high' on all three dimensions. This contrasts with the 'bipolar' unidimensional conceptualisation put forward by Machielse and Hortulanus, who regard autonomy and connectedness as in tension – competing poles of a single dimension.

Developments within the domain of spirituality seem, perhaps almost by definition, to belong within the problematic of existential ageing. We appreciate the thoughtful and wide-ranging consideration of spirituality and ageing offered by Laceulle. At the same time, we suggest that some of the issues introduced in her discussion could benefit from some additional scrutiny and refinement. One quite basic question seemingly unresolved concerns the basic definition of spirituality. This is important because it delimits the scope of the inquiry. Roughly the first half of Laceulle's chapter is not focused on spirituality at all, but on identity development. While clearly these two domains (self-development and spiritual development) are undoubtedly related, we would welcome a clearer articulation of exactly how they are related, and how they are to be distinguished.

What precisely is it that qualifies an experience, a phenomenon, a belief or an act as 'spiritual'? We note that Laceulle's chapter provides no explicit definition of spirituality. We acknowledge that some helpful insights are provided in some of the scholarship reviewed, such as Atchley's experiential 'stages' or Wuthnow's distinction between spiritualties of dwelling and seeking. Yet the precise threshold at which the focus of a problem can be considered to fall into the domain of spirituality rather than self-development remains unspecified.

Clearly, spiritiuality is not coterminous with ethicality and, as Laceulle emphasises, it is not to be identified with established religions or religious institutions. It is not religiosity. If inspired creativity is spiritual, then might active contemplation and generative human activity in general be considered spiritual? Indeed, if spirituality is seen as including ideas and experiences that respond to the human need for meaning and orderliness in life, the institutionalised lifecourse itself may be spiritual. Indeed, Martin Kohli (2007, p 255) has noted the existential value of the life course in assisting individuals in ordering and making sense of their lives:

> The model of institutionalization of the life course refers to the evolution, during the last two centuries, of an institutional program regulating one's movement through life both in terms of a sequence of positions and in terms of a set of biographical orientations by which to organize one's experiences and plans.

Such boundary questions make clear the need for a definition. Our own view is to agree with a caution implied in Chapter One, that spiritual experience and the profound human problems that draw people to it may not be entirely reducible to the terms of research and scholarship, which are inherently limited to cognitive representation and reference. The demonstrated value of the scholarship Laceulle reviews makes clear that this is a field with much to offer and it is certain to enrich an understanding of spiritual experience, but it is unclear that it can fully contain the latter.

Theory and practice

Several of these chapters make clear that the frequently appearing problem of agency is not only a theoretical problem, but also, often, an urgently practical one. In their discussions, Margreet Bruens and Friederike Ziegler and Thomas Scharf demonstrate not only how contingent the opportunities for the expression of agency are on the social and institutional contexts within which people live, but also how well-intentioned efforts at salutary change on behalf of elders has resulted '... in the furthering of policies and practices around ageing which continue to disadvantage certain population groups' (Ziegler and Scharf, Chapter Nine).

We have observed and experienced similar paradoxes in the US, in our involvement with efforts at reform of long-term care and neighbourhood action research. Such reactions may include both simple unintended consequences (stemming in part from the naïveté of policy makers or action researchers) and deliberate corporate cooptation. We offer an example of each.

Beginning with Riley's call for an age-integrated lifecourse (Riley et al, 1994) and related emphases on the dangers of age segregation (Hagestad and Uhlenberg, 2006), an enduring principle in the sociology of age concerns the need for age integration. In general, there can be no question that the potentials and benefits of age integration remain underdeveloped and underexplored, as numerous innovative examples have made clear (Smith, 2001; Dannefer, 2005). Yet we have found, as did researchers in the CALL-ME project, that such potentials are not necessarily endorsed or recognised by seniors. For example, efforts of US nursing home reformers to integrate a visit by daycare children into the daily programming provided for nursing home residents produced in some residents a sense of annoyance and distraction, as well as strong criticism of the small children's behaviour (Dannefer and Stein, 2001). Similarly, efforts to launch age-integrated experiences in community centres prompted unexpectedly negative reactions from seniors, who focused on the general disrespectfulness of children and, at least initially, expressed little interest in interacting with them (Stein and Dannefer, 2002).

In the US, *culture change* has over the past two decades become a social movement and a significant theme of the discourse in the fields of long-term care and elder care more generally. This movement is evident in national organisations such as the Pioneer Network (www. pioneernetwork.net/) and the rapid expansion of the Eden Alternative, founded by Bill and Judy Thomas, in reaction to their analysis of the three pervasive plagues of nursing home life noted above, boredom, helplessness and loneliness. The Eden Alternative has now franchised many nursing homes in the US, Canada, Europe and Australia, who have implemented its model of progressive and humanised nursing home care. Announcement of being an Eden-franchised institution is a prominent example of a culture change cache that represents a form of cultural capital and competitive advantage in the marketplace, and culture change has prominently appeared in RFPs (requests for grant proposals) of both state and national-level agencies funding research on long-term care and elder care. Public awareness of such developments has also grown, and long-term care and elder care facilities competing for residents have rapidly recognised that 'culture change' may be good for residents and public funding, but it can also be a powerful marketing tool. Inevitably, this has led to a cooptation of the critical and humanising impulses that originally fuelled the culture change movement, as for-profit chains and other large lifecourse institutions have announced innovations that provide the more manifest trappings of culture change (such as populating facilities with flora and fauna, and announcing 'resident-centred' programming), without necessarily extending the efforts of innovation to substantial and enduring changes in daily practices of nurshing home life..

At the same time, we note that the culture change movement has both raised the level of debate and has had many salutary effects in changing policy, educating and broadening the visions of nursing home leaders about how to work with the clientele, and hence – in many institutions of long-term care – in the quality of residents' lives and health. Thus it would be an incomplete and unduly dark picture to consider cooptation to be the primary effect of the culture change effort. A redeeming aspect of the US culture change movement – explicit in the principles of the Pioneer Network – is that 'the work of culture change is never done' (see, for example, Fagan et al, 1997), which introduces a self-reflexive and self-critical moment into the core of the culture change enterprise.

In the US, mobilisation of this self-reflexive moment has provided an opening to deal quite directly with problem of the agency of elders that is so searchingly considered in Bruens' chapter on dementia and dementia care. We argue that the agency of elders, including elders with dementia, is not only possible but continuously occurs on an everyday basis, both in long-term care settings and in the community. Of course, elders' sense of efficacy, or even their memory of agentic action, may vary considerably. Under certain conditions, however, it can take an encouraging form – either in lifecourse settings or in the community. Regarding the former, consider our action research projects that have mobilised the knowledge of 'the real experts' on a long-term care facility, those who present in the facility 24/7 and have the most direct and intimate view of its frontline operations. Residents joined weekly 'research groups' which met to consider what could be done to improve the quality of life in the facility, and several specific suggestions were implemented (Dannefer and Stein, 2001; Shura et al, 2011).

A poignant community-based example of agency in the face of dementia comes from the age-integrated daily life of The Intergenerational Schools, which operates in Cleveland, Ohio, but is now being nationally replicated. At its annual meeting of the board, the 'Volunteer of the Year' award was given to a woman with dementia who enjoyed, and was extremely good at, reading to and interacting with young children, and did so on a regular basis – even though she did not remember doing it and had no idea why she was being given an annual 'Volunteer of the Year' award. (Whitehouse and Whitehouse, 2012).

We believe such examples, of which there are many, make clear that agency is a more pervasive, nuanced and subtle phenomenon than is often imagined, even by theorists of agency. We believe such examples offer hope, and make clear that the problems and challenges encountered by Ziegler and Scharf and reported by Bruens, Ray and others can be transcended if thoughtful practitioners and theorists alike continue to seek ways to mobilise the generative potentials that remain present and potentially vibrant, even in elders with dementia – evident, for example, in humour, imagination and expressions of caring even by elders with dementia. As such potentials are discovered in proactive programming, action research and other real-life arenas where they may be nourished, practice may bring new challenges to theory and scholarship in both the social sciences and the humanities, and may suggest new avenues of interaction.

References

Baars, J. (2012) *Aging and the art of living*, Baltimore, MD: The Johns Hopkins University Press.

Broughton, J. (1987) *Critical theories of psychological development*, New York: Plenum.

Chudacoff, H. (1989) *How old are you?*, Princeton, NJ: Princeton University Press.

Crimmins, E., Kim, J. and Seeman T. (2009) 'Poverty and biological risk: The earlier "aging" of the poor', *Journal of Gerontology: Medical Sciences*, vol 64, pp 286-92.

Dannefer, D. (1984) 'Adult development and social theory: a paradigmatic reappraisal', *American Sociological Review*, vol 49, pp 100-16.

Dannefer, D. (1999) Freedom sn't free: power, alienation, and the consequences of action, in Jochen Brandtstadter and Richard M. Lerner (eds) Action & Self-Development. New York: Sage. Pp. 105-131

Dannefer, D. (2005) 'Practicing the best of theory: age integration at the intergenerational school', *Intercom*, vol 12, pp 22-3.

Dannefer, D. (2002) "Whose life course is it, anyway? Diversity and 'linked lives' in global perspectives, in R.A.Settersten (eds) Invitation to the life course. Amityville, NY: Baywood. Pp. 259-268.:

Dannefer, D. (2008-) 'The waters we swim: everyday social processes, macro-structural realities, and human aging', in K. Warner Schaie and Ronald P. Abeles (eds) *Social structure and aging individuals*, New York: Springer. Pp 3-22.

Dannefer, D. and Lin, J. (2012) Opportunity structure and personal agency: the social regulation of healthy and successful aging. Paper presented at the Healthy & Successful Aging Working Conference. Cleveland, OH.

Dannefer, D. and Stein, P. (2001) 'From the top to the bottom, from the bottom to the top: Systemically changing the culture of nursing homes', Unpublished Final Report, Van Amerigen Foundation. New York, NY.

Dannefer, D. and Stein, P. (2002). Beyond culture change: Building the living-learning community. Unpublished Final Report, The New York, State Department of Health. Albany, NY.

Deci, E.L. and Ryan, R.M. (1985) *Intrinsic motivation and self-determination in human behavior*, New York: Plenum.

Deci, E.L. and Ryan, R.M. (2008) 'Self-determination theory: A macrotheory of human motivation, development, and health', *Canadian Psychology*, vol 49, pp 182-5.

Elrod, N. (1992) *500 years of deception: A classic case in the 20th century: Erik H. Erikson's portrayal of the Native American*, Zurich, Switzerland: Althea Verlag.

Ewen, S. (1977) *Captains of consciousness: Advertising and the social roots of the consumer culture*, New York: McGraw-Hill.

Fagan, R.M., Williams, C.C. and Burger, S.G. (1997) *Meeting of pioneers in nursing home culture change*, Rochester, NY: Lifespan of Greater Rochester.

Hagestad, G.H. and Uhlenberg, P. (2006) 'Should we be concerned about age segregation? Some theoretical and empirical explorations', *Research on Aging*, vol 28, pp 638-53.

Hayward, M.D., Crimmins, E.M., Miles, T.P. and Yu, Y. (2000) 'The significance of socioeconomic status in explaining the racial gap in chronic health conditions', *American Sociological Review*, vol 65, pp 910-30.

House, J.S., Lantz, P.M. and Herd, P. (2005) 'Continuity and change in the social stratification of aging and health over the life course: Evidence from a nationally representative longitudinal study from 1986 to 2001/2002', *Journal of Gerontology: Social Sciences*, vol 60, S15-26.

Katz, S. (1996) *Disciplining old age: The formation of gerontological knowledge*, Charlottesville, VA: The University Press of Virginia.

Kett, J. (1977) *Rites of passage: Adolescence in America: 1790 to the present*, New York: Basic Books.

Kohli, M. (1986) 'Social organisation and subjective construction of the life course', in A.B. Sorensen, F.E. Weinert and L.R. Sherrod (eds) *Human development and the life course: Multidisciplinary perspectives*, Hillsdale, NJ: Erlbaum, pp 271-92.

Kohli, M. (2007) 'The institutionalization of the life course: Looking back to look ahead', *Research in Human Development*, vol 4, pp 253-71.

Link, B. and Phelan, J. (1995) 'Social conditions as fundamental causes of disease', *Journal of Health and Social Behavior*, vol 35, pp 80-94.

Marmot, M.G. (2004) *The status syndrome: How social standing affects our health and longevity*, New York: Henry Holt.

Shura, R., Siders, R.A., Dannefer, D. (2011) Culture change in long-term care: participatory action research and the role of the resident. *The Gerontologist*, vol 51, pp212-225.

Riley, J. (2001) *Rising life expectancy: A global history*, New York: Cambridge University Press.Riley, M.W., Kahn, R.L. and Foner, A. (1994) *Age and structural lag: Society's failure to provide meaningful opportunities in work, family and leisure*, New York: Wiley.

Rowe, J.W. and Kahn, R.L. (1987) 'Human aging: usual and successful', *Science*, vol 237, pp 143-9.

Schor, J. (2004) *Born to buy*, New York: Scribner.

Smith, W. (2001) *Hope Meadows: Real life stories of healing and caring from an inspiring community*, New York: Berkley Books.

Thomas, W.H. (1996) *Life worth living: How someone you love can still enjoy life in a nursing home*, Acton, MA: Vanderwyk & Burnham.

UN (United Nations) (2010) *Rethinking poverty: Report on the world social situation 2010* (www.un.org/esa/socdev/rwss/docs/2010/fullreport.pdf).

US Bureau of Census (2012) *Current Population Survey, Annual Social and Economic Supplement, 2012* (www.census.gov/cps/data/cpstablecreator.html).

Wexler, P. (1977) Comment on Ralph Turner's "the real self: from institution to impulse". *American Journal of Sociology*, vol 88, pp 178-186.

Whitehouse, P. and Whitehouse, C. (2012) *Fountain of youth: engaging the brain*. City Club of Cleveland. Cleveland, OH.

Index

Note: the following abbreviations have been used: *n* = note; *t* = table

R

rational conscious awareness 67–8
Read, S. 151
reductionism 24–5
reflection 43, 44–5
reflexive modernity *see* late
    modernity
reflexivity 43, 170–3
relatedness 188
relationships *see* social relationships
religion *see* spirituality
remorse 48
residential care 140, 188, 190, 191
resignation 48
resilience 49
resistance 65, 66, 72
reskilling 35
responsibility 46, 47, 49
retirement age 22
rights-based social work 150
Riley, J. 190
risk
  fraility 18, 56, 58
  individualisation 142, 144
  isolation 126, 128–9, 130
Rose, G. 173
Russell, B. 18
Russia 22
Ryan, R.M. 188

S

Scourfield, P. 146
second order desires 37
secularisation 104–5, 107
selective optimisation and
    compensation 70
'self, the'
  dementia and 83
  self-realisation and 101–4, 106, 112,
    116
  society and 60–1, 63
self-assessment 147
self-care 35, 36–7, 45
self-determination 32, 35, 40, 44, 46,
    188
self-directed support 144–5, 148
self-fulfilment 15, 46, 47, 101
self-harming acts of agency 68
self-identity 14, 98, 103
self-realisation 6, 187, 188

ageing and spiritual development
    106–11
agency and 99, 100
authenticity and 99, 100, 102
dependency and 102, 111
health and 116
individualisation and 103, 104,
    97–101
merits of the spiritual perspective
    111–15, 116
self and 101–4, 106, 112, 116
spirituality and 104–6
self-respect 121
self-worth 17, 18
senescence
  biological 2, 6, 15, 26, 27, 134
  contingent limitation and 25, 26, 27,
    181, 183
  self-realisation and 109, 110, 111
  social relationships and 127, 128,
    131
serenity 47–8, 50
Settersten, R. 19, 25, 59
Sewell, W.H. Jr 67
Shura, R. 70, 71
social competencies *see* personal
    competencies
social contacts typology 125, 126*t*
social exclusion 124–5, 167
social existence 120–1
social gerontology 23, 60
social inequality 8, 19, 22, 144, 146,
    147, 151
social inhibition 132*t*, 133
social institutions: systemic world 21
social integration 7, 46–7, 120, 121,
    122
social isolation 124–5, 128–9, 131,
    132*t*, 133, 159, 185
Social isolation in modern society
    (Hortulanus) 120, 135*n*
social networks 6–7, 103, 113, 122,
    123, 124, 125, 127–8, 131, 135
  typology of contacts 126*t*
social participation: dementia 89
social relationships 119–20, 134–5
  ageing well and 133–4
  changes in social networks 122, 123,
    124, 127–8, 135
  health and 127–8
  independence and 124, 130, 131,
    132, 135